Visionary Observers

Critical Studies in the History of Anthropology

Regna Darnell
Stephen O. Murray

Visionary
Observers

Anthropological Inquiry
and Education

Edited by
Jill B. R. Cherneff
and Eve Hochwald

Foreword by Sydel Silverman

University of Nebraska Press   •   Lincoln and London

Chapter 3,
"A Century of
Margaret Mead"
by Ray McDermott,
previously appeared in
Teachers College Record
103, no. 5 (2001): 843–867.
⊗
Library of Congress
Cataloging-in-Publication
Data
Visionary observers:
anthropological inquiry and
education / edited by Jill B. R.
Cherneff and Eve Hochwald;
foreword by Sydel Silverman.
p.   cm.—(Critical studies in
the history of anthropology)
Includes bibliographical
references and index.
ISBN-13: 978-0-8032-6464-9
(pbk.: alk. paper)
ISBN-10: 0-8032-6464-X
(pbk.: alk. paper)
1. Educational
anthropology—
United States.
2. Anthropologists—
United States.
I. Cherneff, Jill B. R.
II. Hochwald, Eve.
III. Series.
LB45.V57   2006
306.43—dc22
2006009265

Designed by R. W. Boeche.

To our families

Contents

Illustrations

Foreword

Capturing the history of anthropology is a precarious task in a time when institutional memories are short, when publications are forgotten only a few years after they appear (the premium being on currency in citing sources), and when personal papers are routinely discarded as trash. Even more elusive is the unwritten history embodied in the unrecorded aspects of the lives of people who were part of the development of a field and in the recollections of those who knew them. The result is a loss of continuity and of a sense of cumulativeness in anthropological research and practice, which may lead to illusions of "new" discoveries and novel predicaments. While this situation holds for all of anthropology, the difficulties are especially great in those areas on the margins of the academy. If applied anthropology has for too long been regarded as less central to our discipline than the traditional areas of theoretical focus, so also has the history of the public face of anthropology, and the history of anthropology in practice, been treated with benign (or not so benign) neglect.

This collection of essays on pioneers in the field of anthropology and education is thus particularly welcome. It includes both leading figures of anthropology, whose contributions to this field are less well known than other facets of their work, and the unheralded individuals who ventured into new anthropological territory for reasons of theoretical curiosity, personal or political commitment, or accidents of biography—or a combination of these. We recognize Franz Boas, Ruth Benedict, and Margaret Mead to have been early public spokespersons for anthropology, and these essays probe how in this role they laid the groundwork for an anthropology of education. But people like Solon Kimball, Jules Henry, and Eleanor Leacock, who may be little remembered today, carried that enterprise to another level, to create what is now a thriving anthropological specialty.

There was, in other words, an anthropology relevant to education before there was anthropological research on schools. The beginnings of the enterprise were interwoven with the belief—then uncommon in the discipline—that anthropology could speak, and had the obligation to speak, to the social concerns of the time, that research and theory go hand in hand with an involvement in public life. This theme runs through the careers of each of the figures in this book, and in most instances it also implied a strong political stance. As the title of the book indicates, these individuals were trained observers of social life, but they were not detached scientists, and their anthropology carried with it visions of a better world—for their own society as well as for the people they studied.

Franz Boas saw anthropology's role in society as one of educating the citizenry about race, cultural difference, and other social issues, establishing for his successors a link between scholarship and public affairs, activism informed by science. Ruth Benedict continued this legacy, especially in her writing for the public on racial and cultural tolerance, and her interest in cultural conditioning and culture learning had a significant, if indirect, bearing on educational questions. Margaret Mead, of course, took the public role much farther, making it the centerpiece of her career and commenting on virtually every aspect of American life, but especially on matters of gender, family, and child rearing. Mead was also the first anthropologist to focus on educational processes in a primitive society and to draw implications for Western schooling from what she learned in her fieldwork (see *Growing Up in New Guinea* [1930a] and also *New Lives for Old* [1956] on her revisit to Manus twenty-five years later).

Gene Weltfish, a student of Boas as well as of John Dewey, took it as her mission to apply anthropology to public education, initially with a challenge to racism and later by applying her theoretical ideas of a pragmatic anthropology to a community project geared to "relevant" education. Hortense Powdermaker, whose mentor was Bronislaw Malinowski, not Boas, carried out a pioneering ethnography during the 1930s of a community in Mississippi, in which she looked at both Black and White sectors of the society and the ways in which they were interwoven. Her 1939 book *After Freedom* included a chapter on education and the effects of a segregated school system.

The early 1950s marked the beginning of a specific anthropological concern with education as schooling, in contrast to the earlier conflation of socialization, enculturation, and education. Solon Kimball belongs to this transition point because he was appointed to develop an anthropology program at Teachers College, Columbia University. Although his own research background was peripheral to education, a number of his students went on to do ethnographies of schools, and he himself later organized a major project of this kind in Florida. The early 1950s was also the time when Jules Henry shifted his research focus from psychiatric hospitals to schools. Soon afterward Ruth Landes found employment on a project for teacher training in Southern California, in which she developed some innovative anthropological approaches to education. The final figure in this account, Eleanor Leacock, was among the first to do fieldwork in schools, in New York City in the late 1950s, and she became a major theoretical force in what was by then an established field of anthropology.

This field straddles academic and applied anthropology, as well as other familiar contrasts such as theory/practice and descriptive/problem-oriented research. Anthropologists interested in education do all of these, sometimes all at the same time. But one might ask whether the conditions under which anthropologists work and the sources of their research topics and funding matter for what is learned and for the impact of that knowledge. Certainly there is a difference between research in which the anthropologist defines the questions to be asked (usually drawn from current concerns of the discipline) and that in which the questions are posed by others, who also stipulate the kind of answers that are sought. The first—investigator-initiated research—is the luxury afforded by academia under the best of circumstances, although it is never free of subtle institutional pressures or the interests of outside funders. The second situation describes applied research, whether conducted as part of the anthropologist's employment or on contract.

Theoretical advances in anthropology and education have come out of both kinds of research, but probably more work in this field has been done under terms of employment and contract than academic exigency. To a certain extent, the field grew through the work of anthropologists who had insecure career histories or for various reasons had marginal status within anthropology (the cases of Weltfish, Landes, and Leacock come to mind—not coincidentally, all women). It is not clear how these circumstances have shaped the direction of the field or will do so in the future—since they are with us again in this era of diminished academic employment. On the one hand, it is a field in which the theoretician and the practitioner (often the same person) work in tandem, which enriches both enterprises. On the other hand, mainstream academic anthropology may proceed oblivious to developments in an area it defines as peripheral to its so-called center stage.

Whatever the future holds, the stories of the figures in this book are testimony to how "visionary observers" can both affect the course of their discipline and help realize the goal, first articulated by Boas, of an anthropological contribution to public life.

Sydel Silverman

Acknowledgments

This book has evolved from a project begun more than ten years ago by three anthropologists. Committed to preserving our discipline's history, they began to assemble a series of essays on the foundations of anthropology and education. We were invited to be contributing authors. Through this introduction, we subsequently became collaborators on the present manuscript. Our deep thanks go to Richard Blot, Juliet Niehaus, and Richard Schmertzing.

We also wish to acknowledge the many friends and colleagues who encouraged us by persuasion, coaxing, and inveigling to move ahead on this project. Without them we would never have moved so smoothly through the work of assembling this manuscript. This book has been helped, too, by the University of Nebraska Press staff and by the comments of reviewers who took the time to read our manuscript carefully and offer succinct and meaningful clarifications.

We want to thank Rayna Rapp, Sydel Silverman, and Leni Silverstein for advice and encouragement. A special thanks goes to Nancy King and Karen Ray for the editing suggestions they provided, often on tight deadlines. For a lively and thoughtful exchange on the history of anthropology at Columbia University we thank Richard Handler, Judith Shapiro, Rosalind Rosenberg, Nan A. Rothschild, and Robert McCaughey.

For generously providing the photographs included here we thank Allan Burns, Claudia Leacock, Ann Margetson, the Smithsonian Archives, and Mark Katzman at the American Museum of Natural History.

We thank Martin Janal, Roger Laverty, and the other members of our families for proofreading, purchasing countless reams of printer paper, preparing meals, and picking up an unfair share of errands. We are grateful for the patience that led them to give of themselves beyond reasonable limits.

Introduction

This book explores the relationship between anthropology and public policy in the United States. Anthropologists in this country have been attentive to issues of race, democracy, and education since the discipline's early years. In the period from just before World War I to the 1960s, anthropologists emerged as public intellectuals as a consequence of their awareness of the diversity of human societies. Applying their knowledge to domestic policy, they promoted tolerance, racial equality, and social justice.

This volume assembles essays about nine twentieth-century anthropologists—Franz Boas, Ruth Benedict, Margaret Mead, Hortense Powdermaker, Gene Weltfish, Sol Kimball, Jules Henry, Ruth Landes, and Eleanor Leacock—who did research in the areas of socialization, enculturation, and education. They also were public policy activists, who applied what they learned to broader social issues, using illustrations from fieldwork as a basis for alternatives.

During this time the most obvious change in the discipline of anthropology was its expansion—in numbers of practitioners, in the number of academic departments, and in the types, methods, and topics of anthropological inquiry (for overviews, see Darnell 1997, Darnell and Gleach 2002, Goodenough 2002, Nader 2002, Patterson 2001, and Silverman 2004). The expansion was in part the result of new sources of funding from corporate foundations and government agencies. For example, the Laura Spellman Rockefeller Foundation, founded in 1918, was the sponsor of the Institute of Human Relations at Yale University and the Social Science Research Council in New York City. Both establishments and others like them encouraged growing numbers of American students to pursue graduate studies.

With new sources of funding for social sciences came a movement away from the tradition of recording vestiges of past behavior to a new emphasis on contemporary problems and new interdisciplinary approaches. The influence of psychology led to the culture-and-personality theorists exemplified by Benedict and Mead. Contact with sociologists, as well as with British social anthropology, encouraged anthropologists like Powdermaker and Kimball to pursue community studies. Both approaches extended the field through the use of new methods and the study of new populations—children, Europeans, African Americans—enlarging the record of human diversity.

These changes did not affect the anthropological tool kit—the concept of culture, the comparative method, neutrality not ethnocentrism, and participant-observation. The holistic approach to cultural analysis remained the same, even as some of the underlying premises changed. Race became a social, not a biological, category. Culture became ideational, no longer material and object-oriented, but based largely on the transmission of values, symbols, and behaviors. Dissertation research came to mean fieldwork instead of library investigations.

Similarly, after Boas, the units of cultural analysis changed. Boas looked for culture traits. His students Benedict, Mead, and Weltfish tried to find themes and patterns. Powdermaker and Kimball, heirs to a different tradition, uncovered structures and systems. Landers, Benedict's student, was associated with the culture-and-personality approach. Henry and Leacock focused on systemic power relations and a dialectical concept of culture in their research about institutions; their work reflected the emerging concern with economics and power.

New approaches and topics of inquiry led to new specialties. The Depression in the early 1930s made jobs scarce for the increasing number of newly trained anthropologists until the New Deal, when plans for work projects included them in the larger goal of job creation. Both the Department of the Interior and the Department of Agriculture had major programs. The Department of the Interior was searching for ways to return to Native Americans "a degree of political and economic control" (Kelly 1985:126). The Department of Agriculture devoted its staff to matters of conservation and help for farm laborers.

As World War II became inevitable, many anthropologists became more involved in the public arena. Some worked directly for the government. Others spoke and wrote against Fascist and racist doctrines. Still others joined leftist political organizations. Most volunteered to help with the war effort once war was declared. After the war, enrollment in universities increased greatly, spurred by the entry of returning veterans, for whom the GI Bill of 1944 provided financial aid. Existing university programs expanded, and new programs were begun. Applied anthropology was bypassed as an appropriate field of study, as university positions opened for PhDs, and because the atmosphere of Cold War politics discouraged active involvement in programs for the disadvantaged.

However, at the same time the expansion of the field of social studies in general even at the primary and secondary educational levels led to the training of teachers and the creation of curriculum materials by anthropologists. Early anthropological interest in the socialization and enculturation of children in diverse cultural settings was a precursor to research interests more directly concerned with education (see Eddy 1987; Pelissier 1991; Yon 2003). In 1954 George Spindler organized the four-day Stanford University Conference on Education and Anthropology funded by the Carnegie Foundation. Among those taking part were Henry, Mead, and Kimball. The landmark Supreme Court decision *Brown v. the Board of Education of Topeka* outlawing "separate but equal" school segregation had been handed down earlier that year.

The role of education as a vehicle of acculturation and integration, and as a means of making real the ideal of equal opportunity, made it a natural concern of many anthropologists, even before the area emerged as the specialized area of inquiry it has become. In the 1920s and 1930s anthropologists concentrated on the process of educating citizens for democracy, in the context of assimilating immigrants and of the fight against European Fascism. They identified education with progress. In the 1940s they developed curriculum materials designed to combat racial prejudice at home, such as Powdermaker's *Probing Our Prejudices* (1944b) and Benedict and Weltfish's *In Henry's Backyard* (1948).

After World War II, for reasons having to do with the increased numbers of Americans enrolled in school at all levels, with the waning of colonialism, and with the emerging civil rights movement, some turned their attention directly to schools and schooling. Beginning with Jules Henry in the 1950s and increasingly in the 1960s and 1970s, more anthropologists became directly involved in observing and influencing behavior in schools (see Gearing and Tindall 1973). Landes and then Alexander Moore worked on teacher education projects (Moore 1967). Throughout the 1960s American anthropologists increasingly turned to investigations of problems at home, including schooling. Others such as Kimball and Leacock joined Henry in using schools as field sites, and like him, they saw the educational system, not as a vehicle of progress, but as a socialization mechanism for maintaining the status quo.

Organization of the Book

Following the model of Sydel Silverman's *Totems and Teachers* (1981, 2003), four contributors describe the work of individuals with whom they were personally acquainted. Three were students of their subjects (Young of Benedict, Niehaus of Weltfish, and Hochwald of Leacock), and the fourth was a colleague (Moore of Kimball). Some of the essays originally were presented at sessions of the American Anthropological Association meetings. Others were written specifically for this volume. Only one (McDermott on Mead) has been previously published. This book is not intended to be comprehensive. The relationship between anthropology and public policy is complex and could be illustrated in many ways. We have limited the topic by concentrating on anthropologists a great deal of whose work concerned aspects of anthropology and education. Even so, other equally compelling scholars had to be omitted as a concession to the demand of reasonable length.

The chapters are arranged chronologically, in the order of the dates the subjects received their PhDs. Arranging the chapters in this way is intended to show the expansion of the discipline, as it responded to new ideas, methods, and areas of inquiry. Each chapter contains an editors' preface, placing the subject's life in context.

In chapter 1 Regna Darnell writes about Franz Boas, the "citizen-scientist." Franz Boas is the towering figure of American anthropology in the first half of the twentieth century. When he came to the United States at the end of the nineteenth century, the field of anthropology was museum based and object oriented. The assumption of a great divide between our civilized selves and the savage other was rarely questioned. Among his accomplishments, Boas is credited with making ethnology the central component of anthropology, with recognizing that Native American languages were no more primitive than English in their abilities to express abstract ideas, and with the paradigmatic shift from biological to cultural determinism. His courageous stands for social justice depended on scientific evidence for their arguments. Boas asked a fundamental question necessary to scientific understanding: What is the relationship among the independent variables of race, language, and culture?

In chapter 2 Virginia Young, a student of Ruth Benedict, discusses first Benedict's influential concept of "patterns of culture" and then her much less widely known notion of the "area beyond cultural relativity," that cultural arrangements are correlated with social effects on general welfare and sense of freedom. Benedict, writes Young, told her students the question to pursue: Under what cultural arrangements are different ends sought and possibly achieved?

In chapter 3 Ray McDermott analyzes Margaret Mead's contributions and contradictions in two sections: the first, concerning her ethnography in Samoa, New Guinea, and Bali, and the second, about her legacy as applied to the problems of contemporary America, particularly her "rarely noticed contributions to a theory of learning." As McDermott points out, Mead focused on learning in the context of habits developed within social relations and on learning as lateral rather than hierarchical. Mead consistently inquired: How many people, in what levels of organization, are involved in shaping the specifics of anyone's learning?

In chapter 4 Jill Cherneff writes about Hortense Powdermaker, a contemporary of Mead and an innovative fieldworker and ethnographer. Working alone she conducted a community study in the deeply segregated American South. Originally published in 1939, *After Freedom* was her first publication on the subject of race relations, followed by many others. She was one of the first anthropologists to consider popular culture. Her ethnography of the feature film industry, *Hollywood, the Dream Factory* (1950) was a pioneering study. Interested in the relationship between emotions and intellect, Powdermaker asked: What factors in our social environment surround our notions about others different from ourselves, and how do they affect how we act toward one another?

In chapter 5 Juliet Niehaus draws on her personal experience studying at the New School for Social Research in the late 1970s with Gene Weltfish, another of Boas's students. Both Boas and John Dewey influenced Weltfish's "pragmatic anthropology." Weltfish, a social activist who understood anthropology to be a tool for better adaptation of the human species, asked: What can we learn from others, and how can our lives be different because of our science? Her Pawnee ethnography *The Lost Universe* (1965) began by asking: How do we find our way into tomorrow?

In chapter 6 Alexander Moore discusses the work of Solon Kimball, his colleague at the University of Florida. Moore describes how Kimball addressed problems of education after his 1953 move to Teachers College, Columbia University, culminating in a major but unpublished ethnographic study of desegregation in Gainesville, Florida. Kimball, with Conrad Arensberg, coauthored the seminal community study *Family and Community in Ireland*, first published in 1940, in which the aim had been to uncover "maps" of relationships. Then, as later, Kimball posited that social structure is derived from interaction in pairs and sets. When Kimball applied interaction analysis to schools, community remained his key emphasis. Kimball wanted to know: How are social rules and values derived from human activity?

In chapter 7 Richard Handler examines the research of Jules Henry and Ruth Landes carried out in the 1950s and 1960s. Both had been students of Boas and Benedict in the 1930s. Differing in orientation, Henry drew on psychoanalytic concepts while Landes practiced in the "social engineering" tradition of Benedict and Mead. Contrasting their work from the perspective of their differing "subject positions," Handler notes that Henry, tenured at a private university, used his insights into the conformity and contradictions prevalent in classrooms—whether middle class, minority, or working class—to critique mainstream American culture.

Landes, a short-term contractor hired to improve teaching in California schools with rapidly changing racial and ethnic compositions, focused on training teachers to do their own cultural analyses. The teachers saw the problem as underachieving minority students; for Landes, the problem was communication. Her solution was to teach the teachers how to conduct cultural analysis of their own and their students' backgrounds, in order to challenge stereotypes that reinforced class and racial hierarchies. Both Henry and Landes asked: How can students succeed when the avowed value to encourage individualism is pitted against the institutional dictates of conformity?

In chapter 8 Eve Hochwald discusses Eleanor Leacock's contributions to anthropology and education. Hochwald was Leacock's student at the Graduate Center of the City University of New York in the 1970s. Well known for her scholarship on inequality, gender, and Marxism, Leacock encouraged "advocacy anthropology." Studying urban education in New York City she opposed the "culture-of-poverty" stereotyping of the disadvantaged; in Zambia she exposed the "myth of modernization." Always against reductionism, Leacock argued that children, like adults, function at a social and not an individual level of integration. Focusing on dialectical cultural processes, Leacock asked: How do social institutions shape people at the same time as people themselves are shaping social institutions?

In the topics they chose, the questions they asked, and the theoretical approaches they applied, the subjects of the essays that follow reveal differing responses to social issues. More recently, the notion of the dichotomy between the observed "We" and the observed "Other" has been called into question. Contemporary research questions are more likely to include an explicit consideration of power relations, resource allocation, and the anthropologists' relation to those they observe. Yet the fundamental issues—how to link commitment to the discipline with social concerns; how to combine critical assessment and compassion; and how to use anthropological knowledge to effect change in the world—are not different.

We hope that these essays will remind those of our readers who are anthropologists of our own disciplinary history. For others—educators, policymakers, reformers, and social scientists—we want to illustrate some of the ways anthropologists frame policy questions comparatively and holistically. Using examples from other cultures and settings to model change and reform, anthropologists have made contributions as scholars and as social activists. This book is a legacy of past generations of anthropologists who wrestled with the issues and aspects of their times—and continue to influence ours.

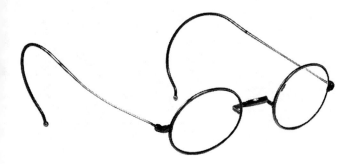

1. Franz Boas

Scientist and Public Intellectual

Regna Darnell

Franz Boas in the American Southwest, 1921. Courtesy of the National Anthropological Archives, Smithsonian Institution (86-1324).

The ideas of Franz Boas (1858–1942) dominated American anthropology for most of the twentieth century. Among them are the distinctions between race, language, and culture; the grounding of culture in specific historic contexts; and the notion that the minds of so-called primitive and civilized humans are alike, sharing the same range of rational and emotional behaviors. In addition to his intellectual legacy, Boas trained generations of students who went on to establish anthropology as an academic field. His influence also continues in the graduate education of anthropologists who learn the four fields of ethnology, linguistics, biological anthropology, and archaeology. This is the approach he instituted at Columbia University, where he taught for nearly four decades.

Born in 1858 into a middle-class Jewish family in Minden, Westphalia (then part of Prussia), Boas trained as a geographer at the University of Kiel. He first left Germany on an Arctic expedition to Baffin Island in 1883. Three years later, in 1886, he went to British Columbia to study the cultures of the Northwest Coast. He then settled in the United States, which brought him closer to the Native Americans in whom he maintained a lifelong interest. Given the rise of political anti-Semitism in Germany during this period (see Richey 1998:242–246), the United States offered more possibility for professional advancement. Also, he was about to marry an American, Marie Krakowizer, whom he had met in the Harz Mountains.

In 1888 the Bureau of American Ethnology published Boas's The Central Eskimo. The following year he began teaching at Clark University in Worcester, Massachusetts, but left in a mass faculty resignation after three years. He then took a job preparing "living cultures" displays for the 1893 World's Columbian Exposition in Chicago. Such human exhibits at world's fairs of the time were a popular attraction (see Breitbart 1997). Boas meanwhile had already returned several times to the Northwest Coast, and in 1896 he received a joint appointment at Columbia University and the American Museum of Natural History. His uncle Abraham Jacobi, a successful New York physician, provided funds for this appointment. At the time private philanthropy, channeled through museums, was the primary source of support for ethnographic research (Stocking 2002:13).

In that year Boas asked the polar explorer Robert E. Peary to bring an Eskimo back to the museum for research. Peary returned with six individuals from Greenland, four of whom died within a year after arrival. The sad life of one of the two survivors, the child Minik, and other details of this sorry episode, in which devotion to science overrode humanitarian considerations, are described in Harper (2000). Boas was also the curator of the Northwest Coast exhibit still on display there, using the rich materials collected by the

Jesup North Pacific Expedition of 1897–1902, which he organized. The principle by which he arranged it—grouping items in cultural context—was innovative and was to govern all his work.

In 1899 Boas was promoted by Columbia University, becoming their first professor of anthropology, and in 1905 he resigned from the American Museum of Natural History. Among his early graduate students were Alfred Kroeber, Robert Lowie, Alexander Goldenweiser, Edward Sapir, and Paul Radin. With the exception of Kroeber, those named were immigrants, although, unlike Boas, they had grown up in the United States. After World War I, most of Boas's students were American born, although one student, Manuel Gamio, was Mexico's first professional anthropologist. Boas's male students of that era, among them Frank Speck, Melville Herskovits, and Alexander Lesser, like their predecessors, went on to build major academic departments. Boas also encouraged women students, some of whom like Ruth Benedict, Margaret Mead, Zora Neale Hurston, Gene Weltfish, and Ruth Landes, became well known. Nonetheless, even the best-known women anthropologists trained by Boas—Benedict and Mead—had professional careers that were more peripheral to academic centers of power than those of their male counterparts.

The extent to which the immigrant and/or Jewish background of many of the Boasian circle influenced both the development of the field and its reception, as well as their social activism, has been debated (see Hart 2003; V. J. Williams 1995). Perhaps their outsider status was a factor in their opposition to the dominant ideology of social evolutionism. Refuting the claims of a presumed hierarchy of development that justified domination by the so-called White race, the Boasians distinguished the variables of race, language, and culture and separated the concepts of "culture" and "civilization."

Boas's own prolific work spanned the four fields. In addition to his teaching and other commitments, he edited and contributed to numerous scientific publications, including the Handbook of American Indian Languages, the Journal of American Folklore and the International Journal of American Linguistics. He wrote extensively, both for academic and popular audiences, always challenging assumptions of cultural and racial superiority.

By training and inclination a natural scientist, he came to the United States at a time when the dominant anthropological task was to document and understand Native American cultures in their entirety before they vanished completely. This became his and his students' goal. It was also the time when immigration to the United Sates and the nativist reaction to it were at their peak. In an often-cited and still disputed statistical study Changes in Bodily Form of Descendants of Immigrants (1912), carried out in

Worcester, Massachusetts, Boas concluded that the measurements of immigrant children tended to conform to those of the general population. This was critical evidence undermining racial typologies and countering strict genetic determinism.

As Regna Darnell discusses in the next chapter, Boas took public stands throughout his career on behalf of academic freedom, civil rights, and liberal education. During World War I he was a pacifist, defending the claims of international science over those of nationalism in an intensely patriotic climate unfriendly to such views. After the publication of his 1911 work The Mind of Primitive Man, which argued that there was no pure or superior race, he was, and still is, attacked by White supremacists (see Baker 2004). In acts of "intellectual philanthropy" (Baker 1998b:17), he thereafter freely lent his name for use by organizations fighting for racial equality such as the National Association for the Advancement of Colored People (NAACP). Even within the anthropological profession he was personally attacked. In December 1919, in a letter published in the Nation, he accused unnamed anthropologists of spying and thereby betraying their profession. This act led to his censure by the American Anthropological Association, an astonishing rebuke from an organization that he had helped found and of which he had been elected president twelve years before.

Toward the end of his life he was an outspoken opponent of Fascism and Nazism, again refuting claims that one so-called "race" was superior to any other. He led a successful campaign to gather signatures for a "Scientists' Manifesto" to counter the Nazi regime's dissemination of their pseudoscientific ideology of Aryan superiority. Published in December 1938, a month after Kristallnacht, the manifesto was signed by almost 1,300 scientists from 167 universities. Among his projects was a study of high school textbooks examining the misuse of the concept of "race." In 1939 he popularized the findings through press conferences, radio shows, and publication of a pamphlet Can You Name Them? intended to reform how public schools taught about racial difference (Burkholder 2005). Still active, Boas died at lunch with colleagues in 1942.

After his death his civic influence continued. His collaboration with his friend and colleague W. E. B. Du Bois laid part of the intellectual foundation for the historic decision in the 1954 Supreme Court case Brown v. the Topeka Board of Education outlawing segregation in public schools. The NAACP legal team used Boas's work establishing the scientific basis of racial equality, but as Baker (1998a, 1998b) points out, not his relativistic contention that a culture must be judged on its own terms, because that position might have supported the "separate but equal" justification for segregation. Rather, they advocated assimilation into the dominant culture, along the lines advocated by liberal re-

formers for immigrants. American Negro culture was not independent of general American culture, they argued, but deficient because of its systematic exclusion from it.

In this and other ways, the controversial Boasian legacy extended well beyond the academy. Through their scholarship, the Boasians transformed anthropology in the United States and shaped the way culture is now viewed within and without the profession: relative, holistic, and pluralistic. In their practice, they combined moral commitment, scientific evidence, and new insights to challenge mainstream assumptions and create an anthropological tradition of involvement in political and social issues.—Editors.

Franz Boas (1858–1942) was without question the preeminent American anthropologist of at least the first half of the twentieth century. Beginning with his pedagogical mission in the ranks of his adopted science and adopted country, Boas moved anthropology from the aegis of government and museum to the academy, where his stringent standards of professional training and peer judgment could be implemented more effectively (Darnell 1998; D. Cole 1999; Hinsley 1981). To characterize Boas as a public educator in a broader frame requires a rather dramatic reassessment of the discipline's inherited understanding of Boas and his role in the history of anthropology.

Boas's first commitments to public education were focused in the great educational museums with which he was associated, the Field Columbian Museum in Chicago and principally the American Museum of Natural History in New York City. When the scientific standards of professionalization clashed with those of public edification, however, Boas chose to resign from the American Museum of Natural History, retreating to his teaching position at Columbia University. His was what George W. Stocking (1992:98) has called "pragmatic academic activism." He made this choice in full realization of its likely costs, at least in the short term, for his own organizational control of the increasingly professionalized discipline of anthropology. And he was prepared to wait for a wider public voice until it could be grounded in adequate science. Boas was laying the groundwork on multiple fronts: his first generation of students was filling newly available academic and museum positions at the same time that the scientific community and the general public beyond it were coming to acknowledge the significance of a Boasian paradigm for the scientific study of race, language, and culture. Boas perhaps concentrated his efforts as a public intellectual within his discipline because anthropology was a small science speaking from the margins of the academy. Scholars such as Thorsten Veblen and John Dewey, for example, had access to broader audiences, as did Margaret Mead for a later anthropology.

Nonetheless, Boas's position of scientific authority was consolidated during the years between the world wars, allowing him to emerge as a public intellectual of a stature unequalled in the social sciences in the years leading up to World War II. His outspoken commentaries on Nazi racism in Europe were built on his much earlier immigrant studies including those demonstrating human biological plasticity and the influence of culture on environment, as well as on his longstanding commitment to the emancipatory struggles of [African] Americans, Native Americans, and other minority groups. In the final years of his life, Boas chose to put aside his scientific work in order to pursue social justice, but still the social justice he envisioned remained indelibly anchored in the scientific methodology of his lifelong studies of human biology, culture, and language. He believed passionately in the role of the scientist as public intellectual and was uncompromising in pursuing the positions he championed. Boas had come to America to escape anti-Semitism, which he equated with seeking freedom of thought. The more he lamented the absence of such freedom, the more eagerly he harangued his fellow anthropologists and his fellow citizens to refashion a world in turmoil around the principles of anthropology. An examination of Boas's biography, publication record, and personal correspondence (available from the American Philosophical Society in Philadelphia on microfilm) would seem to make obvious the above characterization of Boas's pedagogical commitments across a wide range of venues and social or professional issues. But the intellectual successors of a seminal scientist often distinguish themselves from their mentor by deploying a rhetoric of discontinuity. Boas himself did so (1904) in rewriting the history of anthropology to begin with his own position.

Boas's reputation suffered considerable eclipse during the postwar years, in a rapidly changing scientific and social climate. Scientific positivism dominated an academy expanding to absorb returning veterans who were drawn to anthropology in an effort to come to terms with their enforced cross-cultural encounters abroad. The Cold War era initiated government support for research on a global scale in defense of American hegemony, with the study of the American Indian relegated to an increasingly marginal position, leading many among the new generation of anthropologists to dismiss "Boasian" anthropology as merely antiquarian, a descriptive rather than a theoretical enterprise. Now important action was thought to reside in the dismantling of colonial empires around the world. Theoretical and methodological parallels between the internal colonialism of North America and the emerging postcolonial nation-states of Africa and the Pacific were rarely explored. The majority of anthropologists seemingly ignored the non-Americanist Boasian ethnographic field sites and public commitments. In fact, however, the Americanist tradition actually cast its net far more broadly than the stereotype of nonjudgmental and apolitical relativism would suggest, both in terms of ethnographic forays outside native North America and use of ethnographic data to critique American society (Hymes 1972; Valentine and Darnell 1999; Darnell 2001).

Consensus among the postwar Boasian revisionists was that Boas had set back American anthropology by half a century because he was not a theoretician (among the most virulent of critics, see Wax 1956; White 1963, 1966; Harris 1968). Boas was alleged to have eschewed the possibility of scientific "laws" in anthropology, to have restricted his attention to descriptive facts about specific American Indian cultures culled from texts and informant memory rather than from observation of contemporary behavior. "Historical particularism" was not a compliment. Although Boas was acknowledged to have performed a useful service for anthropology by his late-nineteenth-century critique of social evolution, he was accused ex post facto of remaining mired in the negativity of deconstructing an inadequate paradigm.

The complexity of Boas's actual position has returned to professional visibility only recently, in great part through a persistent strain of Americanist work acknowledging its continuity with the Boasian paradigm (for examples of this reflexive building upon it, see Valentine and Darnell 1999; Darnell 2001; Hymes 1972; H. S. Lewis 1999). More nuanced interpretations of Boas's role in the discipline have certainly been around for a while, particularly from an historicist standpoint in the work of George W. Stocking Jr. (e.g., 1968, 1992, 2001) and from an Americanist and linguistic viewpoint in the works of Dell

Hymes (1983) and Stephen O. Murray (1994). It is remarkable then that Douglas Cole's posthumous biography of Boas's early years (from his birth in 1858 to 1906, when he resigned from the American Museum of Natural History) ignores a whole line of scholarship suggesting a more theoretical and activist Boas, accepting instead at face value an atheoretical and outmoded character to Boas's anthropology perceived to be a result of his "temperamental difficulty with making sustained and sweeping generalizations" (D. Cole 1999:160).

In actuality Boas was a theoretician, educator, and public intellectual of major significance in this historiographic context. His skills as an organizational leader built the premier department of anthropology in North America at Columbia, set a standard of professionalism and credentialism for the discipline, put a stamp on the emerging national institutions for anthropology, entrenched the four-subdisciplinary structure of the discipline, and maintained himself at the center of a close group of students and protégés who increasingly controlled the discipline. The Boasians were perceived by outsiders in terms of in-group identification, exclusionary practices, and cohesiveness in pursuit of common interests around Boas as patriarchal father figure.

Indeed, Boas was a positivist with a skeptical approach to explanation or generalization. He was not a systematic theorist, and his theoretical paradigm remained largely implicit and internal to the emerging discipline. But his theoretical ideas were influential both within and beyond anthropology. Transcending a narrow definition of education, Boas more broadly insisted that science must speak to social values, must function pedagogically. In museum exhibition, he interpreted this to mean that tribal rather than typological (evolutionary) classification alone could meet this educational function: "the main object of ethnological collections should be the dissemination of the fact that civilization is not something absolute, but that it is relative, and that our ideas and conceptions are true only so far as our civilization goes" (Boas 1887a:589). The disputes that these beliefs evoked with the American Museum administration centered around his opinion that the museum-going public should be educated through the exhibits to understand unbowdlerized science. Ultimately these differences led to his retreat to Columbia in 1906.

Boas was outspoken even before he had the power to effectively make his case when confronted with the scientific establishment. Documents from the time reflect "what would become Boasian thought" (Hyatt 1990:22). Both in his debates with Otis T. Mason and in his insistence on research as well as popular education at the American Museum, Boas displayed considerable courage, with the outcome by no means certain.[1]

Hyatt (1990:61) contends that Boas "was reacting to his own experiences with prejudice," attacking social evolution because it merely justified White Western Christian superiority, a sensitive rebuke to an upstart Jewish immigrant. Indeed, the anthropology Boas was to develop would establish common cause for Jews, women, Blacks, and immigrants. Hyatt contends that Boas's inclusive science arose from personal career disappointments of these early years (see D. Cole 1999), and that his activism targeted bigotry toward [African] Americans "rather than call attention to his own plight and risk accusations of subjectivity. . . . This camouflage became part of Boas' raison d'être for attacking all forms of human prejudice" (33–34).

Whatever his personal motivations, Boas continued taking political positions that made him unpopular in powerful circles. Prior to American entry into World War I, Boas energetically supported neutrality. Science for him was rational, whereas nationalism and patriotism were irrational. During the war, however, he was utterly silent and thus did not suffer active persecution for his views. He did attempt to protest the dismissal of various academics opposed to the war effort, including J. McLean Cattell at Columbia. The faculty "revolted" in support of the dissident faculty when Columbia threatened to investigate faculty "political sentiments" (Hyatt 1990:126); Boas's contribution to the revolt was to read six principles of science and the interests of mankind to his classes.

In 1919 he wrote a letter to the *Nation* in which he scathingly attacked scientists who had acted as spies in Mexico. The allegations Boas made were accurate, but not popular at the time. He saw such action as a perversion of science; the remainder of the scientific establishment in American anthropology labeled it as sedition (see Stocking 1968; Darnell 1998). Boas's political enemies within the discipline used his letter as an excuse to curb his increasing organizational power across American anthropology. In this case, however, the issues were also external. Hyatt (1990:134) argues that Boas became "disturbed with America" after this incident and that his "public respect for science" suffered as a result. At this time he had not yet achieved the role of "scientist-statesman" (131). This would only come later, during the prelude to World War II.

After the peace, Boas's next "crusade" was against the unjust settlement at Versailles (Hyatt 1990:134); he correctly identified a legacy of mistrust and dissension. His protests against the restrictive immigration act of 1924 identified it as a "new destructive type of nationalism" (136). Boas appeared personally before the congressional immigration committee without effect. But social Darwinism was in the ascendancy in the United States, with many Americans feeling threatened by the decreased homogeneity of their own society as a result of immigration and the wartime breakdown of isolationism. Boas's position was that racism restricted individual self-actualization and had undesirable consequences for society. The underlying ideology of American anthropology thus became one of cultural pluralism even though this agenda was superficially marked by a language of objectivist science (MacDonald 1998:22–23). Boas's larger pedagogical role in American society became increasingly important, however, as his professional stature increased and his discipline brought its message of cultural pluralism and tolerance to a general public caught up in an ever more complex world, both internally and internationally.

Boas was an organizational leader par excellence, creating a national network of his students that effectively controlled the discipline by about 1920 (Darnell 1998; Stocking 1968). Many were ambivalent about the control Boas maintained over former students and protégés in what he perceived to be the larger interests of American anthropology, about his sink-or-swim pedagogical method of graduate training, and about his lack of openness to some of their forays away from the shared paradigm (Darnell 1998, 2001). He was tireless in insisting that students repeat courses, study each subdiscipline, and receive training "in all facets of research" (Hyatt 1990:75). The students' discontent, however, was articulated mainly in private correspondence and must be interpreted in the context of an overarching loyalty both to Boas as mentor and to anthropology as he understood it.

Edward Sapir wrote to Robert H. Lowie (20 May 1925: R. H. Lowie Papers, George and Mary Foster Anthropology Library, University of California, Berkeley) characterizing their former teacher in terms of C. G. Jung's psychological types as a feeling introvert for whom science continually struggled to exclude personal subjectivity and to value thinking over feeling. Stocking (1992:110) has also privileged ambivalence in reading Boas's personality and personal style, with the "ice-cold flame of truth" warring with the emotional and irrational facet of his character as scientist and activist. Margaret Mead reported that she persuaded Boas to let her go to Samoa for her first fieldwork in 1925 by accusing him of behaving like a Prussian autocrat rather than the liberal democrat that was his ideal and self-image (MacDonald 1998:24).

In "The Study of Geography" (1887a) Boas made it clear that the sides of his temperament were inseparable from the sides of his science. Methodologically and theoretically, he distinguished the purportedly objective sciences of the natural world from the historical or cosmological approach to science characteristic of geography, the discipline from which he most immediately came to anthropology. Stocking (1968) has documented the continuity from Boas's disillusion with materialist physics to incorporating an observer effect in his human geography among the Eskimos and to his rejection of environmental determinism in favor of ethnology (with its inherent cultural specificity). Boas's first point was that science (producing "laws") and history (producing interpretations) were equally legitimate enterprises; the problem came only when their differences were not distinguished. Logic or aesthetics provided a proper discipline for science, whereas affect, feeling, and emotion came to the fore in the social sciences. The cosmographer "lovingly tries to penetrate" the secrets of the phenomena studied "until every feature is plain and clear. This occupation with the object of his affection affords him a delight not inferior to that which the physicist enjoys in his systematical arrangement of the world" (1887a, quoted in Stocking, 1996:14).

Despite the warmth of the erotic metaphor, however, it would be a mistake to assume that Boas intended to restrict his anthropology to a science of the subjective. The necessary other side of the coin was the rationalism of science whereby even social activism must be judged. There is no question that he saw himself as speaking for science, in method as well as content, to a general public. But to choose between the two forms of "science," a cover term on which he always insisted, was for Boas a matter of personal "standpoint" or "mental disposition" (Stocking 1996:15). His own disposition encouraged him to shift his standpoint systematically, from the historical to the psychological, from the analyst's model to what he called "the native point of view" (Darnell 2001).

Boas grew up with the ideals of the failed 1848 revolution in Germany, accepting without question the ideal of Bildung or self-realization (Liss 1996).

He acquired in childhood the idea of the importance of an intelligentsia, of public intellectuals who would serve as avatars of cultural change (see Stocking 1992:105). Boas was drawn to America by the "freedom of the American intellectual world" (Herskovits 1963:7) although he was soon and often to find it illusory.

The charge that Boas's work was atheoretical can be countered easily by noting his dual paradigm statements of 1911—the introduction to the *Handbook of American Indian Languages* (1911a), in which he distinguished race, language, and culture as analytically independent variables, and *The Mind of Primitive Man* (1911b), in which he attacked the scientific validity of racial types and consequently the hierarchical distinction among human races and cultures based upon them (see Stocking 1974b).

Boas had been building toward this theoretical synthesis of race and culture for some time. Surprisingly to many of his intellectual heirs, his argument began with the biological and universal rather than with the cultural and historically particular. As early as 1894, Boas tackled the "Human Faculty as Determined by Race" in his vice-presidential address to the American Association for the Advancement of Science (Boas 1895). The critique of evolutionism was soon to be thoroughly grounded in Boas's substantive studies in *Changes in Bodily Form of Descendants of Immigrants* (1912)—primarily in head form or cephalic index—for the Immigration Commission, then underway. The conclusions he drew from his work, doubtless expected by its sponsors to justify exclusion of immigrants, subverted the agendas of eugenics and scientific racism dominant in the first decade of the twentieth century. Boas discovered that head form could change in a single generation, leading to the inescapable conclusion that environment strongly modified heredity and thus that racial types were arbitrary. Consequently, the study of race gave way to the study of racism, the social construction of a purportedly biological category. At the time, however, Boas's work was ignored by government officials in favor of eugenicist agendas and his work received only limited attention in university circles; changing the dominant paradigm would take time (Baker 1998a:106). Baker argues persuasively that the paradigm shift usually attributed within anthropology to Boas in fact depended upon the conjunction of his empirical work and academic stature with the political economy of race as articulated by African American activist W. E. B. Du Bois and others (107).

In fact, it seems clear that Boas was only one among a group of liberal reform intellectuals in America, not all of them native born, who challenged what they perceived as a smug isolationism and melting-pot image of potential homogeneity based on social Darwinism. Baker (1998a:99) identifies Boas in anthropology, Du Bois in sociology, Charles A. Beard in history, Louis Brandeis in law, Thorsten Veblen and John R. Commons in economics, and John Dewey in education as "muckrakers in an ivory tower." Their pedagogy was aimed at educating the general public to join them in seeking social reform.

Although most anthropologists remember Boas primarily as a largely apolitical student of the American Indian (for exceptions see V. J. Williams 1996; Baker 1998a), his collaboration with Du Bois and early activism on behalf of the American Negro apply a shared German "methodological orientation that emphasized inductive reasoning and the empirical gathering of descriptive and historical data" (Baker 1998a:119).

Baker further suggests (119) that the reason Du Bois and Boas clicked so well in their balancing of scholarship and activism was because they both had "firsthand experience with persecution and discrimination." Boas's Jewishness has been raised in discussions of his activism, perhaps because he and many of his early students were Jewish and immigrants and because he became a powerful critic of Nazi anti-Semitism in the final years of his life.

Framing Boas's public statements of political position alongside those of his intellectual contemporaries, however, makes the Jewish explanation less persuasive. Boas's immigrant studies focused on southern Europeans more than Jews and his activism centered around African American political struggles; anti-Semitism did not become his primary target until the rise of the Nazis. Whatever the sensitivization entrained by personal experience, Boas was consistent in his commitment to unmasking racism and bigotry in all their forms.

Nor can the anthropological contribution to liberal reform be attributed to a Jewish bias among the Boasians and their allies across the social sciences. John Dewey, philosopher and educator, espoused anthropological relativism in its Boasian form, arguing that enculturation or socialization should be the focus of pedagogical attention. Education and science could lead to positive reconstitution of society. Dewey wrote the forward to Paul Radin's influential *Primitive Man as Philosopher* in 1927. Although both Boas and Radin were Jewish and were anthropologists seeking to foreground culture rather than biology as the root of human differences, Dewey and Boas's sociologist colleague at Columbia, William Fielding Ogburn, were not Jewish. Along the same lines as Baker, Eric Wolf (1972:256) emphasized in the link between Boas and Dewey that Boas's intellectual defense of liberal reform required attention to the practical constraints of power in order to have any real-world effects.

In his foreword to the 1963 reissue of *The Mind of Primitive Man*, Boas's former student Melville Herskovits stressed the importance of the volume when it initially appeared. Like Boas, Herskovits turned from race to culture (of African, Caribbean, and [African] American worlds), finding Boasian precedents at each stage of his career. Boas's introduction was, in Herskovits's view, the "first single work which, in the best scientific tradition, derived its conclusions from measured, objective analysis, and presented its data in terms of their wider implications, marshalling the known facts to bring them to bear on disputed questions" (1963:6). Boas was concerned to attack American racial bigotry and muster science in support of equality. Boas challenged racial determination of "human faculty" and the influence of physical on mental processes. His final chapter deployed history to tackle the problem of race in American society.

Although the term *racism* was coined only during World War II, Boas had long protested "the utilization of the concept of race for political ends" (Herskovits 1963:5). Boas rewrote the book substantially to incorporate new research and new social applications in a changed political context. He waged a campaign directed to the general public to prevent the spread of Nazism to America, speaking widely "to attack anti-Semitism, pseudo-scientific race theory and the suppression of free thought" (Hyatt 1990:146). These issues were all interrelated, part of his long-standing contention that race, language, and culture must be treated as distinct variables. But now Boas was explicit about anti-Semitism rather than prejudice in general. Hyatt (147) argues: "No longer was he able to appear the detached, objective scientist, for he was no longer utilizing a surrogate cause to mask his true concern." This accusation belies the fact that the critique of scientific racism of the end of Boas's career also targeted the persistent aftermath of Negro slavery in the United States, as well as assertions of Aryan superiority in Europe. Interestingly, Boas was never particularly interested in American Indian political issues, apparently content to leave this side of his work to ethnological "science" rather than its activist interface. He protested the Canadian legislation outlawing the potlatch and intervened in local matters affecting George Hunt and other Northwest Coast collaborators. But he did not make political activism a tenet of ethical Americanist fieldwork. Since most of his students were Americanists, his omission of Aboriginal issues from his definition of American cultural politics doubtless contributed to the retrospective sense that Boas was fundamentally apolitical. Furthermore, politics, like theory, was implicit and unsystematic for Boas almost to the end of his life and the Nazi critique.

The Mind of Primitive Man weathered well, and Boas did not change his argument over the rest of his career. He concluded in his preface to the 1938 edition, as he had in 1911: "There is no fundamental difference in the ways of thinking of primitive and civilized man. A close connection between race and personality has never been established. The concept of racial type as commonly used even in scientific literature is misleading and requires a logical as well as biological definition" (in Boas 1938b:17). Therefore, environment and culture still must be considered inseparable from race. Boas might well have taken pride in the burning of the German edition (published in 1914 under the title Kultur und Rasse) by the Nazis in 1933. The danger of ideas was clearly recognized within a totalitarian regime.

There are, of course, difficulties with the position articulated in 1911 and consistently maintained throughout Boas's career. The paramount critic of evolution was ironically trapped in some of its categories. Herskovits (1963:10) argued that Boas's definitions of "the primitive" and of "race" retained evolutionary overtones that his own argument should have rendered obsolete. Boas maintained a commitment to progress, to a distinction between culture(s) and civilization, which would seem to contradict the cultural relativism that has been the hallmark of the Boasian position. Cultural relativism, in this reading, reflects the characteristically Boasian dualism of science and history. On the one hand, the surface diversity of culture forms resolves itself into a universal humanity based on scientific studies of race, language, and culture. On the other hand, "the role of emotional association in shaping judgments" led Boas to the threshold of a "comparative study of values" that would soon be constructed upon his pioneering work (10–11). Boas's intellectual heirs would finally transcend the lingering remnants of his evolutionary certainty about the nature and ownership of civilization.

The Mind of Primitive Man is not an easily accessible book for a lay audience. Boas was disinclined to compromise "in his feeling that no concession to his readers should obscure the stark scientific quality of his data and his concepts" (1911b:xi). Even as a public intellectual, Boas insisted on scientific credibility and detailed evidence. The evidence was necessary to support rational scientific conclusions. His conclusions were based in science.

In the book's 1938 preface, however, he shifted attention from the conclusions of his scientific research to issues of academic freedom and the public's right to apply science to the persistence of racism in American society. He aspired to educate Americans about the critical importance of freedom of thought and the need for a politics of science. Crucially, science could not be separated from its supporting social infrastructure; Boas simultaneously lamented the increasingly disturbing events in Europe and worried that similar dangers could threaten American society:

> Still worse is the subjection of science to ignorant prejudice in countries controlled by dictators. Such control has extended particularly to books dealing with the subject matter of race and culture. Since nothing is permitted to be printed that runs counter to the ignorant whims and prejudices of the governing clique, there can be no trustworthy science. When a publisher whose pride used to be the number and value of his scientific books announces in his calendar a book trying to show that race mixture is not harmful, withdraws the same book after a dictator comes into power, when great [en]cyclopedias are rewritten according to prescribed tenets, when scientists either do not dare or are not allowed to publish results contradicting the prescribed doctrines, when others, in order to advance their own material interests or blinded by uncontrolled emotion follow blindly the prescribed road no confidence can be placed in their statements. The suppression of intellectual freedom rings the death knell of science. (1938b:17–18)

Boas's position rested on the applicability of scientific method to the study of human culture. His argument was both theoretical and remarkably contemporary in its openness to continuous scientific revision of contingent and provisional results:

> In scientific inquiries we should always be clear in our own minds that we always embody a number of hypotheses and theories in our explanations, and

that we do not carry the analysis of any given phenomenon to completion. If we were to do so, progress would hardly be possible, because every phenomenon would require an endless amount of time for thorough treatment. We are only too apt, however, to forget entirely the general, and for most of us purely traditional, theoretical basis which is the foundation of our reasoning, and to assume that the result of our reasoning is absolute truth. (1938b:201)

After the limited public response to the original edition of The Mind of Primitive Man, Boas directed his next theoretical statement of his paradigmatic method, the 1928 work Anthropology and Modern Life, to a more popular audience. He defined the science of man (taking for granted its relevance to "modern life") before plunging into the core of the matter: "the problem" of race and the interrelations of races, dealt with scientifically. Boas then discussed nationalism before turning to eugenics, the nation-state's perversion of the scientific study of race and to abuses of racial typing in criminology (lamentably reminiscent of the "ethnic profiling" of our own day). Somewhat more than half the book preceded its turn to culture. Although the rate of change in so-called primitive societies was quite gradual, culture could be understood as stable. Moreover, both "primitive" and "civilized men" [sic] were wont to rationalize the forms of their culture. Rational and irrational elements coexisted in both.

Boas turned next to education, in the narrow sense of schooling and socialization, gradually broadening his definition to include the continuing education of citizens. This redefinition of education immediately followed the all-important topic of race and racism. Boas emphasized variability within groups and the pedagogical needs of the individual, citing positively "the pedagogical anthropology" of Maria Montessori (1928a:168) on behalf of the Bildung of the individual student. Evidence of physical growth was related to social class and sex, with a view to "laying out a standard of demands that may be made on boys and girls of various ages and belonging to a certain society" (177). It is impossible to sort out the relative roles of environment and heredity (thus, the question ceases to be interesting for issues of social reform and educational policy).

"Anthropology throws light upon an entirely different problem of education" (Boas 1928a:184). Individuals in "primitive tribes" were trapped by their "customary forms of thought" but considered themselves free. Our own society as well followed habits learned in childhood. Educational methods were dependent upon "our ideals" (187), despite rare consciousness of the conflict in democratic society between individual freedom and the teaching of shared symbols restricting such freedom. Boas argued, in the same year that his former student Margaret Mead published *Coming of Age in Samoa* (1928), that traumatic adolescence might be a product of such cultural conflict for the individual rather than a cultural universal. Boas cited Mead's work among several others by his students or protégés. He seemed to believe that a stable society, changing slowly, would avoid such conflicts. His position was contrastive: the children of immigrants to America had no such sense of continuity and security. American pluralism raised challenges that the so-called primitive society need not face.

Traditional teaching was insidious even within scientific specializations, because established ideas were acquired by "infusion" (1928a:195), especially through socialization within a small-scale and presumably homogeneous society. The "critical faculty" was entrained within a narrow range, leaving the educated classes without an overall critical standpoint (196). Even intellectuals were inclined to be "conventional" because "their thoughts were based on tradition"; only a few escaped to true freedom of thought (197). This was more likely in a heterogeneous society. Education, then, should be a continual process of evaluating the past and breaking free of it to create new ideals. The major problem of modern society was its "conflict of ideals," which might be avoided in a simpler, more homogeneous society (202). He largely ignored rapid cultural changes and increasing complexity of Native American societies relative to change in the mainstream. His second generation of students (such as Herskovits) would move to incorporate such change.

The method of the anthropologist demanded "emancipation from our own culture," which was difficult because everyone was inclined to see his or her own behavior as natural. "Scientific anthropology" began with the physical or organic side of things in order to determine universals. The "objective study" of historically distinct traditions produced "a standpoint that enables him to view our own civilization critically, and to enter into a comparative study of values" (Boas 1928a:207). Boas equated "freedom of judgment" with the ability to distinguish cultural and biological causes, always a fraught task because of the observer's own standpoint. The social sciences could never become exact

or predictive because of the complexity of variables and our inability to experiment on human societies. But the anthropologist could understand, if not explain, social phenomena—the very distinction of science and history that Boas
had embraced in 1887. Absolute progress was impossible, although some re-
current tendencies in values and moral standards could be identified across
civilizations. "Simple tribes" and "closed societies" could offer alternatives
for the critique of the anthropologist's own society. Anthropology could guide
policy in modern life (245) even though there was no single theory to which
social phenomena could be reduced. Boas asked his targeted popular audience to accept a remarkably postmodernist view of knowledge and science.
The moral commitment of the anthropologist as social critic acknowledging
and amplifying voices from the margins of the dominant society guaranteed
that the practice of anthropology would be a profoundly political—and pedagogical—endeavor.

Anthropology and Modern Life appeared in 1928 before the traumas of the Nazi
rise to power in Germany and the virtual inevitability of war. In the late 1930s,
Boas continued to seek an anthropological voice in the public domain. Although the wartime and postwar work of Margaret Mead and Ruth Benedict
on cultures at a distance now seems more salient, Boas took his legacy seriously. Education was at the core of his last political commitments.

After Boas was forced to retire from teaching in 1936 because of his age,
he became increasingly critical of the academy, first at Columbia and later
beyond. He urgently believed that power should be retained in the hands of
teachers because administration limited freedom both to teach and to learn
(Hyatt 1990:149). Education, centered within the academy where public intellectuals were most often produced, was the most effective way to counteract
prejudice. His academic politics, however, remained closely tied to his anti-
racism. University education was a means to this end.

> It was in the area of race that Boas had his greatest impact on American society
> and on future intellectual thought. By emphasizing the importance of each
> culture's values and by promoting "an understanding of the human misery,
> degradation and demoralization that can result when one people imposes its
> way on another," Boas changed many minds both within academic circles and
> in the general community. (Hyatt 1990:155)

In 1938 Boas consolidated his position in a textbook, *General Anthropology*, with some of the chapters written by former students and protégés. He suggested that it was impossible for a single person to cover the full scope of anthropology but asserted that the collectivity could do so and could be taken to speak with a single [Boasian] voice:

> Anthropology covers such a wide range of subjects that it is difficult for one person to be equally conversant with all its aspects. For this reason cooperation of a group of students, most of whom have worked in close contact for many years, seemed a justifiable solution of the task of preparing a general book on anthropology. Thus a greater number of viewpoints could be assembled, and the unavoidable divergence in the handling of diverse problems by a number of authors is, we hope, offset by the advantage of having the special points of view in which each author is interested brought out. (Boas 1938a:iii)

Taken together, the papers encapsulated the Boasian paradigm. The volume simultaneously co-opted the collaborators to maintain their shared position with Boas as the intellectual center and *pater familias*. Despite his disclaimers of sole authority, Boas reserved a number of key positions for himself: the brief introduction on the scope of anthropology, plus the chapters on race; language; invention; literature, music, and dance; mythology and folklore; methods of research; and the conclusion (considerably more elaborated than the introduction).

In 1940, two years before his death, Boas collected his major papers into a single volume, entitled *Race, Language and Culture*—the triangulation of independent classificatory variables identified in 1911, which remained crucial to his theoretical thinking thereafter. The collection included twenty papers on race, five on linguistics, thirty-five on culture, and three miscellaneous. The definition of race, succinctly stated in the brief preface, presumably on the assumption that the papers spoke for themselves, reflected changing language in biological anthropology but remained consistent with the substance of the immigrant head-form studies of the early century: "The terms 'race' and 'racial' are throughout used in the sense that they mean the assembly of genetic lines represented in a population" (Boas 1940:v).

Professional opinion of the quality of Boas's immigrant head-form studies remains hotly debated today, on ideological as well as methodological grounds. Sparks and Jantz (2002; see also Wade 2002) attribute to Boas an environmental determinism, which they believe is disproved by contemporary sociobiology. They seek to rehabilitate cranial typology as an accurate method for both fossil and living human studies. Their reanalysis of Boas's results invalidates his conclusions about plasticity of bodily form in descendants of immigrants. In contrast, Gravlee, Bernard, and Leonard (2003) praise Boas's studies of human plasticity for their effective challenge to scientific racism. Their reanalysis of Boas's data confirms his results and even strengthens some of them using inferential statistics and computational methods not available to him. For these authors, Boas remains a heroic figure, both in his science and in his politics.

Whatever the intentional legacy of Boas's pedagogy, within the academy and beyond its gates, the historiographic question of continuing influence remains. I identify only three such continuities here, although many other exemplars could have been chosen.

First, Dell Hymes's edited collection *Reinventing Anthropology*, published in 1972 and still relevant to contemporary practice, suggests that Boasian activism is best remembered among Americanist anthropologists and linguists but defines anthropology in terms that apply more widely: "interest in other peoples and their ways of life, and concern to explain them within a frame of reference that includes ourselves" with a view to "ultimate fulfillment of human potentiality" (Hymes 1972:11). The volume as a whole reflects a 1960s optimism that anthropology has something to say to the larger world and that anthropologists can move effectively between scholarship and activism, between observation and participation. Such political and scholarly commitments are being reclaimed by many in recent years.

Second, Eric Wolf's *Envisioning Power* (1999) builds on the insights of his contribution to the Hymes volume, calling politically committed anthropologists to consider relations of power as well as to respect the diversity and integrity of all cultures. This political economy approach was lacking in the early Boasian work but is not inconsistent with the refashioning of global society that Wolf envisions.

Third, Michael Ignatieff's summary of human rights issues (2001) reflects contemporary stresses in the anthropologically designed United Nations Declaration of Human Rights but nonetheless accepts a useful continuity to the

Boasian positions on citizenship, public responsibility, and activism informed by science. This Boasian package has become so commonplace that it is hardly acknowledged as having Boasian roots, politically or methodologically. Paradigmatic success often engenders "invisible genealogies" (Darnell 2001).

These contemporary works, representative of many others that could have been chosen, suggest that the Boasian legacy is alive and well. Anthropologists today are reexamining their Americanist genealogies (Darnell 2001) and finding in Boas a theoretical sophistication, methodological rigor, pedagogical commitment, and political activism that is far from outdated. Rewriting the history of Boas as public intellectual and model for anthropological praxis has been long overdue.

Notes

1. Editors' note: Otis Tufton Mason (1838–1908) was the first curator of ethnology at the U.S. National Museum (now the National Museum of Natural History) and later its head curator. He was associated with the museum, part of the Smithsonian Institution in Washington DC, from 1884 until his death in 1908. Boas criticized Mason's method of displaying objects based on an "evolutionary" rather than "functional" paradigm. Similar objects from different cultures were displayed together as inventions rather than in holistic and specific cultural contexts. Similarly, Mason's pioneering *Women's Share in Primitive Culture* (1894), although important as an early record of women's economic, ritual, and political roles, suffers from the same fault because its scattered references are taken out of historic and ethnographic context.

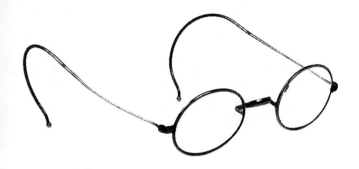

2. Ruth Benedict

Relativist and Universalist

Virginia Heyer Young

Ruth Benedict in the American Southwest in the 1930s. Courtesy of the National Anthropological Archives, Smithsonian Institution (86-1323).

Among the many accomplishments of Ruth Benedict (1887–1948) are developing the concept of cultural configuration, applying psychology to the study of culture, and using anthropological insights to interpret complex cultures. Closely associated with Franz Boas, her teacher, and Margaret Mead, her student, she shared with them the belief that the anthropological perspective is vital to understanding human behavior and to improving our own society; and a commitment to scientific activism that furthers tolerance, democracy, and human acceptance of difference based on culture but not race.

She wrote two influential books, which were among the first to bring the anthropological perspective to a wide reading public. Neither was an ethnography, nor was Benedict a dedicated fieldworker. Patterns of Culture (1934b) grew out of her experiences among Native Americans in the Southwest, where she spent about eight months in the field during the 1920s. The Chrysanthemum and the Sword: Patterns of Japanese Culture (1946a) was based on secondary sources, since she had not visited Japan nor could she read Japanese. Their enduring popularity attests to her skill in interpreting and making accessible seemingly remote cultures. Both deal with Benedict's major themes of the psychological integration of cultures and the variability between them, and the relationship between emotions and culture.

Benedict was born in New York City in 1887 to Bertrice and Frederick Fulton; her mother was a teacher educated at Vassar College, her father a homeopathic physician and surgeon. Both her parents were from upstate New York farming families and were Baptists, with deacons on both sides of the family. The death of her father when she was less than two years old and its shattering effect on her mother were traumatic events from which the family never recovered. Adding to her difficult childhood, she was partially deaf due to an illness in infancy. She later wrote that she learned to live in the world of her imagination from an early age (1935, posthumously in Mead, 1959a:97–117). She grew up on her maternal grandparents' farm and then in Buffalo, New York, where she and her younger sister were educated in an Episcopal girls school. They both attended Vassar College on full scholarships provided by a family acquaintance. After graduation, Ruth taught school, and five years later, in 1914, she married Stanley Benedict, a professor of biochemistry at Cornell University Medical School.

During the early years of her marriage she completed a biography of the early feminist Mary Wollstonecraft, but the manuscript was rejected for publication. She also did volunteer social work. She began to write poetry, and over her lifetime much of it was published pseudonymously. When her marriage proved childless, she sought a career, studying first educational philosophy with John Dewey at Columbia University, then anthropology with

Elsie Clews Parsons at the New School for Social Research. She transferred to Columbia University in 1921 to work under Franz Boas. Her PhD dissertation, "The Concept of the Guardian Spirit in North America," completed in 1923, written when she was in her thirties, discusses the cultural implications of an individual religious experience, a topic that foreshadowed her later interest in the culture-and-personality approach she pioneered.

Benedict and her husband separated in 1930; soon after she began a happy acknowledged lesbian relationship. Boas hired her as the first full-time member of the Columbia Department of Anthropology in addition to himself. She remained on the faculty the rest of her life. She was promoted to full professor only a few months before her untimely death in 1948, which occurred during her term of office as president of the American Anthropological Association.

Patterns of Culture, her first book, was a landmark in anthropological theory because she described cultural integration, rather than documenting cultural elements or traits. She contrasted three cultures—the Zuni of the American Southwest, the Dobu of Melanesia, and the Kwakiutl of British Columbia—characterizing them as "Apollonian," moderate, or as "Dionysian," excessive. She introduced psychological terms into her analysis, identifying the Dobu as paranoid and the Kwakiutl as megalomaniac. Although her depiction of these cultures, particularly the Apollonian Zuni, has been challenged (Li An-che; Leacock 1972b:24–25; Goldfrank 1978), her approach to personality and culture—by which she meant that a culture was a "personality writ large"—and to cultural configurations was new and quickly adopted by other anthropologists, among them her students Margaret Mead and Jules Henry. Ruth Landes, also her student, collected life histories, another method Benedict advocated.

As Virginia Heyer Young points out in the next chapter, despite the academic and popular impact of Patterns of Culture, this book's message of cultural relativism often is oversimplified. Although Benedict claimed that cultures must be understood as a whole in their own terms, she did make judgments. In fact, a historian of the field suggests that Patterns of Culture can be read as an implied criticism of the United States. Two of the three cultures she studied could be seen as pathological parodies of the worst aspects of the Puritan and robber-baron traditions, while the Apollonian integration of the Zuni presented a sharp contrast to the waste and wanton destruction that threatened the future of Western civilization (Stocking 2002:48).

In the 1930s Benedict became well known as a public intellectual. Her many articles and book reviews in general periodicals continued to bring the anthropological point of view to the public. She wrote often about the equal endowment of different races, and she spoke out in her classes against homophobia. Her book Race: Science and Politics (1940) was part of her and Boas's involvement with the fight against fascism, racism, and Nazism, in the context of the threat to democracy posed by global war. Like Boas, Benedict argued that there was no scientific basis for racism or racial discrimination. The scientific evidence to the contrary reached a large audience when Benedict and Gene Weltfish used it as the basis for a Public Affairs Committee pamphlet, The Races of Mankind (1943).

Explicitly refuting Nazi propaganda, Benedict and Weltfish called for a "Science Front" to counter claims of Aryan superiority (1943:2). Discussing the variables of height, blood, head shape, and skin color, they concluded that there is only one human race. Jews, they wrote, physically resembled the populations among whom they lived. The term Aryan, as used by Hitler, had no meaning—racial, linguistic, or otherwise (11). To demonstrate that there was no difference in intelligence by race, Benedict and Weltfish included a chart of scores from intelligence tests taken by American soldiers in World War I. Because it showed that the scores of northern Negroes were higher than those of southern Whites, a Kentucky congressman caused the pamphlet's distribution to the U.S. armed forces to be blocked. The ensuing controversy brought a wider readership.

During World War II Benedict worked for the Office of War Information in Washington DC. Her insightful but little-known analysis of Romanian culture, discussed by Virginia Young, is an example of the "culture-at-a-distance" approach she pioneered. Another is her much-cited The Chrysanthemum and the Sword. A best seller, it was credited with shaping and moderating government policy and public opinion toward Japan after the war. Studying culture at a distance continued at the Columbia University Research in Contemporary Cultures project, also under government sponsorship, directed first by Benedict and then by Rhoda Metraux and Margaret Mead.

Young focuses on Benedict's later work, the "area beyond cultural relativity," a concept Benedict planned to develop further. As Young shows, Benedict was not only interested in personality and individual types, but also in social organization and human behavior. She used the comparative method to yield subtle insights into which system provided the greatest good for the greatest number. Benedict also explored cultural contradictions, such as that in the United States between slavery and a political system based on professed democratic ideals. Although the notion of "cultural relativity" is sometimes misused as a justification for moral neutrality, this was not Benedict's intention. She herself was outspoken about the fallacy and harm in stereotyping groups such as the poor, youth, or minorities. Her analyses of cultural configurations, culture and personality, and culture-at-a-distance went well beyond "cultural relativity" to add new dimensions to anthropology.

Ruth Benedict excelled at describing the inner logic and fundamental humanity of other cultures. She delved deeply enough into their values to discern their
virtues and faults, even as she advocated cultural relativism to overcome ethnocentrism and to comprehend contrasting norms of behavior. She wrote of the
rich diversity of cultural patterns, differently imagined ways of thinking and
arranging social life. She also wrote that some cultures undermine the security
of some of its members, whether by depriving them of access to things valued
or severely restricting whole categories of persons. Yet when some cultures
reputed mainly for their weaknesses were studied more deeply, they might be
seen at the same time to celebrate human dignity and give voice to universal
human anxieties, thus enabling their members to achieve resolution of common problems of social life. Understanding cultures in the many-faceted way
Ruth Benedict described them may help in easing the confrontational cultural
clashes that occur in a multicultural society.

Benedict's methods directly address problems now recognized in American
education. For example, she identified the discontinuity in culture learning
that arose when contradictory patterning had to be learned at different stages
of the life cycle, a situation she showed was structured into many societies. She
explored the uses of shame as a sanction for reinforcing the codes and patterning of culture, a sanction different from guilt. Benedict was prompted by the
crisis of totalitarianism in her time to reevaluate the weaknesses and strengths
and the distinctive characteristics of American society. She thought in terms of
overarching culture patterns and also had the ethnographer's eye for the mi-
nutiae of behavior in which she often saw actions and reasonings that were the
key to analysis. Her observations on several aspects of American culture made
during the 1940s still signal useful models today. Benedict set up frameworks
for posing problems in American society and education.

This chapter takes many of its illustrations from Benedict's seldom-dis-
cussed writings. Her first book, *Patterns of Culture* (1934b), is the only work
cited in most references to her. It had a great impact in anthropology; yet her

articles that followed it and developed her theory of culture beyond the 1934 book appear to be unread. This has led to misunderstanding of her thought. Moreover, advocates of universal human rights who hold that relativism and universalism are antithetical have labeled her an extreme relativist (Zechenter 1997). Benedict believed that relativism was an essential perspective in understanding cultures and in overcoming ethnocentrism; and she also weighed, with the comparative method, which social arrangements promote human rights and which allow exploitation of the many by the few. To label her an extreme relativist overlooks her publications on the subject. Her last book, *The Chrysanthemum and the Sword: Patterns of Japanese Culture* (1946a) extended the concept of culture pattern from kin-based societies to a stratified and hierarchical society. Although it has been influential in the field of Japan studies, one important part of that book was less noticed, a more clear differentiation of individuals from the culture pattern than in much of the work on personality and culture at the time, which she phrased as a self within culture. She had developed the concept of self in her four national culture studies done for the Office of War Information (hereafter OWI); it was a new way of thinking about the relation of individuals to culture. Her death in 1948 at the height of her productivity precluded the writing she planned about her more developed approach. A book précis indicates her plans and the ideas from her articles that she intended to pursue further. This chapter takes illustrations from her overlooked publications and from her manuscripts to present a fuller picture than is generally available of her contribution to anthropology, much of it still relevant to contemporary educational research.

I studied with Ruth Benedict from 1946 to 1948. She taught the full field of classical cultural anthropology, including social organization, religions of primitive peoples, history of culture theory, area courses on Australia, Melanesia, and American Indians, carefully preparing a new generation of anthropologists. She taught personality and culture for the first time as a lecture course in 1946–1947, previously having taught it as a seminar, a format for exploring the subject. She missed class only the few occasions when she was lecturing out of town. She could always be found in her office, and she took a close interest in students' work, their questions, their financial needs, and in them as individuals. Her own devotion to her work spurred students to match her drive.

Her courses were so packed with knowledge, with interpretive discourse, and with statements of her own position and of the direction she wanted students to take, so overflowing, that I never could throw away my notes, although eventually I discarded all my other graduate course notes. Aware that her book *Patterns of Culture* was being stereotyped by a later generation of students, I began researching her unpublished manuscripts and collecting the many ideas that she broached there and in her courses, but that remained scattered or unexplained in her published works. I then sought other students' course notes and found three sets that had been saved. They happened to be from the same years as mine, narrowing the time range, but bringing an authenticating overlap of text. All the sets had the fullness of raptly attentive students, and some caught points others had missed. I collated the four sets of notes into a "text" for each course, not verbatim texts, but very close approximations. These course notes make up a lengthy appendix in my book *Ruth Benedict: Beyond Relativity, Beyond Pattern* (Young 2005). I think these course "texts" even today give a good education in anthropology. They help today's readers understand Ruth Benedict's published and unpublished works by adding her commentaries on many points. A few passages from these course texts are included in this chapter and are identified by the name of the course and the date of the lecture. In this way the interested reader can look up the lecture to find the context of the quoted passage.

Patterns of Culture

Ruth Benedict's greatest influence was through her first book, *Patterns of Culture*, published in 1934. She wrote that cultures integrate themselves through the psychological factors in a people's habits and attitudes. People choose to adopt or reject cultural practices they learn about through neighboring peoples, often reinterpreting these practices in accord with their own ways, and they adapt their institutions to accommodate their own psychological makeup, thus developing a distinctive pattern of culture. The pattern is enacted, reinforced, taught, and affirmed, and it is elaborated as external and internal forces call for change. Pattern in this book was not uniform or static, but was a product of human agency. *Patterns of Culture* also demonstrated the great differences in attitudes and values in the multitude of cultures and advocated tolerance of the full range of cultures. Each was a solution to common human problems, and all that continued to reproduce themselves were work-able, more or less, in their context. The basic points—the relativity of culture, the psychological basis of cultural integration, and the large range of workable cultural solutions—were developed from their initial foreshadowing in Franz Boas's anthropological work.

The impact of this book among anthropologists and other social scientists was immediate. It was recognized as a persuasive formulation of the central aspects of Boasian cultural anthropology and a new argument for the force of psychic aspects of culture as well as an expansion of anthropological inquiry to the relation of individuals to culture. The first criticisms proposed revisions in her examples of patterning and did not challenge the cultural and psycho-logical framework she had posed (Bennett 1946). Later criticisms came from the perspective of economic determinism and denied any causative influence on culture from psychological factors (Harris 1968; Diamond 1969). Benedict continued to speak and write in opposition to economic determinism and ma-terialism, which were increasingly employed as what she considered a reduc-tive platform in anthropology in this period. *Patterns of Culture* was acknowl-edged widely as a landmark, and its influence in anthropology and outside it continued. Forty years after its publication a historian of the field wrote it "remains today the single most influential work by a twentieth century Ameri-can anthropologist" (Stocking 1974a:73).

Beyond Cultural Relativity

Benedict moved on to several new investigations, among them problems se-lected for discussion here, including the discontinuous learning of culture and the sanctions employed in different cultures to reinforce codes and patterning. Her principal investigation after *Patterns of Culture* was what she called "an area beyond cultural relativity." By this she meant that "cultural arrangements" could be correlated with their "social effects" such as promotion or disruption of general welfare and security, and promotion or denial of a sense of being free. She had posed this problem, briefly and in less developed terms, in the penultimate chapter of *Patterns of Culture* (1934b:229), and she soon launched into research on the topic. As her ideas on problems of universal conditions of a good society matured, the rise of fascism in Germany and Italy confronted social scientists with an obligation to address immediate social crises in our own society. Benedict delayed an intended book on the area beyond cultural relativity and devoted a 1939 sabbatical to writing the widely read and influential *Race: Science and Politics* (1940). With Gene Weltfish she prepared an abbreviated version, *Races of Mankind* (1943), which was briefly distributed to the U.S. armed forces before being withdrawn for political reasons. Later condensed and retitled *In Henry's Backyard: The Races of Mankind* (1948), it was republished with illustrations from the animated film produced with the backing of the United Automobile Workers (CIO). In both its book and animated form, this work was distributed to an even wider audience. *Patterns of Culture* was also put out in an armed forces edition, further enlarging its readership.

A statement of some of Benedict's findings on "an area beyond relativity" was published in an *Atlantic Monthly* article, "Primitive Freedom" (1942a). A more theoretical and fuller presentation of the work was included in a lecture series that she gave at Bryn Mawr College in 1941. There she illustrated how various social institutions promote or disrupt the general welfare and security in societies. She referred to institutions having social effects of high and low synergy; however, she did not thereafter use the word *synergy* and instead used other phrases for the idea of a free and beneficial society.[1] She probably intended to return to the problem of describing conditions for security and freedom in human cultures. She told her students that the question to pursue was under what cultural arrangements are different social ends achieved (Theory 1/15/48).

The crisis of World War II made urgent a need to understand state societies that were allies or enemies of the United States. Anthropologists and other social scientists were enlisted to draw up background analyses of these societies to assist government policymakers. They played a large role, particularly because the field later called area specialization was slightly developed at that time. The idea of a holistic pattern of culture, which Ruth Benedict had cogently presented in her 1934 book, was one of the tools sought out for this task. She spent a year and a half with the OWI in Washington on intensive research and analysis. The work was thought to be urgent for survival of the Western democracies. She noted problems in democracy as a system of organization more than some other influential thinkers of the period,[2] and pointed to difficulty in self-protection in primitive democratic societies, as well as impediments to social reform in the workings of American democracy. She also noted that some hierarchical cultures combined stability with respect for different statuses. Her work on the area beyond cultural relativity was put aside for the most part in the huge leap from descriptions of small relatively independent societies to the study of nation-states contending militarily for territory and wealth.

One question Benedict had taken up, of how cultural values and prescriptions are sanctioned, was a relevant background for understanding the controls that governments exercised over their peoples. Discontinuous learning was equally at issue in the changes demanded in dynamic state societies and in the ethnic multiplicity incorporated into many states, and in anticipated problems of social disruption and change after the war ended. These topics reappear in Ruth Benedict's analyses of state societies. OWI assigned Benedict the analysis of the cultures of Rumania,[3] Holland, Thailand, and Japan. Her reports on these nations are all substantial in length and quality.[4] In addition she wrote advice for pro-American propaganda to these peoples, advice on how to encourage enemy soldiers to surrender, on how to lessen clashes of culture in postwar occupation of these countries, and on enlisting the people's tolerance of Allied troops. OWI also assigned her the problems of assessing German morale, predicting problems of military government in Italy while the assault on Germany continued, and the question of how Finland could be kept out of the Soviet orbit. How an anthropologist produced insights for these problems bears some lessons pertinent to the problems of schools.

Ruth Benedict's deep relativism allowed her to project herself into other cultures. Her quest for nonrelative cultural arrangements, for universal values, did not lessen her commitment to relativism as a principal for understanding the great variety of human cultures and for overcoming ethnocentrism through education. Rather, the point of view of cultural relativism provided the essential frame of mind for finding the logic, values, and functioning of culture. She also had a technique for representing cultural patterns that struck her students in the 1930s as particularly her own. One of her students quoted her in class in the mid-1930s: "We need to *penetrate* these societies." He went on to say, "I particularly enjoyed in her a certain hesitancy . . . uncertainty. . . . She was an honest woman" (Irving Goldman, in McMillan 1986:203). Another student wrote: "Ruth Benedict taught us to read an ethnography . . . delving beyond the interpretive words of the writer, till we savored the culture. She taught us meticulous attention to detail because to her mind no detail was trivial" (D. Lee 1949:346). Benedict could see herself as an individual in other cultures. There is a brief undated manuscript in her papers entitled "If I were a Negro." In it she itemized many everyday occasions when she would "meet that steely or insolvent rebuff," and she went on, "If I were a Negro . . . thousands of whites would have conspired to teach me a passionate demand for human decency. . . . I should know something that they do not know, . . . in its simple eternal essentials, what it is that makes human life decent: that men respect each other" (RFB Papers, Box 54). The habit of mind of identifying with persons in other cultures opened up to her the experience of the cultures she studied. Empathy with other cultures is a critical step toward improved ethnic relations.

It is a tenet of anthropology that every culture has a reasonable code that can be deciphered to open up the consistency and the human experience of that culture. The culture of family, kinsmen, and communities, if not the state organization—which is so often subject to idiosyncratic programs, so often inattentive to the common welfare—in many cultures is based on some formula for sharing, for gratification, and for attachment, based on vision beyond the mundane. Often it is this area of culture where values are likely to persist in circumstances of culture change. This conception of culture was always found in Ruth Benedict's work. The method and framework for making a different culture understandable to persons who have not lived it are not so readily perceived or easily learned, and they require study. Two examples from Benedict's work for the OWI demonstrate her ability to transform initial stereotypes by finding admirable aspects in a previously barely known and negatively viewed culture. At this point simple tolerance becomes genuine appreciation.

Ruth Benedict adapted her OWI paper on Japanese culture for the American public in The Chrysanthemum and the Sword: Patterns of Japanese Culture (1946a). She described the civilian background of the enemy soldiers who had been enlisted to accomplish the aggressions of a militarist state. They and all Japanese were bizarrely depicted in U.S. media, but she described the culture that had been commandeered and distorted by militarist leaders. The institution of emperorship symbolized the hierarchical relations in the family and the elaborate codes of obligation in the society and was not in itself militarist.[5] Japanese values when separated from the pursuit of war could be readily admired. The culture placed moral expectations high and nurtured self-development in ways different from our own culture, but in a motivational and moral sense understandable to American readers. Different as they are, Japanese and American cultures share a drive for achievement, self-discipline, delayed gratification, degrees of group solidarity, among other traits.

The book sold 350,000 copies in the United States, a substantial sale but low compared to the 2.3 million copies sold in Japan over fifty years (Fukui 1999).[6] Its influence on American opinion is hard to measure; however, the book probably reduced prejudice against Japanese Americans after the severe wartime internment they underwent, and reduced prejudice against Japan (Suzuki 1985). It helped prevent the kind of prolonged resentment against the enemy that had dogged German Americans following World War I. The problem was not just with enemy nations—political alliance was not enough to bring about empathy for Chinese Americans during and after the war—but with all foreign cultures. Americans needed to understand the meanings in a foreign culture, including the systematic relationships of what they take to be "bad" parts of the culture with the elements that they recognize as gratifying or elevating, or as qualities that they have in common.

Rumania: Self-Gratification, Pride, Corruption

Rumanian culture, one of Benedict's OWI assignments, a scarcely known European culture, honored and institutionalized values about which American culture was highly ambivalent. Rumanians overtly valued hedonism and self-centeredness and tolerated bribery, qualities Americans usually expected to keep in check and disavow. American government and army personnel had expressed prejudice against Rumanian culture in clichés: "They think they are big shots; Rumania is a comic opera; corruption runs throughout the society." Benedict drew up a detailed historical and cultural analysis.[7] Unlike her analysis of Japanese culture, this work has never been published, although it is available from the National Archives. Therefore I summarize it in more detail to convey her method and mode of thought.

Rumanian culture retained the symbolism of harmony with nature and individualism expressed in the metaphors of its sheepherder forebears. A succession of native and foreign overlords never owned the lands of the herders and cultivators but taxed them heavily in kind and in labor. A state had been imposed in 1878 by joint Russian and German power, but it never asserted effective leadership, and the sheepherder tradition lacked institutions of community and leadership. The upper class was not hereditary, but based on current and former wealth. The middle class was made up largely of state officers. In villages the mayor, teachers, priests, notary, and chief of police were appointed by the state. These positions had come to be available to educated or prosperous peasants between the world wars; thus, village outsiders still often filled them. The state appointees all had an allotment of fifteen acres of land and the right to command peasant labor on it, a tax peasants deeply resented. They were in a position to receive *baksheesh*—the Turkish word for oiling the palm—as was the innkeeper, who managed the government monopolies of tobacco, matches, and salt. A proverb said, "Trust the Rumanian only so long as his shirt hangs out," that is, so long as he wears peasant costume (Benedict 1943c:17).

Since all offices were state appointed, state salaried, and claimed land rights allotted by the state, even when they were filled by successful peasants, there was no village corporateness. Nor was the church a unifying institution. If the priest was from a peasant family, he was more honored than when he was an outsider, as in the past. Still, older attitudes persisted; for example, after greeting and passing the priest, one threw a curse at his back. Mass brought few worshipers—Sunday was for dancing the *hora*—and mass was a service to be sought only in rites of passage and then only secondarily to peasant customs for marriages and funerals. Priests did not hear confessions or absolve sins. Instead numerous practices for atonement, such as many fast days and many confessional or protective ritual sayings, were part of daily life. Priests were reputed to be venal, and a proverb said, "Do as the priest says. Do not do as he does" (1943c:22).

Social solidarity was weak even among kinsmen, and even in nuclear families. There is a proverb: "'Why is your wound so deep?' 'My brother gave it to me'" (Benedict 1943c:62). Not only was the practice of *baksheesh* omnipresent, but "the struggle for property and preferment is perhaps the most prevalent adult Rumanian preoccupation. . . . The phrase, 'Mine shall live and yours die' is common in towns and cities and referred to the nature of the struggle for financial betterment—a struggle with few holds barred if a man is clever or powerful enough to get away with it" (37). Yet "to a student of Rumanian culture the entire openness of all Rumanians about corruption is more striking than the admitted venality" (50). Sayings such as "'No one can live without political protection' and 'you can buy anyone in Rumania' are matter-of-fact summaries of conditions from Rumanians who like life in their country better than any other life in the world. As one such man said, 'Rumanian life gives one a chance to indulge all the human weaknesses. . . . There you feel really free'" (37). To feel really free was illustrated in the values of hedonism and attitudes toward the self:

> Rumanians are extreme both in the degree to which they exalt their joy in another person and the degree to which they repudiate a person and all its ways whom they regard as interfering with the good life they should have. . . . This paramount pursuit of pleasure in interpersonal relations has been strong enough to rule out many customs which are "duties" and "obligations" in surrounding countries. The Rumanian brother does not postpone his own marriage to earn his sister's dowry as the Greek brother does. The role of the older generation is not to "sacrifice" itself for the younger. One of their riddles runs: "Where is the center of the earth?" "Here where I am. If you don't believe it, measure." (Benedict 1943c:50–53)

Personal pride was given free rein. There were few bars to opportunism and aggression. No group consensus imposed shame. Guilt was managed by observing numerous rituals of atonement.

> The interpersonal hostility that accompanies this opportunism is of course great. One of the most constantly recurring proverbs in Rumania is "Kiss the hand you can not bite." This proverb is particularly impressive in a country where the young kiss the hands of their elders, the laity kiss the hands of the priests and subordinates kiss the hands of their superiors. This submission is hostile, but hostility is not confined to this relationship of inferior to the superior. Any person readily becomes, in any other's eyes, the frustrator of his wishes and his will. (Benedict 1943c:55–56)

Individualism was well served, and the costs were not as socially destructive as in some other cultural contexts. Indulgence of human weaknesses, pride, and feeling really free were open to all. They were peasant and herder patterns, not reserved for a privileged class. Pride and personal agency prevailed even at death and funerals, in most cultures a time of fear, remorse, and disruption of interpersonal relations. Rumanians hated aging with its prescribed passing on of the land to the sons, and even denied decrepitude, saying "He would push his grave-covering aside just to watch [his 'fair one'] going out of the cemetery" (Benedict 1943c:52, referencing Vacaresco 1908:105). However, at death Rumanian folk poetry portrays the individual calmly managing beautiful ceremonies for his own burial and funeral. The dead was supposed to say to the earth:

> I am giving you now,
> Without ever taking them back,
> My shoulders in your arms,
> And my face under your green grass.
>
> (Benedict 1943c:38, from Gaster [1915]:344)

In the most famous of all Rumanian ballads, the man to whom his sheep foretell death accepts it without comment and proceeds to instruct his lambs:

> Of the murder Thou shall not tell them.
> Only say that I married a proud Queen,
> The bride of all the world;
> That at my wedding a great star fell.
> The sun and moon held the wreath.
> Firs and young maples were my guests,
> Priests, the high mountains,
> Fiddlers, the birds, thousand of little birds,
> And torches, the stars.
>
> (Benedict 1943c:39, from Patmore 1939:72)

To call one's death murder here is anger, not an accusation of sorcery, not fear. This lone sheepherder constructs a proud and beautiful scenario of his death. A proud unsubmissive folk culture relished enjoyment and festivities, was burdened by taxation but not by respect for any authority, and was unburdened by supernaturalism; people carried young trees in processions instead of figures of saints. There is a way of life here that plays also in some of the imagery of American culture. Americans attend to the anticipated cost of their funerals, and for some this is still done through lifelong payments into a Friendly Society that will provide a funeral often lavish in relation to the payees' personal expenditures during their life. The newly possible medical fight against death brings an active element to dying. But the removal of the corpse to the funeral parlor and the orchestrating of the ceremonies even in the church by the personnel of the funeral parlor is a procedure in which the living are passive at the death of loved ones. The rupture of relatedness at death is depicted in the viewing of the corpse, if done at all, without leave to kiss it as many central Europeans and Middle Easterners do. Rumanian poets tell how to take charge of one's own death. Americans seem to want to do so, but our culture does not provide customs and imagery for a self-assertive death ceremony.

Appreciation of a part of a culture and recognition that there is good and bad in their culture, and in ours, can open up a relativist view. Empathy for a culture can penetrate racial prejudice as can be seen in White America's fascination with the language, music, religious expressiveness, dancing, and sports ability of African Americans. Multiculturalism can mean valuing different ways of living, not just tolerance of differences among cultures.

Learning to Grow Up

The learning of culture was a new problem, among several, that Ruth Benedict took up after *Patterns of Culture*. Although that book became identified with the personality and culture school, she considered it a background statement only, with the real problem of the new field the learning of culture. She had closely followed Margaret Mead's work on learning culture. She was much interested in the contrast between lifelong consistency in the expected behavior in Samoa and Arapesh cultures and the Manus culture's requirement of reversal at adolescence from childhood freedom and immunity from danger to adult restrictions, obligations, and vulnerability to sorcery attacks (Mead 1928, 1930a, 1935). She generalized the discontinuity in Manus by reconsideration of the extensive literature on age grade systems, as in Masai and Arapaho cultures, and the initiation procedures for girls and boys in Africa and North America. She had discussed variations in life cycle transitions in *Patterns of Culture*, but she later took up the question of how, in some other cultures but not in our own, ceremonies and ritual instructions brought an end to behaviors and identifications of childhood and initiated the expected behaviors and identities of adolescence and adulthood. She wrote on this subject for the journal *Psychiatry* (1938), addressing psychotherapists, most of whom at that time took no account of culture. In the Arunta tribe of Australia boys' total identification with the women's world was transformed through a series of stages and a final rebirth through men's "baby pouch" into adult male prerogatives and responsibilities. As the adolescent boys stoned the women's camp at the close of one of the stages, they acted out the end of childhood and their assuming new behavioral expectations and responsibilities. Another example of discontinuity in the life cycle came from the Keraki tribe of New Guinea in which boys had to be the passive homosexual partner until the age of ten; then to protect them from pregnancy lye was poured down their throats, and after this ritual they became the active partner to the younger boys. In the next stage they were expected to begin heterosexual behavior and to father children. Male homosexuality was not interdicted in later life, nor was its practice prominent. These societies successfully bridged discontinuous cultural expectations in behavior through marking stages and ceremonially conducting the child and adolescent from one stage to the next with clear enactment of the meaning of the transitions.[8]

The discontinuity in personal motivation that had to be learned was one point. In addition Benedict also showed that a pattern could encompass a wide spectrum of behavior, that symbolically powerful procedures could bring about fundamental changes in individuals' orientation and view of the self as they matured, and that a pattern could structure radically different forms of behavior into a consistent whole. It is a major misreading of Ruth Benedict to attribute to her the idea of "culture as uniform" (Varenne and McDermott 1998:164).[9] Such attributions survive because *Patterns of Culture* is the only work of hers referenced by most of her critics. Her later articles go unread, and several of them are statements of developments in her theory.

Benedict saw discontinuity in the arrangements of the American life cycle. American children have little opportunity to see the principal form of productive labor in their society, which at that time was industrial. Children cannot begin contributing to real productivity, in contrast to many primitive societies where the young child observes much of the production process and is given strength-appropriate tasks that adults recognize as a contribution. Examples are the Ojibwa boy's accompaniment of his father on the trapping line and the meal made of the Cheyenne boy's first successful shooting of a bird. While young American children are expected to play instead of work, in other societies children are continuously conditioned to responsible social participation (Benedict 1938).

In an article about schools in our society Benedict noted that adult authority over children hindered them in learning the initiative and the responsibility to make moral decisions that are rights and duties in our democratic society.

> The transmission of our democratic heritage means, then, preparing children in our schools to act as adults with initiative and independence. Our culture does not go about this with the directness that is characteristic of many tribes which set this same goal. With us, children are dependent, and yet as adults they must be independent. They are commanded as children, and as adults they command. This is in strong contrast to those societies which make no qualitative difference between children and adults. The qualities they value in grown men they boast of also in little boys even if the child flouts his father and even strikes him. "He will be a man," his father says. . . . [In our schools] the training is overwhelmingly in docility rather than in self-reliance and independence. (1943d:725)

She then again made her point that in societies like ours where adults should behave very differently from children the change in expectations is best taught by a clearly marked transition to a new stage, a leaving of docility and dependency and entry into the new responsibility of taking initiative. Where were the instructive graduation ceremonies to effectively end identity as a passive child? And where was the point of introduction of an expectation of initiative?

Humiliation and Shame

In a paper (1939) prepared for a conference for mental health specialists Benedict focused on a severe sanction for behavior practiced in America and in some primitive societies: the use of humiliation. In some cultures the novice in male adolescent initiation ceremonies was subjected to humiliating treatment,

sometimes as an assertion of authority of the men. However, a ceremony of closure of childhood and the initiate's assuming a higher status or entry into adult prerogatives appeared to wipe out the humiliation. It was appropriate only to a transitional ritual. Humiliation was widely used in our society, she noted. It was humiliating to be unemployed in our society and for adults to be dependent. To be part of the productive group was usually assured in non-industrial societies, and dependency was managed without humiliation in some societies by honorable giveaways, by an ethic of hospitality, or by attributing positive characteristics to dependency.

Like the United States, Chukchi society in Siberia honored only the owners of valuable property, reindeer herds. Chukchi men who did not own herds had to hang around the camp of a herd owner, hoping for a humiliating hand-out for their families. Young men had no property since their fathers held ownership of herds until death; furthermore, after marriage the bridegroom had to live for a year with his father-in-law as his herdsman and dependent. Thereafter he would gradually acquire reindeer to gain status. Chukchi society experienced much psychic instability, murder, and suicide and projected interpersonal hostility onto their image of the spirit world, in which evil and implacable spirits controlled human events.

Kwakiutl culture on the Northwest Coast of Canada managed humiliation differently. It also elaborated humiliation, interpreting every mishap small or large as a humiliating insult. Since individuals were representatives of kinship lines, insults were to the whole kin group. However, the Kwakiutl had a means to overcome humiliation: the chief of the group distributed manufactures— blankets or canoes made by the kinsmen, or if the man was a great chief he distributed beaten sheets of copper shaped in a symbolic form not very different from a European coat of arms—and the humiliation was wiped out, his dignity restored. The "psychic vigor" of the Kwakiutl, shown in their effective management of the human vulnerability to shame, was a lesson for therapists. This lesson, Benedict reminded the therapists, was found in studying the great variation in cultural ideas. Later, when she studied Rumanian culture, she found a cultural elaboration of the polar opposite of humiliation: pride. The Rumanians structured marriage, and even death, as proud occasions. For the Manus in New Guinea marriage was the acceptance of humiliating subordination by the bride to her husband's family and acceptance of heavy debt by the groom. Rumanians asserted pride throughout their culture, and it was not a culture that employed shame or insult. These examples illustrate Benedict's use of opposites in human attitudes as a principal analytic tool. Drawing contrasts is seen in much of her work.

When Benedict later described Japanese culture, she found the Japanese were vulnerable to insult to an unusual degree. The shame inflicted by insult was extreme and had to be avenged. Clearing one's name from insult was an adult preoccupation. Well aware of this problem in their culture, Japanese elementary school teachers carefully eliminated competition and the humiliation that it brought, but the examinations for entrance to middle school at age nine introduced children to this anxiety, which sometimes had led to suicide. Benedict went on to discuss variations in cultural uses of shame. The necessity in Japan to clear one's name "is not, as the phrase goes, Oriental. The Chinese regard all such sensitivity to insults and aspersions as a trait of 'small' people—morally small. . . . The Siamese have no place at all for this kind of sensitivity to insult. Like the Chinese they set store by making their detractor ridiculous but they do not imagine their honor has been impugned" (1946a:147).

Benedict observed that studies of American and German working men showed they performed better under competition. In some New Guinea tribes insult was a goad to reciprocity; indeed, all inter-village hospitality in these tribes was initiated by the rival village shouting insults about the inability of the debtor village to stage a feast. Shame and humiliation could be extremely disruptive. If the culture had also devised a procedure to show insults were undeserved, they could be managed successfully, and they could be goads to heightened personal and social activity. Shame was fraught with difficulty in Japan, but it was the principal enforcer of the ethical code and a motivation for achievement. Shame was the emotion felt with loss of self-respect.[10] Benedict explained to her readers (1946a:222) the psychoanalytic view of shame and guilt, in which shame was a less compelling emotion than guilt because it was felt only when others knew of one's fault, but guilt was an internalized emotion, felt whether or not the social group knew the transgression. She noted that this concept had been used in describing societies as shame societies or guilt societies.[11] She did not find this distinction useful for Japanese culture, and instead she stressed the internalized aspects of the Japanese sense of shame. She criticized other psychoanalytic views as bound by culture as well (Benedict 1949).

Benedict began her paper on the sanction of humiliation (1939) with the point she made in *Patterns of Culture* (1934b) and in "Anthropology and the Abnormal" (1934a) that symptoms psychiatry considers indications of mental illness are to a great extent those behaviors American culture defines as abnormal. What is considered abnormal differs, and symptoms such as visions and hallucinations have been valued in numerous cultures as signs of ability to communicate with supernatural powers. Mental illness was a culturally defined state. Some societies considered as mentally ill those persons who denied hospitality to travelers. Such persons put themselves outside the group of mutual obligation and mutual credibility. The abnormal is not a consistent category cross-culturally, but is variable and culturally defined, just as the normal is culturally variable. Furthermore, persons considered abnormal may not be ostracized from communities and may find rewarding places in society.

These lessons are relevant to school problems, for all cultures have deviants, and multicultural societies contain varied concepts of who is deviant. The way schools define level of attention and activeness determines the conditions known as attention deficit disorder and hyperactivity. Varenne and Mc-Dermott (1998) made a similar and much broader point concerning school definitions of success and failure. Benedict's inventory of different cultures' handling of shame, insult, and competition could be a lesson in education theory. If Americans, Germans, and New Guineans are spurred to achievement by competition, could competition be employed more in schools, opening up sedentary classroom routines? And schools may consider whether it is better for groups of equals to insult comparable groups than for authorities to evoke shame in subordinates.

The Method of Cross-Cultural Comparison

The method of cross-cultural comparison had long been employed by nineteenth-century anthropologists and was much refined by the standards for fieldwork introduced by Boas in the United States and Radcliffe-Brown and Malinowski in England. Ruth Benedict used the comparative method to clarify differences and to pose contrasts in order to define basic patterning more precisely. She made use of contrasts in almost all her work, first borrowing Friedrich Nietzsche's contrast of Apollonian and Dionysian types of behavior in *Patterns of Culture* to compare Pueblo to Plains Indians. She later compared societies on many dimensions, as has been discussed here—on the allotment of dominant and subordinate statuses in families and in internal hierarchical arrangements; on the contrast of responsible and nonresponsible roles; on the contrast of passive and initiatory behavior; and on the contrast of the sanction of humiliation and the allowance of pride. She compared political systems found in the modern world as background to anticipated postwar military government and political reform in areas ravaged by World War II.

In an article titled "Recognition of Cultural Diversities in the Post-War World" (1943b), she addressed a general audience and made a case for recognizing the legitimacy of different political systems. She advised against trying to introduce Western systems of national government in areas with traditional local political systems. She did not discuss Japan in this article, the nation that would be most at issue because of its differences from Western political traditions, but she chose a broad context of Eurasian local systems, comparing them to North Atlantic national representational systems. She again selected points on which pattern could be clearly differentiated and set up opposite categories. Strong community orientation in the Eurasian pattern allowed local leaders to negotiate consensus or to impose it as a condition for the benefits of group membership, and while Eurasian systems differed in specific form, they had in common institutions for achieving political consensus. She described village councils in China, the Punjab, and Poland and referred briefly to the Russian mir, the traditional village council. She contrasted the North Atlantic pattern of two major national parties, which represented diverse and conflicting viewpoints, operated through statewide elections, and accepted the principle of majority rule—which is very different from requiring consensus. However, the North Atlantic pattern, particularly in the United States, had weak local organization. In the Eurasian system, acceptance of consensus usually carried with it the protection and social stability achievable when high-status persons fulfilled the culturally specified obligations to low-status ones, but the system failed to accommodate dissent; dissatisfied families and clans were ostracized from the group. If dissidents became numerous and if they amassed as authoritarian movements, the local system was subject to external takeover.

Eurasian systems differ in how far the states of that period, whether colonial or indigenous, reached down into local affairs. A half-century after this article was written, the political situation in Afghanistan that accompanied the United Nations–sponsored national interim government has illustrated the strength and the weaknesses of the Eurasian system. A national leader was affirmed in an assembly of many leaders from tribal areas. Tribal consensus has been a stabilizing factor, but warlords have traditionally moved outside the tribal system to extend their rule by violence, just as a religious faction, the Taliban, superseded tribal authority and imposed totalitarian rule. A locally achieved consensus can seldom be extended to a nation that includes diverse groups, and local political solidarity weakens national negotiations.

By describing the widespread Eurasian political pattern in 1943, Benedict made the point for the American public that a vacuum of traditional popular political organization should not be assumed where national organization was weak or autocratic. Furthermore, any attempt to impose a national elective system must respect the existing local modes of social order. Later ethnography on several Eurasian societies that hold assemblies for the purpose of arriving at affirmation of values and leaders has shown wide variation. For example, Pashtuns of Pakistan and Afghanistan have quite different types of local leadership from the Jains of northern India, although both regularly assemble in large numbers to affirm consensus (Ahmed 1980; Barth 1959; Carrithers and Humphrey 1991). However, strong local organization can impede centralized authority and national political systems. The problem is as real today as in 1943.

American Culture Patterns

Benedict's commentaries on American culture during World War II concerned principally political organization and behavior. Large-scale contrasts in political structure had been drawn up by Emile Durkheim in the categories of segmentary, organic, and hierarchical society, which she employed in her lectures on social organization. She elaborated on Durkheim's implied contrast of the behaviors that accompany these types of social organization, a contrast anthropologist Gregory Bateson (1936) had also elaborated: the symmetrical behavior in segmentary societies, where persons respond to others with behavior like that of the others, and complementary behavior in hierarchical societies, where different behaviors prevail between an upper-status person and a lower-status one. The interactions between persons of different status are complementary acts of dominance and subordination. At the same time the dominant person assumes the obligation to preserve the rights of the subordinate as they are defined in a particular culture. The expectation to receive protection from above and the obligation to give fealty and service upward are familiar as noblesse oblige in European parlance. Segmentary societies, those with locally similar units and without centralized organization, were likely to expect egalitarian behavior of individuals, that is, A and B should behave similarly toward each other. In describing the Orokaiva of New Guinea and its segmented units as being "like equal pieces of a pie," Benedict quoted one of their phrases to illustrate symmetrical behavior: "All men they walk abreast" (Social Organization 10/31/46).

Benedict wrote about the social basis of symmetrical behavior in the United States (1946b). American colonies set up egalitarian relationships in their formative period and during their political growth and enjoined egalitarian thought and behavior among free men. At the same time, they withheld this egalitarian status from slaves. The ethic of "being as good as the next person" prevailed in American development, but our society also embodied the principle of hierarchy, particularly in its social classes and in race relations. The two principles were contradictory; the contradiction exacerbated social relations and caused rending conflict at several periods of American history, yet it remained an integral component of the culture of the United States. The comparativist looks for parallel cultural situations, and Benedict cited in her courses several examples of primitive societies that had contradictory patterns causing ambivalence; yet the societies were not immobilized (Social Organization 12/17/46). This was not a condition like discontinuity in the life cycle, which could be bridged by instructive transitions to move individuals from one pattern to the next. Hierarchical forms impeded movement in status, and egalitarian principles were denied in hierarchically arranged relationships. Deeply embedded contradictory principles had not immobilized some other societies. Recognizing them provided a map, which was better than pursuing culture change blindfolded. She thought that much social gain could come from hierarchical relationships in which responsibility and respect were honored.

Benedict explained aspects of culture in the United States to newly arrived foreign students at Columbia University and to United Nations staff members, a lecture in a series on America that the university faculty sponsored (1948). Regarding relations of immigrant minority groups with mainstream Americans, Benedict compared their goals to ethnic minority groups' widespread objectives of maintaining separate settlements, keeping their own language in schools, and safeguarding their traditional customs and celebrations within Europe. In contrast, American immigrants intended to become Americans. This was accurate for most of the national groups that arrived from the mid-nineteenth century until the exclusionary laws of 1924. Only Bulgarian, Montenegrin, Serbian, and Chinese immigrants showed high rates of return to the countries of origin (Archdeacon 1983:138–139). The American people also expected that the immigrants wanted to become American. Benedict noted that immigrants here wanted their children to be taught in English.

Educators and linguists primarily initiated the programs of bilingual teaching, not immigrant groups. Minority group parents have frequently opposed such programs. School systems that use foreign-language instruction initially for immigrant children and then move them as quickly as possible into English-language classes have met with parents' approval. Parental protests against bilingual programs, saying they track their children in second-rate standards of achievement, are a telling indication that becoming American, in the sense of gaining access to full achievement in the United States, is still a characteristic of our immigrant populations. Practices in immigrant families and communities indicate that ethnic customs can be maintained and adapted to American circumstances, along with participation in work and public institutions. Bicultural adaptations rapidly develop and rapidly change.

In speaking of immigrants wanting to become American, Benedict told this foreign audience: "The American people have hardly deserved this attitude of our minorities. . . . Americans are indeed guilty of great sins against the dignity of minorities." Americans err, she also said, in thinking that other nations will want to adopt our way of life, just as immigrants to America have. She asked these foreign students and UN staff members to "teach Americans the truth about the devotion other nations have to their own ways of living" (1948:4,7). She went on to explain American organizational principles:

> The American melting pot has had an influence upon another kind of characteristic behavior in the United States: the kind of political parties and fraternal

organizations and the kind of churches we have here. . . . People with the most opposite opinions stay together in great organizations in the United States. . . . [B]ut it is an odd way of organizing society. I think it can be fully understood only in terms of the great American drive toward assimilation in this country. People whose goal is to achieve membership in a nation do not stake everything on the particular way it shall be run. . . . People who are not quite sure they are accepted into membership do not split that club. They are content that it should be ideologically quite amorphous. . . . Americans are not revolutionists. (1948:6–8)

She noted that trade union ideology showed similar amorphousness. Her points all concern social organization, and while she observes attitudes, her explanations are in terms of social behavior, not personality. Her perception of patterning connects different aspects of American social structure and attitudes. Her large-scale institutional focus was characteristic of her use of the comparative method and differs from the "thick description," the "unpacking," the reflexivity, the dilemmas of accuracy, which later characterized anthropological writing. The comparative method fell out of favor in some quarters in anthropology, but recently it is again defended and practiced (de Munck 2002). The method brings important cross-cultural insights, and it served Benedict well.

Ruth Benedict gave many good leads for understanding American culture and the processes of education. The most important were her active writing and speaking on the equal mental endowment of the races of humankind and on tolerance of different cultures. She promoted tolerance by describing the inner logic and humanity of different cultures. Her American readers could feel a greater identity with aspects of another culture, even recognizing shortcomings in their own. Ruth Benedict's work was very large scale, leading to concern about "thick brush strokes":

It seems to make sense to assume that cultural coherence is the result and cause of people being the same psychologically or experientially. It makes common sense to write phrases about people "being members of a culture," of their "belonging to a culture," . . . At home, it is not similarity that stands out but discord and disagreement. From our point of view the coherence of culture . . . is constituted in the long run by the work we do together. Human life . . . is made

*of the voices of many, each one brought to life and made significant by the
others, only sometimes by being the same, more often by being different, more
dramatically by being contradictory. (Varenne and McDermott 1998:137)*

If discord and disagreement are to be taken as a principal description of mainstream American culture, it must be remembered that Americans share as narrow a range of experience as do many in other cultures, even more so in view of
their participation in mass media and consumer culture. The viewpoint is less
accurate for ethnic minority cultures in the United States, which may have a
greater emphasis on cooperative and consensual behavior in their homes and
less participation in mass media and consumer fare. As for contradictions in
culture, Ruth Benedict opened the way to analyzing them. She did make very
large brush strokes, but she also used the idea of culture instructively. Much
insight would be lost if the concept of culture were to be abandoned as though
it were a chimera.

Notes

Archive Abbreviations

MM:	Margaret Mead Papers. Library of Congress. Washington DC.
RFB:	Ruth Fulton Benedict Papers. Special Collections, Vassar College Libraries. Poughkeepsie NY.
RISM:	Ruth Benedict File. Research Institute for the Study of Man. 162 East 78th St., New York NY.

1. This section of the lectures was published posthumously by two of Benedict's students (Maslow and Honigman 1970). She intended to include this section, which in
its full form was a statement of her theoretical view of culture at that time, in a general
textbook, but she delayed the project for her wartime research and never prepared the
topic for publication. Furthermore, the published version of the lectures, incorrectly
thought to be the only record of them, does not represent her full presentation of the
topic, and the full texts of five of the six lectures have been located in Benedict's papers.
Margaret Mead, who was Ruth Benedict's literary executor, wrote, in her letter transmitting Benedict's papers to Vassar College Library Special Collections, that she could
not find copies of Benedict's Bryn Mawr lectures in the papers and that she assumed
Benedict had disliked the lectures and destroyed them. Four of the six lectures were
found much later in Benedict's papers by the Vassar archivist. A copy of another of the
lectures was found in the small collection of Benedict's papers in the Research Institute

for the Study of Man, New York City. Comparison of the manuscripts with the version published by Maslow and Honigman shows that the published version was taken from a few of the lectures only and omits some sections of those lectures, but that it is verbatim for the sections selected (Young 2005).

2. See, for example, the addresses of John Dewey and Margaret Mead at the Conference on Science, Philosophy, and Religion (Bryson and Finkelstein 1942).

3. Now Romania; this chapter retains the older spelling used by Benedict.

4. Benedict's paper on Thailand was distributed in mimeographed form by the Institute for Intercultural Studies and by the Cornell University Southeast Asia Program (1952[1943]). Her report on Japan was the basis of The Chrysanthemum and the Sword. Her reports on Holland were very favorably discussed by Dutch anthropologist Rob van Ginkel (1992). He compared Benedict's work with other writing on Dutch national character and found it to be the best and most substantial among these writings. I do not know of any commentary on Benedict's paper on Rumania or of any reference to it.

5. Later research has shown greater involvement of the wartime emperor Hirohito in the decisions of government and war than Benedict's interpretation implied, but it also showed decisively that the emperorship rather than the person was symbolic of the country and the culture, and thus accorded with Benedict's representation. This opinion was echoed by Japanese leaders of the time in their attempts to influence the terms of surrender (Bix 2000).

6. Pauline Kent (1999) has assessed Japanese views of The Chrysanthemum and the Sword. There has been some criticism, but Kent's extensive study of opinion shows the admiration and fascination with the book on the part of Japanese intellectuals and general readers, as well as the wide attention it continues to receive. Suzuki (1999:219) makes an important point in his detailed and informed account showing that Benedict's "perspective on Japanese suicide has been widely accepted by contemporary Japanese suicidologists." Kent (1996) also has written a careful assessment of two articles by Douglas Lummis in Japanese and published in Japan, articles that are highly critical and dismissive of Benedict's analysis, and that Kent considers both misconceived and unrepresentative of Japanese opinion of Benedict's work. An article in English by Lummis (1980), which predates the two articles in Japanese by several years and which was published in a non-peer-reviewed journal, seriously misrepresents Benedict's book (Young 2005). It makes the same point Kent describes for his articles written in Japanese.

7. Benedict's paper "Rumanian Culture and Behavior," approximately 35,000 words in length, was based on interviews with twenty-five Rumanian Americans and cited twenty works of Rumanian history, sociology, folklore, proverbs, and tales. She specified that her account applied to the area of the Old Kingdom and Bessarabia. Other provinces, which Rumanians considered ethnic brothers and rightfully part of Rumania, had been influenced by central Europe and differed somewhat in folk customs and in class relationships from those in the Old Kingdom. She called attention to urban and rural cultural differences and to the attitudes toward the minority Jews and Gyp-

sies. She also wrote a condensed version of the paper in the format of OWI with the title "Basic Plan for Rumania: Background and Suggestions for Psychological Warfare" (1943a). The suggestions for psychological warfare had four parts: Weaning Rumania from Germany; Eliciting Active Assistance for the United Nations; Maintaining Good Relations in Rumania in the Event of United Nations Occupation; Basic Cautions in Rumanian Psychological Warfare. Initially classified "restricted," both papers were declassified in 1947 and became available from the National Archives. They are also available from the Institute for Intercultural Studies. Benedict planned to include her paper on Rumanian culture in a book she contracted for in early 1948, as indicated in her outline and précis for the book, but other chapters were unwritten at the time of her death in September 1948. The Rumanian study and other national culture studies were never published.

8. Benedict's bibliographic references on these points were Ruth Landes, *The Ojibwa Woman* (New York: Columbia University Press, 1938); Geza Roheim, "Psycho-analysis of Primitive Cultural Types," *International Journal of Psychoanalysis* 31 (1932):1–224; W. B. Spencer and F. J. Gillen, *The Arunta*, 2 vols. (London: Macmillan, 1927); Francis E. Williams, *Papuans of the Trans-Fly* (Oxford: Clarendon Press, 1936).

9. Earlier Varenne published an enlightening paper on Ruth Benedict's thought (Varenne 1984).

10. Modell notes also the positive effect of shame in Japan: for Benedict "shame *as a concept* demonstrates the synergy of the Japanese nation" (1999:198).

11. Piers and Singer (1953) later reviewed studies of cultural variations in regard to shame and guilt.

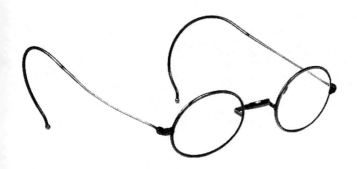

3. A Century of Margaret Mead

Ray McDermott

Margaret Mead. Courtesy of the American Museum of Natural History Library, 334029.

For fifty years Margaret Mead (1901–78) was an extraordinary presence on the American stage. Social commentator, adviser to civic organizations and governments, and the recipient of many honors, she was the most widely recognized anthropologist in the United States. She authored approximately 1,500 books, articles, occasional pieces, and films, aimed at both professional and popular audiences, and she was outspoken on the many issues she cared about, among them child rearing, sex roles, nutrition, education, nation-building, technology, and social change.

Mead was born in Philadelphia in 1901, the oldest child of parents who were both social scientists. Mead discovered anthropology at Barnard College, where she studied with Franz Boas and Ruth Benedict. In 1923, the year she graduated from Barnard, she married Luther Cressman, a theology student who later became an archeologist. Mead continued to study anthropology with Boas and Benedict at Columbia University. She chose the field, she said, because it offered work that had to be done before the opportunity was lost (Spindler 1978:87).

One of Boas's few graduate students not to write a dissertation on American Indians, she decided instead to go to the South Pacific. Leaving Cressman behind, she went to American Samoa on her first field trip, which led to her best-selling first book, Coming of Age in Samoa (1928), and to her PhD in 1929. Mead addressed the question of whether the biological changes of adolescence led inevitably to emotional turbulence. Based on her observations and interviews, she concluded that in Samoa they did not; culture, not biology, defined and determined the transition to adulthood.

Aboard ship on her way home after five months, Mead met the anthropologist Reo Fortune, a New Zealander whom she married in 1928. During the seven years of their marriage their joint fieldwork led to three books for Mead, Growing Up in New Guinea (1930a), The Changing Culture of an Indian Tribe (1932), and Sex and Temperament in Three Primitive Societies (1935). In 1936 Mead married her third husband, Gregory Bateson; their daughter, and her only child, the anthropologist Mary Catherine Bateson, was born in 1939. Bateson and Mead collaborated on fieldwork first in Bali and then in New Guinea, using film and photography in innovative ways. In Bali they focused on socialization and mother-child interaction, the subject of their pioneering Balinese Character: A Photographic Analysis (Bateson and Mead 1942).

During World War II Mead worked for the National Research Council's Committee on Food Habits, analyzing American attitudes toward food rationing. She joined Ruth Benedict and others in national character studies, intended to help the United States understand both their allies and their enemies by studying "culture at a distance." Mead's contribution was a 1942 portrait of the American character, Keep Your Powder Dry. After the war Mead's influence continued to grow. Although she taught at various institutions, her base continued to be the American Museum of Natural History, as it had been since 1926. In addition, she became the director of the Columbia University Research in Contemporary Cultures project, where she continued the applied work of studying culture at a distance until 1953. Her marriage to Bateson ended in 1950. She then set up a household with her wartime colleague, Rhoda Metraux, with whom she was to collaborate on various projects, including the study of European nations and revisits to several of her field sites. In 1951 she wrote a second book about the United States, The School in American Culture.

Always interested in extending the audience for anthropology, she wrote a didactic children's book, People and Places (1959b), advising her young readers to use science and social science to end war. In that book she also advocated bringing the Western standard of living to the rest of the world, learning how to learn so that lifelong learning could occur, and ensuring that every child grow up in close relationship with loving adults. She counseled civic organizations and governments on a variety of topics, among them civil rights, leadership, population, mental health, and the environment. In her own version of the "kula ring" ceremonial exchange system, everyone was a potential donor and recipient of information and interventions, the roles being alternated by the situation (Dillon 1980). She used numerous forums, including television and the mass-circulation magazine Redbook, to project her views. Mead's contacts even extended to Santa Claus, whom she "interviewed" for another children's book (Mead and Metraux 1978).

In 1971 the American Museum of Natural History opened the new Hall of Pacific Peoples, which was planned and constructed under her direction, and which now bears her name. Yet Mead was not universally applauded. Although her prominence benefited all anthropologists by attracting attention to their work, she was often not taken seriously within the profession because of her easy generalizations and willingness to offer superficial opinions on any subject. A quickly produced book in the form of a dialogue with the noted writer James Baldwin, A Rap on Race (Baldwin and Mead 1971), followed by a series of appearances on late-night talk shows, did little to enhance her academic standing (see Diamond 1971b). Surprisingly, she never took a public stand against nuclear testing in the Pacific, despite its harsh effects on Pacific Islanders.

Within the discipline she was faulted for her role in an ethics dispute during the Vietnam War. Two members of the Ethics Committee of the American Anthropological Association (AAA), Eric Wolf and Joseph Jorgensen, published an article in which they described, without naming names, various instances and degrees of anthropological cooperation in

Cold War research projects (Wolf and Jorgensen 1970). Antiwar activists had provided the two with documentary evidence about recent cases in Thailand. Declaring that the age of the "naïve" anthropologist was over, Wolf and Jorgensen called for anthropologists to disengage from clandestine research and colonial aims. Simply put, the issue was whether it was ethical to supply anthropological data for purposes that would harm the people under study.

Despite the fact that Mead's study of European cultures in the Columbia University project had been funded by a grant from the Office of Naval Research, and that this had been mentioned in the Wolf and Jorgensen article, the AAA Executive Board appointed Mead to head an investigation. Not surprisingly, her committee's report defended the work of "applied" anthropologists, saying that "counterinsurgency" was only a new label for "community development," and condemned the Ethics Committee for publicizing charges against fellow anthropologists. However, in a floor vote at the next annual AAA meeting in 1971, the members voted in favor of the Ethics Committee, repudiating Mead.

Five years after she died at the age of seventy-seven, Mead again became the object of controversy. Derek Freeman, an anthropologist from New Zealand, questioned both her methods and conclusions in Coming of Age in Samoa. Influenced by sociobiology, Freeman accused her of misrepresentation, arguing that, contrary to her idyllic portrait, Samoan life in reality was characterized by rape and violent behavior. Mead, he claimed, had been deceived by her informants. In the ensuing furor Mead was generally supported by anthropologists, who rejected the biological determinism implicit in Freeman's attack.

Summarizing Margaret Mead's achievements is not easy. In addition to her rich contributions to Oceanic ethnography, she taught the first-ever course in field methods at Columbia University in the 1920s. As Ray McDermott shows, she was instrumental in creating four distinct anthropological subfields—psychological anthropology, visual anthropology, applied anthropology, and anthropology and education. For the public she personified the discipline of anthropology. As she summed up her life's work, writing in the third person shortly before her death: "During her fifty years of sequential field work in Oceania, she tried to combine the insights gained from small homogeneous primitive societies and the needs of the emerging world community in accord with her acceptance of the task to cherish and protect the lives of all human kind and the life of the world itself" (Spindler 1978:87–88). To an admirable extent, she accomplished the task she set for herself.

She had known for half a year that she had cancer, but she came to help. So much of what is being remembered about her seems to have that theme: She came to help.

Dell Hymes, "To the Memory of Margaret Mead"

From the publication of *Coming of Age in Samoa* (1928) to her death fifty years later, Margaret Mead (1901–78) relentlessly pounded away at whatever she thought did not make sense in American culture. She traveled the world, living for months to years at a time in eight different cultures, always in search of cultural patterns that would put into high relief the arbitrariness of the life Americans considered natural and plain good sense. She was particularly incensed by the foolishness of American gender arrangements and child rearing. In the tradition of her teacher, Franz Boas, she was present in the fight against racism, and in the long run, she would resist the arms race and the violation of our ecology. In none of these battles was she alone, nor always right-headed, but she was often predominant. In the early years her writings made the difference, but for the last twenty years of her life, she was a highly visible media event on the pages of *Redbook* and the talk shows of late-night television. Her Columbia University colleague Robert Murphy used to like to say it was difficult to have an opinion about Margaret Mead, for she was like the air we breathe.

America has not had a Margaret Mead for more than twenty-eight years. James Boon says it directly: "There'll never be another Mead" (1990:181). She is an elder sorely missed. She was a moral force who gave direction and guidance to all, whether they wanted it or not. As she traveled through America, she asked her audiences to write down questions, and the hundreds of articles she did for *Redbook* offered the answers. Most questions required more information than she had available, but little deterred her from expressing an opinion. The following examples are Mead at her *Redbook* best, disrupting the commonsense categories of middle-class America:

Are young people more realistic about love than their parents? "Young people today are typically the children of their parents. . . . Far too few people in these two generations have thought very intensely about the seriousness of taking responsibility for another person's happiness or of the mutual responsibility of parents for the happiness of children." (Mead 1979:100)

Will men get over feeling threatened by women's liberation? "It isn't really a question of men's 'getting over it,' but of men's and women's finding a new balance in their relationships." (1979:47)

In other cultures, are women valued for their appearance? "Why just women?" (1979:41)

Should fathers share kitchen chores? "There is very little to be said for letting fathers 'share the kitchen chores' or, for that matter, do any work at home defined as chores. It is denigrating not only to the man who is asked to do them but also to the woman who defines homemaking tasks in this way." (1979:39)

Are you a cautious person or a risk taker? "Caution and risk-taking are not paired opposites." (1979:273)

She was always in search of a new angle. Her popular writings taught a way of thinking. It is not enough to answer the questions given by our culture. It is necessary to reformulate the key terms of the culture. It is necessary to get a new place to stand, to get a fresh point of view, to get not just a solution to a problem, but a way of erasing the problem from its place in the culture. Should men help out with kitchen chores? "No!" she said. No one should do chores. People should do serious work. Kitchen work is serious and should not be denigrated. Margaret Mead did things for a reason. In her wonderful memoir Mead's daughter, Mary Catherine Bateson (1984:69–70), described their nightly dinner ritual: everything in their kitchen was done seriously, with a purpose, to get the best for the human relationships at hand. Activities and values inherent in either the private, intimate kitchen or the exposed, public lectern validated, informed, and made good sense in terms of the other. She did serious work, not chores.

There are only a few roads to a new angle on issues of the day. First, look at the world until it releases new patterns for analysis; some call this science, others literature, but all agree it is a slow way to proceed. Second, for a quicker pace that takes courage, make change, keep track of how the world resists, and develop a new angle of vision along with the kicks in the shins. Mead opted mostly for a third road: she crossed into other cultures, discovered the arbitrariness of our way of life, and brought the news home. In Samoa, she found a different way of organizing adolescence; in New Guinea, different ways of organizing arrangements among genders (three of them, at that); and in Bali, different ways of organizing one's body. Between 1928 and 1942 she published eight volumes reporting on life in eight cultures, and in each case she had the same news: we do it this way, they do it that way; sometimes it seems they have a better handle on life. In what Clifford Geertz calls the "Us/Not-us" school of anthropology, from Jonathan Swift to Ruth Benedict or Margaret Mead, "There confounds Here." From Lilliput to Zuni or Samoa, "There confounds Here. The Not-us (or Not-U.S.) unnerves the Us" (1988:106).

By age twenty-seven, Margaret Mead was unnerving us. Her wisdom came quickly and easily, and her conclusions were sometimes wild and without warrant. She was a good fieldworker, not the best, and recent controversies aside, certainly one whom anthropologists have felt free to ignore.[1] She was a good enough fieldworker to bring home important news. It is increasingly popular for commentators to make Mead look bad, and quotations from her work can make things worse. Still, there is much to be gained from her work and especially from an examination of her life of trying. Both positive and negative critiques have expanded over the past twenty years.

The United States that made Margaret Mead possible provided a language of democracy, modernization, and science for self-reflection, each a positive development, and each also an efficient cover for the country's aggressive capitalism and colonialism. In this chapter the term America refers to a larger level of analysis, covering not just the United States but the America that was alive at its borders, gobbling up other cultures for exploitation and explanation. The America that is now without Margaret Mead includes, in various ways, Samoa, New Guinea, and Bali. Not only did she bring them home to the United States, but she found a market for them. In the years from the Depression to the end of the Vietnam War, America needed a Margaret Mead to locate what it could hardly imagine being. Her take on public issues such as adolescence and learning emerged from an effort to define cultural differences that could circumscribe what was intrinsically American. Not only does her world of the middle decades of the century no longer exist, but it perhaps never existed in ways she presumed. Certainly, it should have never existed in the ways she presumed. As much as she fought for cultural relativity, she rarely doubted that American democracy—by which she meant also Western capitalism and science—was in practice the yardstick by which cultures might measure their progress. She helped to build that yardstick by defining its edges.[2]

This chapter offers an analysis of Mead's contributions and contradictions in two sections, one on her ethnography, the other on her legacy applied to the problems of contemporary America, particularly her rarely noticed contributions to a theory of learning.

Margaret Mead, Anthropologist

It is difficult to imagine starting a career more dramatically than Margaret Mead. Coming of Age in Samoa (1928) was her first book, and it captured the popular imagination immediately with its account of a Samoa that allowed young girls more freedom and access to sexual experience than most Americans thought possible. This was not the first such news brought home by anthropologists,[3] but Mead made life in Samoa appear so sensible, so emotionally soothing, that it became, with reservations, a recommended way of life. The book was warmly greeted in academic circles. Franz Boas was the most influential anthropologist of the time, and he praised its dual contribution to anthropological theory, first for showing the influence of culture on what had been thought to be a universal, biologically induced, and socially suffered stage of life called adolescence, and second for showing so thoroughly the "personal side of the life of the individual" normally "eliminated" from anthropological treatments "of rigidly defined cultural forms" (1928:vii).

Two years after Coming of Age, Mead published a technical volume, The Social Organization of Manu'a (1930b), based on the same Samoan fieldwork, and a second volume designed for a popular audience, Growing Up in New Guinea (1930a), this time from her fieldwork with the Manus in the Admiralty Islands. The New Guinea volume received a negative review for its version of the kinship system, and four years later, she answered the complaints with a more technical monograph, *Kinship in the Admiralty Islands* (1934). In 1935 she published the still popular *Sex and Temperament in Three Primitive Societies* (starring the Mountain Arapesh), and over the next fourteen years she added five book-length technical articles based on the Arapesh data (Mead 1938–49). This pattern of doing everything twice, once for the public and once for the academy, lasted for the first half of her career but gradually gave way to a more total concern for the American public. Stephen Toulmin has fashioned a generous parallel: "For Margaret Mead, anthropology was thus what ethics had been for Aristotle: a field less for theorizing about abstract issues than for practical wisdom in dealing with concrete problems" (Toulmin 1984:6). She had to give answers. She had to offer solutions.

Although attention to the public eye made her academic anthropology's ambassador to the wider world, it also contributed to a declining place for her work within the discipline over the second half of her life, and she has not been essential reading for students in anthropology for decades. Some of her preoccupations within the field did not help matters much. Her strong emphasis on the cultural patterning of mother-infant relations had her making large generalizations from tiny experiences among the tiniest of people. She thought nothing, for example, of explaining her own success with an account of her being a wanted and properly, on-demand, breast-fed baby. She even claimed that "the temporary advantages or political preponderance of one tribal group in a new nation over another, as in Nigeria or Indonesia, may be likewise attributable to the repercussions in early childhood of differences in historical experience" (Mead 1968:172–173). Even a good idea can be pushed beyond usefulness, and in a discipline of "real men" studying the "real stuff" of life in other cultures—kinship structures, power relations, and economic strategies—Margaret Mead became disparagingly known as a "diaperologist."[4] Attention to children was not the only problem. During World War II, she stretched anthropological good sense beyond its limits, even by national defense standards, by organizing projects on "studying cultures at a distance," and many people in the world's most powerful nations were made a little less human by her stereotypes (Mead and Metraux 1953).

Strangely, Mead's best fieldwork—in Bali, with a strong supporting team of husband and natural historian Gregory Bateson, artist Jane Belo, musician

Colin McPhee, and some extraordinary European aficionados of Balinese cul-ture[5]—has been mostly ignored. J. Stephen Lansing (1995) wrote that Bateson and Mead's *Balinese Character* (1942) was interesting, but irrelevant, and that seems to summarize the book's place in Balinese studies. Although a hand-ful of the most prominent names in anthropology—Clifford Geertz, Hildred Geertz, James Boon, Fredrik Barth, Unni Wikan—have worked in Bali in the decades following, until recent criticism, there has been surprisingly little discussion of *Balinese Character*. Like a number of experimental ethnographies from the early 1940s, the Bateson and Mead work focused on the details of the personal and interactional order in search of the logic that guided relation-ships inside a culture. In most cases, what was won by detailed attention to the behavioral environments in which people lived their lives with each other has been overwhelmed by complaints about what was left out. The complaints are not completely unjustified, particularly those critiquing descriptions that moved too quickly from surface behavior to in-depth psychology for an ex-planation of a national character.[6] It is certainly true that an analytic focus on the orifices of the body as the key not just to child rearing but to the whole drama of people living with each other in Bali can certainly look silly without a corresponding analysis of the politics of the family in the wider social struc-ture. This is particularly true, warns Tessel Pollmann (1990), in the context of a colonial police state with an explicit agenda of showing off a traditional Balinese culture devoid of political intrigue, of which, says Clifford Geertz, there was a great deal (1980). Hildred Geertz is typical of modern anthropolo-gy's impatience with a strong diaperological version of analyzing children to gain a prediction of what they will look like as adults: "Bateson and Mead . . . present a complex hypothetical model of the character of the Balinese, based on the premise that the people of every nation, ethnic group, or culture have common personality configurations due to commonalities in their early child-hood experiences. This premise, popularly held among many still today, has been rejected by anthropologists since the 1960s" (1994:126). When phrased in terms of psychological character gained early in life and maintained without circumstance and variation through adulthood, the theory is not worth taking too seriously.[7] When the theory is phrased in terms of a patterned constancy in how people relate to each other, as a constancy newly experienced by young-sters and old-timers alike across multiple settings, data from child training

"Stimulation and Frustration" (plate 47) by Gregory Bateson and Margaret Mead. From *Balinese Character: A Photographic Analysis.* © 1942. Courtesy of the New York Academy of Sciences, United States of America. 148–49.

appears more interesting. Although Bateson and Mead sometimes wrote as if they were analyzing the behavior of toddlers only in search of the psychological roots of the next generation's adult behavior, methodologically they were attempting much more: they were trying to describe the ongoing organization and maintenance of character types in terms of the behavior of many people within and across various scenes inside a frame they call culture.

So there is much to complain about, but much to admire as well. *Balinese Character* is written in two parts. The first is an essay by Mead describing Balinese culture primarily through the lens of child rearing. The second is a photographic tour de force by Bateson in which he delivers sequences of behavior for readers to share his impressions of the play of life in Bali. Bateson was an excellent photographer and natural historian.[8] For every statement made about Bali, Bateson and Mead wanted pictures and ideally sequences of pictures to make their point. An example should help us appreciate the method. Under the heading "Stimulation and Frustration" (plate 47), they offer a sequence of nine photos of a mother and her toddler covering about two minutes of interaction.

First, the mother brings the child into a stimulating interaction, then she lets her attention wander until the child gets refocused, then the two of them look out together into space. Bateson and Mead had a strong sense that the Balinese often arranged ways to be together, but unengaged, to be in each other's presence, but unavailable. Bateson and Mead called this "awayness."[9] Potentially, "awayness" is a messy category for analyzing a people's behavior. From the ethnographer's sense of how behavior might work to a written description of an attitude is an analytically treacherous road. Bateson and Mead limited the treachery by describing how the Balinese could teach each other to do "awayness" across a lifetime. They tried to display the behavioral shape of "awayness" in photos. The last photo captures "awayness" on the faces of the mother and child. The previous eight photos show how it is orchestrated by the participants. Just what "awayness" might be, how it connected to the rest of Balinese life, and how it should be interpreted—all that remains unsettled, but something has been described and must be attended to in future accounts of the society.[10] That was their intention, and it is still worthwhile.

Bateson's picture of Bali was built up behavior by behavior, scene by scene, and stood in marked contrast to Mead, who offered Bali in broad brush strokes. Her picture was easier to read and easier to attack; his was easier to ignore.[11] Together they present a seldom acknowledged breakthrough in how to do ethnography and how to worry about its adequacy.[12] Despite a focus on socialization to the exclusion of politics, economy, and colonization, Bateson and Mead delivered enough documentation that they can still have influence on debates about the nature of culture, learning, and behavior analysis more than sixty years later.[13]

After Bali, Mead's focus on fieldwork gave way to a concern for public duty, initially in the war effort of the early 1940s and then, for the rest of her life, in a more dispersed effort to straighten out everyone. Ethnography, except for revisits to old sites, particularly to the Manus (1956), gave way to policy, but anthropology was still her calling card. Whatever anthropologists said about Mead privately, publicly she spoke for the discipline. Even if they did not read her, anthropologists had to know her opinion. Dramatic to the end, she passed away during the annual meetings of the American Anthropological Association. The drama was returned, and the association dedicated an issue of its journal to assessing the influence of Mead, the only person ever accorded the honor.[14]

Mead's legacy hit an unfortunate low in early 1983 with the announcement of a forthcoming volume on *Margaret Mead and Samoa* by Derek Freeman (1983). The book claimed that Mead's Samoan ethnography was terribly flawed by her own naïveté, her desire to find a paradise with sexual freedom for all, including women, and her theoretical bias in favor of culture being more important than biology. Where Mead saw free love, Freeman counted rape; where Mead saw generosity and detachment, Freeman found jealousy and aggression; and where Mead saw cooperation, Freeman found hierarchy and ambivalence. The book was announced on the front page of the *New York Times* weeks before it was available to reviewers, and Mead's scholarly virtues were dragged through the mud, momentarily without redress, in the public press.[15] A great debate ensued. Although there is reason to thank Freeman for some correctives, anthropologists have been overwhelming in their support of Mead, her field work, and even some of her overly enthusiastic conclusions.[16] The Freeman volume was mean-spirited and filled with its own biases.[17] In addition, because Mead and Freeman worked mostly in quite different parts of Samoa (under the control of different colonial powers) and did so separated by at least fifteen years of intense social change, many of the comparisons revealed less about her work than would be implied by all the variants of Samoa being called Samoa.[18] Perhaps most importantly, the restudy of Mead's own Samoan village by Lowell Holmes has been overwhelmingly in Mead's favor:

> Despite the greater possibilities for error in a pioneering scientific study, her tender age (twenty-three), and her inexperience, I find that the validity of her Samoan research is remarkably high. Differences between the findings of Mead and myself that cannot be attributed to cultural change are relatively minor. . . . I confirm Mead's conclusion that it was undoubtedly easier to come of age in Samoa than in the United States in 1925. (1987:103)

Coming of Age is filled with details. When we are told about the children learning to work, we are given the content of the jobs, the materials used, and the expectations of all others on the scene. When we are told that young girls must learn to weave, we are told what they weave, with what materials, learned in what order, and with what eventual outcome. The young Mead delivered a picture of both the pleasures and the problems of growing up in Samoa. In a careful reading of the book, Richard Feinberg (1989) shows that she delivers two Samoas in her text, the Samoa of her conclusions and the Samoa of Freeman's counter-conclusions, the Samoa of freedom and abandon and the Samoa of constraint and ambivalence. The news from the book was in fact the freedom and abandon, and so it was summarized, presented, and easily taken by the world. But as little as a cursory reading shows Mead displaying the constraints and struggles with which Samoan adolescents had to deal.

As good as the details are for the careful reader, Coming of Age deserved much of its misreading. Mead insisted on it. In an appendix to his magnum opus, Bronislaw Malinowski (1935, vol. 1:452), with characteristic arrogance, warned that the ethnographer has no right to "have nothing to say" to any question about the people with whom the ethnographer has lived and worked. Strong words, an impossible recommendation, and now terribly out of style—but good ethnographers, ever humble in the face of the complexity of the people under study, must try to get as much detail as possible. Along with documenting everything they can ask about, ideally they should record their failures and then circumscribe their topic of focus with a statement about what they are not studying. At her worst, Mead tried to look as if she had all the detail anyone

might want. This was apropos of the times, of course, but *Coming of Age* is filled
with a false, confident authority on many points of description: "And you will
see that his eyes are always turned softly on the girl. Always he watches her
and never does he miss a movement of her lips" (1928:96). What would an
ethnographer have to know to make such statements? "Always," "never," and
"only" are difficult terms and should appear rarely in ethnographies of people
engaged in complex activities like courting and love making.[19] Nor did she shy
away from ascribing motives: "Nine times out of ten her lover's only motive is
vanity" (1928:103). Can we say she was likely wrong nine times out of ten?[20]

In her account of Japanese culture, Mead's teacher and close friend, Ruth
Benedict (1946a), argued that even if no Japanese behaved according to the
principles she described, her conclusions could still be accurate; as long as
she could show that the Japanese, in not behaving according to principle,
nonetheless worried about the principles they were not following, her description could stand.[21] By this score, ethnographic certainty comes from inside
the worries of a people, and not from the predictive assurances of an outside
observer.[22] Assurance, not humility, was Mead's trademark. When focused on
details, her assurance pays off; when wildly concluding that people "always,"
"never," and "only" do one thing or another, her assurance leads to trouble.[23]

By the same desire to generalize, Mead's conclusions about the cultures
she worked with were often overdrawn. Her sometimes friend, Edward Sapir,
complained that she confused "the individual psychology of all members of
society with the 'as-if' psychology of a few" (Sapir 1994:181).[24] As she grew further from her fieldwork over the decades, this problem grew; with hindsight,
complex patterns became simple behaviors, ambivalent attitudes became
simple desires, and quick observations became central to stating how people
in other cultures were essentially different. In an evaluation worth repeating,
James Boon says that Mead "wrote incisively, yet repetitively, almost always in
duplicate, almost always in duplicate, and often all over again, whether soon
after or years later" (Boon 1990:175). As she grew further from the data, detail grew thin, and conclusions conformed less with the lives of Samoan and
New Guinea children and more with her message to America.[25] Both Samoans
and Americans were unduly simplified in Mead's comparisons (Marcus and
Fischer 1986). For her work on America and in other cultures, we have reason
both to praise her and to critique her for new purposes. On both accounts,

we have reason to miss Margaret Mead, anthropologist. In a presidential address to the American Anthropological Association, Annette Weiner (1995:17) reminded her colleagues: "Even today, at every association meeting, someone always declares how much Mead's presence is missed, saying with passion, 'if only Margaret were here, she would set things right!'"

Margaret Mead, Educator

It is inviting to critique Margaret Mead. Much like the America she represented so fully and forcefully, she was often simultaneously on the right and the wrong sides of key issues. She spoke with authority in a country dominating and colonizing other parts of the world, and just by virtue of that position she made compromises that turned into political mischief in the lives of those for whom she claimed to speak. In an account of the sexism and racism latent in Mead's writing, Louise Newman displays how much "opposition movements retain residues of that which they oppose" (1996:235). American sexism and racism are so tightly fitted to American colonialism, militarism, and economic domination that it is difficult for anyone speaking from *within* the system, never mind Mead speaking *for* the system, to get clear about what is being opposed, when, in what circumstances, and with what effect. Whatever her accomplishments, we can always turn to Mead as a display board for the difficulty of using the materials of one's own culture to fix the problems of that culture.

Gilliam and Foerstel (1992) have pointed to occasions when the residue of opposed prejudices swayed Mead's activities from her stated positions, whether by commission, omission, or mere association. The positives greatly outweigh the negatives, but the missteps are significant. Gilliam and Foerstel offer examples: despite her commitment to the peoples of the Pacific and her public work against nuclear armaments, her long-term engagement with national defense policy making kept her strangely silent on the use of Micronesia for nuclear testing; and despite her commitment against racism, her willingness to talk about a group of people sharing personality characteristics often had her sounding racist (as in her comments on Melanesians, whom she found bellicose and easy to despise, or on African Americans, whom she found without self-esteem).[26] It is not hard to imagine how, in trying to do the right thing for the most people, she gets stuck in positions invidious to her own cause. In each case she struck out for new ground, worried about how to fit her position into the institutional realities of the day, and wound up back home, conceptually and politically having gone nowhere. Other women around Boas and Mead—for example, ethnographers Ruth Landes and Gene Weltfish and folklorist and novelist Zora Neale Hurston—found it less easy to compromise, and they had much harder lives.[27] A comparison with the less fortunate careers of the women around Mead could be used to call into question her courage, but it might better highlight the treachery of the constraints facing women going against the grain and the difficulty of their communicating with the powers that were.

Mead's position on gender is a clear case of an advance reverting to a status quo. It is ironic Freeman has attacked Mead for choosing culture over biology in her explanations of human behavior. Freeman is wrong twice: first, Boasians, Mead included, did not deny biology as much as they wanted to know "the exact conditions that biology imposed" (D. Schneider 1983:10; see also the excellent discussion in Rappaport 1986); and second, of the Boasians, it is possibly Mead who stays closest to a determinist biology—of the kind, for example, that keeps women essentially different from men. To a biological essentialism that has men and women acting as men and women simply because that is how they are, there is a politically necessary and usually right social constructivist corrective, namely, that the arrangement between the sexes is just that, an arrangement, an arbitrary and likely bad arrangement, with its only saving grace being that it can be rearranged. Mead took such a step (well, mostly) with *Sex and Temperament* in 1935. To a social constructivist essentialism that has men and women acting as men and women only because others have told them how to behave, there is a politically backward and usually wrong corrective, namely, that men and women act as men and women simply because that is how they were born. Mead took such a step (again, well, a little) with *Male and Female* in 1949.

Given that males are restless, achievement motivated, and quest driven and that women are more content, pliant, and care giving, what would a useful arrangement between the sexes be, and is it possible some societies (Samoa, for example, and not America) play more satisfying and realistic tunes on nature's keyboard of genders and temperaments? This had become, unfortunately, her question, and to answer it she had to make the conspicuous assumption she knew the real characteristics of males and females. First comes biology, then culture; first core, then frills—the essentialist song.[28] Throughout the world, people repress each other with accounts of biological gender as destiny, and it is crucial in escaping such foolishness to remember gender, once born into the world and wrapped in pink or blue, is mostly made up. Thank you, Margaret Mead, circa 1935. To say something is socially constructed is not to claim it is without constraints. Biological determinism and social construction are not paired opposites in scientific explanation. Gender, easy to say, is in every nuance socially constructed and made consequential on a moment-to-moment basis by people in interaction, but this is not to say it is made up from thin air, as if according to whim. Thank you, but much less so, Margaret Mead, from 1949 on. Remembering biology counts does not have to drive a theory back to an inherent essentialism rooted in the drives of the individual person. Remembering that biology relentlessly presents problems for people in cultures to solve does not have to invite a view of individuals as slaves to motives established in phylogeny. Ever present biological issues—sexuality, procreation, the helplessness of infants—present part of what humans must deal with in organizing societies together, but biology is not well conceived as a determinant of individual behavior without a full accounting of the world in which the individual makes a life.

The America of Mead's time was in need of an overhaul. Not long before Mead passed away, Eric Wolf identified her America as hungry for a liberal image of itself (1972) but unwilling to acknowledge the economic and political power differentials that originally created the problems in the first place. It was a time to add nurture to nature and to celebrate human diversity as so many tunes played on the same piano. For Mead's generation, intellectual and political advance required documenting enough diversity to shrink the role of nature in the explanation of behavior. Nature was assumed to be the stable core left after cultural layers were removed, as if from an onion. The Boasian program showed the human situation played out primarily in outer layers and not determined by a biological core. This was a worthy program and necessary still to each new generation's struggle with genetic theories of intelligence, school achievement, sexual orientation, and whatever other cultural systems scientists claim to find a gene for every week. It remains an essential program, but it is not enough.[29] Adding cultural diversity to presumably stable and natural forms does not go far enough.

Nature and nurture should not stand as conceptually opposed and only in the real world sometimes interactive. The dichotomy itself has to be challenged. The very existence of a category called human nature has to be challenged. The very category of natural never comes to us free of history, never free of the intentions of others. Just how the category of natural has been used by people pushing each other around must be examined for a record of political intrigue and a call for change. Mead came of age in an America excited about the question of variation in how people were naturally gendered, raced, coming of age, and ready to learn. That same America has delivered to the present a new set of questions about how people use ideas of what is naturally inherent to mark areas of life where there are inequalities and no means to negotiate them: by folk accounts of nature, yes, women are less than men, Blacks are less than Whites, adolescents are virtually nuts, and everyone knows school is only for the best and brightest, and all this is naturally so. Mead's accounts of diversity in how nature could be handled were a first freedom. Calling into question the whole platform for "naturalizing inequality" is an exciting next step.[30]

For Mead moving beyond nature and nurture to the details of life, we can turn to her seldom acknowledged work on learning. Mead did not write much about learning theory, at least not directly, but it would be easy to reshape her ethnographies into accounts of what the people studied were learning from each other about how to behave, be it about adolescence in Samoa, gender among the Arapesh, "awayness" among the Balinese.[31] Her version of the social actor, that is, the unit of analysis in her ethnographies, was in constant need of guidance from others. In her photographic study of growth and development among Balinese children, she states her theme well: "Cultural analysis of the child-rearing process consists in an attempt to identify those sequences in child-other behavior which carry the greatest communication weight and so are crucial for the development of each culturally regular character structure" (Mead and Macgregor 1951:27). She was trying to describe how Balinese children learn balanced and flexible whole-body postures, with dissociated hands and eyes that attend to side issues in interpersonal relations. She used hundreds of photographs to analyze the "sequences in child-other behavior" in which everyone learned from everyone the proper displays of "regular character." If we were to translate all her work into an account of what everyone has to learn from everyone else, this quote shows how her cultural and interactive learning theory might be phrased. For any event in which learning seemed to occur, her question would focus on *how many people, in what order and by virtue of what levels of organization, are involved in shaping the specifics of anyone's learning.*[32] Among Samoans and the Manus, Mead did not yet know how to ask this question, although her descriptions can be used to fill in partial answers. In Bali, with Bateson's help, she both asked the question and attempted an answer. Thereafter, she only pointed at the importance of the question.

She was almost always able to hold the line against an essentialist theory of intelligence and learning. In her master's essay she defended Italians against claims drawn from their performance on IQ tests that they were of lower intelligence than people of Northern European extraction.[33] In Samoa, she administered intelligence tests and noted that Samoans seemed little interested in the tasks and performed with little variation across persons. Among the Manus, she found the children unimaginative, but smart, and noted that:

> *personality is a more powerful force . . . than is intelligence. . . . And it is this very manner of force, of assurance, which seems so heavily determined by the adult who fosters the child during its first seven or eight years. . . . The leading lines of the community represent the inheritance, not of blood, not of property, which is mostly dissipated at death, but of habits of dominance acquired in early childhood.* (Mead 1930a:140)

The biological inheritance of a natural intelligence was of no interest to the Manus and of mostly negative interest to Mead, particularly in the case of low IQ scores that, whether in New Guinea or the United States, whether in 1927 or 1978, "can be attributed to such a wide variety of factors that they do not have comparative significance" (1927:468). Against a rampant essentialist theory of intelligence, she sought an alternative account of how learning was organized by a people building a culture together.

As we restate her theory, we can appreciate how it can be used. Then and now, it stands in contrast to how most Americans think about learning. It is particularly different from how learning has been institutionalized in American schools. Where Americans focus on learning as hierarchically organized, from teacher to student, Mead focused on learning as laterally connected among people doing things together. Where Americans focus on learning as cognition stuck inside the head just in case the organism might have to do something, Mead focused on learning as habits developed in the context of social relations. She was early influenced by the Gestalt psychology of Kurt Lewin (1951) and later by the cross-cultural work on stages of identity development by Erik Erikson (1950). But the main influence, by far, is the work of Gregory Bateson, natural historian, husband of a decade, and one-time, and almost only one time, coauthor. Bateson's main treatise on the systematics of human learning did not appear until 1972, but he wrote little in the thirty-five years before that was not about the organization of contexts for communication, in his terms, contexts for learning.[34] For Bateson, there is little reason to distinguish communication and learning, and this is usually true for Mead as well. Learning is the on-going engagement with the details of life. As life moves on, so is learning relentlessly necessary.

The Bateson and Mead model of learning anticipates much of what is currently under debate in the ethnographic study of learning. Suppose that, instead of a model of the mind in isolation, we are in need of a theory of how children actually learn inside the complex institutions that carry their lives, across multiple pathways, into maturity. Most learning theories do not—indeed, cannot—begin to address the issue of learning in the real world, for they have both a theoretical and, more importantly, a methodological commitment to understanding not just the single child, but the single child only when interfaced with tasks well defined in the psychological test. The real world, as psychologists like to say, is rough and messy, out of control really, and the psychologist's well-defined task brings order, experimental control, and a corresponding set of constraints on interpretation. To the extent learning theories are based on the well-controlled experimental task, that is the extent their findings are irrelevant to what people do with the hard-to-define and constantly shifting tasks of everyday life, including, of course, everyday life in school (M. Cole, Hood, and McDermott 1978; D. Newman, Griffin, and Cole 1989). Bateson and Mead demanded much more than an account of the workings of heads in isolation from the world.[35] They wanted instead a theory of how sequences of child-other behavior were arranged, made consequential, and fitted into more general patterns well structured across the institutions of society. We are still in need of such a focus.[36]

In Bali, says Mead, "the child is fitted into a frame of behavior, of imputed speech, imputed thought and complex gesture, far beyond his skill or maturity" (Bateson and Mead 1942:13).[37] The frame is like a Vygotskian "zone of proximal development," a fast action guide to the appropriately perplexed in search of pattern, in search of connections that enrich an engagement with the world (Vygotsky 1987). The framing may be different for Balinese babies and American babies, but there is a frame nonetheless, and description of a learning child requires a description of the framing work: "Where the American mother attempts to get the child to parrot simple courtesy phrases, the Balinese mother simply recites them, glibly, in the first person, and the child finally slips into speech, as into an old garment, worn before, but fitted on by another hand" (Bateson and Mead 1942:13). Words are the garments of the mind. They come to us close to fully formed, already patterned, well used by others, and available only with a heavy price of conformity. The road to maturity is well traveled; it takes us mostly to places where others have already been, places thick with connections, much like Mead's prose, again and again, to what has already happened and will still happen. Mead could be so taken with patterning that she could easily forget about the ingenuity it took for participants to squeeze into or out of the patterns even a little change. She was so taken with the patterning, she would often write as if, once socialized, the person is nothing more than an internalized pattern. Then she would flip-flop and give, first, the details of the behavior and the complexity of the persons involved and, second, the cultural pattern as if it described the behavior of socialized robots.[38]

Mead's theory of learning may be her most radical move, because it disallows an analytic separation between individual and culture, between nature and culture, and, most importantly, between those condemned by the world and those doing the condemning. By her theory of learning, the units of analysis are engagements, sequences of engagement, and patterns of sequences of engagement. Left aside are theories of inherent intelligence and motivation free of the world in which they are played out; left aside also are theories that permanently fix a child's learning trajectory in traits developed by early experience as if there were no world holding the trajectories together. Just as in her work on gender and adolescence, Mead could not always stick to her own insights, and she easily gave way to more established ideas about how a child's career line could be decided by, say, an overly scheduled bottle feeding. But when she did stick close to behavioral detail, she had the theoretical material to undermine how Americans think of knowledge and its distribution.

This is a crucial issue in contemporary America, where we send our children to school not to learn to read and write, but to read and write better than each other.[39] The school test has become our measure of how each child is to move through the world. As our population is increasingly divided between the few who have and the many who do not, school failure is attributed earlier and more completely to those on the bottom. Underlying this trouble is a theory claiming that small differences among children at early ages are signs of their inherent potential. Mead knew how such a theory could be misused. If a country organizes for half of its citizens to get educated, precise tests can be designed for the purpose, and they can be legitimated by a competition of all against all until the top half (in a sequence of top-half cuts) emerges as the rightful heirs to success. Individual performances on standardized tests with little relation to reality have become the cement that keeps American social structure in place. Mead knew better, and she struggled to develop a descriptive language that would analytically place each child in the push and pull of cultural forces that shaped their lives far more than the small differences that could be observed in the psychologist's laboratory. She never did say what has to be said, but she could have: America is that well organized place that arranges for individual children—about fifty percent of them—to be analytically isolated and institutionally condemned to failure in school and often in the rest of life; and this job is done by everyone in a series of engagements in which the cultural materials available to the participants are structured to allow a student to look good only at the expense of others.

Conclusion

When Margaret Mead started writing, her America needed redirection, and she went to what she thought were new worlds and brought back what was needed. She could not have made up better stories to challenge American common sense. She needed the help of the Samoans, the Manus, the Balinese, and others she found at the edges of an ever-expanding America. With them, she developed counter examples to American beliefs on how people were naturally supposed to be.

Mead's America was marked by an adolescence that made teenagers outsiders to their own society and, to add craziness to a potentially difficult time of life, in ways orchestrated by that same society. To this mess, she could remind everyone that more emphasis on responsibility—for no one worked harder than Samoan children taking care of younger siblings—and less emphasis on repression just might net us young adults who could build a better society.

Mead's America was marked by theories of learning that separated measured knowledge from intelligent activity in ways that gave those with access to schooling unfair advantage in every public arena. To this mess, she could show that all learning was a matter of alignment with others—everyone did it, and even those who appeared not to learn were, in fact, learning to look that way with the help those around them.

Although this is a great deal to have delivered, Mead's counter-examples did not change her America. She could not have developed her examples without the American frame, not just in the sense America helped cast her net to distant shores, but in the more important sense that her examples were developed explicitly to speak to Americans. As she took away, she also gave back; as she took away core American beliefs about adolescence and learning, Mead confirmed science and democracy as their frame without an acknowledgment of the even wider frame of capitalism and colonialism. At the same time she defined variation in how children grow up in different cultures, she generally failed to notice that her Samoa, Bali, or America cannot be talked about without taking a systematic account of Western systems of signification that come with guns and money, certainly, and modes of self and presentation, perhaps just as certainly. Inside the American frame, she could challenge one category after another and make things more lively and up for discussion, but she never developed a critique of the American frame. She never developed a systematic critique of the capitalism and colonialism that supported her version of either anthropology or public service. We still have her work to do and then some. Received ideas of adolescence get worse. Adolescence gets longer, school performance is increasingly the only measure of the young person, and employment opportunities denied to the young poor are matched only by employment opportunities offered to educated adults to care for alienated adolescents. Received ideas of learning fare even worse as our sense of how to measure knowledge and intelligence has been narrowed to fit the heightened competition that allows children of plenty to continue to lord over the rest. Margaret Mead would be terribly disappointed. The problems were more difficult to solve than she had thought. As we get on with her work, we can appreciate that she always brought so much for us to work with and reapply. She always came to help. No wonder we miss her.

Notes

This chapter exists because Denis Philips asked me to teach a short seminar on Mead for the Continuing Studies Program at Stanford in 1993. Paula Fleisher helped to teach the class. Robert McDermott and Richard Blot encouraged two write-ups. The essay first appeared in the Teachers College Record in 2001 (103[5]:843–867) and is reprinted here with small changes. Sessions at the American Anthropology Association annual meetings in 1989 and 1990 organized by Richard Blot, Juliet Niehaus, and Richard Schmerzing were a major stimulus. Bernadine Barr, Eric Bredo, Shelley Goldman, Meghan McDermott, Mica Pollock, and two seminar groups at Stanford asked for changes in early drafts. Reviewers for the University of Nebraska Press offered an excellent handful of corrections and extensions.

1. Although there were only a few attacks on her work before she passed away, Mead (1976, 1977, 1978a, 1978b) nonetheless spent her last years reminding everyone of the value of her fieldwork.

2. The role of America in Mead's theory and rhetoric is discussed brilliantly in Varenne (2000).

3. In 1919, Elsie Clews Parsons taught a course at the New School on Sex in Ethnology. Ruth Benedict was in that course, and a few years later Mead was in Benedict's course. Parsons's book *The Family* (1906) used ethnographic data to argue for an assault on received arrangements governing premarital sex. The topic and mode of presentation were in the air (Lamphere 1989; Zumwalt 1992).

4. A history of the issues and the times is available in Bock (1980) and Spindler (1978). An example of Mead at diaper wild is her 1951 film *Bathing Babies in Three Cultures,* in which Balinese, American, and New Guinea cultures are defined by small differences in how mothers in the three cultures handle their baby's bath. The bathing scenes do not deliver the differences to which Mead points, and her conclusions feel forced. This is unfortunate, because interaction rituals are a great starting point for cultural analysis. Ironically, a good example is the still photograph analyses Bateson and Mead (1942) produced with Balinese materials, discussed below.

5. For a sampler of the team's work, see Belo (1970). Along with Covarrubias (1937), de Zoete and Spies (1938) and McPhee (1947), the books make Bali in the 1930s a classic field site. For intercultural intrigue, intellectual verve, and international politics, the group is worth a study. Mead's own accounts in her autobiography (1972) and *Letters* (1977) are interesting, but not as juicy as the stories in Jane Howard's biography (1984) or the biting exposé by Pollmann (1990).

6. Mead liked to stereotype members of a group with a partial account of their char-

acter and its hardships. In Baldwin and Mead (1971), she picked on the Irish because they get angry when "they're in love. It was one of the things that I used to watch with my child when we shared a household with a family where the wife was Irish. . . . So my daughter was beginning to learn that anger and love are the same thing, which she wasn't supposed to learn, because she wasn't Irish, after all" (42). Oliver Cromwell could not have had a better reason to rid the earth of the Irish.

7. For the demanding position that the past lives on in the present not because it is determining but because it is behaviorally re-created ad nauseum in present circumstances, nothing is stronger than Bateson (1971).

8. For a celebration of Bateson's photography, see Hagaman (1995); for a heated disagreement between Mead and Bateson on how to work with cameras, see Bateson (1976). For a restudy of their careful photographic work, see Sullivan (1999).

9. While Bateson and Mead were working on "awayness" among the Balinese, James Joyce, in *Finnegans Wake* (1939:100), coined the term "attenshune" to cover his experience among the Irish (it works better without the final "e"). Bateson's ideas on the push and pull of "awayness" or "attenshun," what he called "schizmogenesis," were taken from his reading of Butler, *The Way of All Flesh* (1903).

10. In a pair of books, an American psychiatrist and a Balinese mental health worker have criticized Bateson and Mead's description of "awayness" and other personality traits. They believe national character traits to be ethnographically interesting but think Bateson and Mead failed to capture the Balinese from inside (Jensen and Suryani 1992; Suryani and Jensen 1992). Bateson and Mead's generalizations, particularly relating Balinese character to schizophrenia, left critics much to attack, but the depth of their observations remains unparalleled.

11. Clifford Geertz (1988:4) rejects Mead's "culture-and-personality speculations" in *Balinese Character* (Bateson and Mead 1942) but reports that they do not "seem to detract very much from the cogency of her observations, unmatched by any of the rest of us, concerning what the Balinese are like." To this high praise, he adds that, though Mead believed Bateson's photographs "demonstrated her arguments, hardly anyone, including Bateson, much agreed with her." Bateson's half of the book had little influence on the study of Bali or on anthropology in general, but was a major influence on the development of behavior analysis. Erving Goffman (1979:34), with characteristic ambivalence, said *Balinese Character* "brilliantly pioneered in the use of pictures for the study of what can be neatly pictured."

12. *Balinese Character* (Bateson and Mead 1942) is one of two landmark books for the study of body movement as communication as practiced by Ray Birdwhistell (1970) and Adam Kendon (1990). The second book is by another student of Boas, David Efron (1941), on the gestural world of Jewish and Italian immigrants to New York City. After her rich experience with film in Bali, Mead would often write as if it were simple to record, "scientifically," the behavioral patterns of a people. She sometimes knew the

difference between a good description and a set of pictures; see, for example, Mead and Byers (1968).

13. Boon is more willing to celebrate the methodological importance of Bateson and Mead: their "extraordinary field methods (involving photographs, filming, and several varieties of simultaneous writing) deserve a study in their own right" (1986:223).

14. *American Anthropologist* 82 (1980). Franz Boas had an AAA memoir dedicated to him at a time when members received both the journal and occasional memoirs.

15. The next year, biographies by J. Howard (1984) and M. C. Bateson (1984) revealed some of the details of Mead's sex life, including affairs with Edward Sapir and Ruth Benedict. It is nice no one seemed to care about the revelations, and it is even nicer to think Mead's work on sexual mores in different cultures was in part responsible for the shift in sensitivities. It is amazing that Margaret Mead's fieldwork methods were more important to newspapers than her sex life. The Benedict-Mead relationship now has its own study (Lapsley 1999).

16. For a quick response from six Pacific specialists, see Brady (1983). A later collection by Foerstel and Gilliam (1992) is more critical, as is the volume written by the Samoan Chief Malopa'upo Isaia (1999). An insightful critique of the Boasians, including the early work of Margaret Mead, is the testament to long-term fieldwork by Paul Radin. He accuses Mead's ethnography of "a pretentious impressionism, and a counsel of perfection," and more importantly complains that despite all the rhetoric given to the importance of the individual, Mead, among others, rejects the "individual in favor of psychological catchwords, such as unconscious development, patterns, psychological sets, and configurations" (1987[1933]:44).

17. Freeman's self-involvement in writing the book is revealed by the title of the second edition, *Margaret Mead and the Heretic* (1995). If we add his second volume of complaints (1998), we can estimate that Freeman spent about as many years critiquing Mead in Samoa as she spent weeks in the field, and she is still more convincing. Even if Freeman is right about Mead being the victim of a hoax, there is still no reason to accept the naive realism of his biological arguments.

18. A previous great controversy in anthropology, between Robert Redfield and Oscar Lewis on Tepoztlán, was mined by the next generation for accounts of how divergent methods generate divergent results. Lewis was more interesting than Freeman, but the terms of his debate with Redfield are echoed by Freeman's attack on Mead. Read Lewis in a letter to Redfield (June 11, 1948) and experience how Freeman might write to Mead: "Much of the unity and bonds of family life in Tepoztlán flow from what might be called negative factors rather than positive ones. . . . It would be missing many of the crucial aspects of Tepoztlán not to see the great amount of internal tensions and conflict that exist, as well as frustrations and maladjustments. . . . The idea that folk cultures produce less frustrations than non-folk cultures or that the quality of human relationships is necessarily superior in folk-cultures seems to me to be sheer Rousseauian romanticism." A subsequent letter (May 13, 1954), in response to a paper by

Redfield, gives a more complete description of Tepoztlán: It "made me keenly aware of the shortcomings in my version of Tepoztlán with its accentuation of the negative aspects of life. It is true that I had often thought of how far 'we' had come compared to Tepoztlán, especially in terms of the potential of our civilization. But I was never really satisfied that I had conveyed the 'wholeness' of Tepoztlán life and you have put into words and thoughts more beautiful than I had ever conceived the very aspects of peasant life that I had left out. In my next community study, if I should ever do another, I must strive for the 'good and the bad' as you have put it." Both letters appear in Rigdon (1988:205, 213). Lewis's next fieldwork stayed tuned to the hard side of life, but rarely seemed as crass as Freeman.

19. What counts as sex in Samoa is a point of controversy (Grant 1995; Shankman 1996).

20. On Mead and Freeman not giving readers the detail to evaluate who is wrong or right, see Orans (1996).

21. Wise methodological advice aside, Benedict's wartime description of Japan (1946a) has been subject to much critique. The Japanese do not always behave as she suspected from a distance, nor do they worry about it much (Lummis 1980; see Kent 1996 for a defense of Benedict and a critique of Lummis; for an intriguing reading of Benedict, see Varenne 1984).

22. It is not the ethnographer's job to predict how people will behave, for they are always too complex for that. The alternative is to predict when people might be surprised with each other's behavior (Frake 1980).

23. Critical literature on Mead has moved beyond Samoa. Freeman's attack was followed by the complaints discussed above on her Balinese effort. The same year delivered Foerstel and Gilliam (1992) with complaints by the grandchildren of Mead's New Guinea informants, some of them anthropologists, on how much she was a part of the America that has constrained their lives unfairly. A recent critique (Roscoe 2003) and response (di Leonardo 2003) on Mead's comments on Arapesh warfare shows the intensity of feeling involved.

24. Sapir (1994:181–182) goes on: "The presumptive or 'as-if' psychological character of a culture is highly determinative, no doubt, of much in the externalized system of attitudes and habits which forms the visible personality of an individual. It does not follow, however, that strictly social determinants, tending, as they do to give visible form and meaning, in a cultural sense, to each of the thousands of modalities of experience which sum up the personality, can define the fundamental structure of such a personality."

25. Victor Barnouw says, "Mead had an unfortunate tendency, of which Freeman takes advantage, to make stronger and broader assertions in later publications than she did in her original study" (1983:428) Samoans are more uniformly peaceful and noncompetitive in her later summaries than in the early ethnography.

26. Gilliam and Foerstel write that Betty Lou Valentine said Mead claimed, at a talk

in the early 1960s, that African Americans have low self-esteem (1992:110). The idea
was in the air in liberal circles, although it left obscure why there was so little self-
esteem to go around and why White liberals seemed to acquire so much of it. See, for
example, Kardiner and Ovesey (1951) on the effects of poverty on the psychic life of African Americans. At the same time, Deutsch (1967) was writing essays about "cultural
deprivation" as the reason for African American children not doing well in school, and
Oscar Lewis (1970) was pointing to "a culture of poverty" to explain the psychic life
of poverty across generations. For a critique, see Charles Valentine (1968) and Mead's
unfortunate response (1968).

27. For an account of Landes's harsh life in anthropology, see Park and Park (1989)
and Sally Cole (2003). Weltfish's life was only a little less difficult (Pathé 1989; Niehaus,
this volume). Hurston's story is as complex as her talent was extraordinary. It is now
popular to praise Hurston by pointing to how Boas and Mead, by their style of work
and their personally not lending a hand, suppressed her talent. Some critiques go beyond the facts. Hurston should be praised, but no more so than either Boas or Mead.
Together, their strong points offer a three-part impulse for reorganizing America. For
one discussion, see Gordon (1992).

28. Mead grew up surrounded by a public discussion of the rewards and dangers
of coeducation (see Tyack and Hansot 1990 for a masterful overview). A glance at psychologist G. Stanley Hall's ideas on the potentials of women would have kept Mead
opposed to the biologically phrased essentialism of the time. Her slip back to an essentialism was subtle, more the move of a person who had not given up on nature as an
explanation of individual behavior than of a person who thought there were things that
women could not do if they had to.

29. John Dewey thought of nature and culture as contexts for each other and not
an appropriate contrast set: "the true antithesis of nature is not art [read: culture] but
arbitrary conceit, fantasy, and stereotyped convention" (1934:152). For Dewey, nature
and culture are to be studied together as the setting for "relationships that determine
the course of life." Mead shared a campus and milieu with Dewey for decades, but with
little direct influence. Their ideas overlap enough that it is hard to believe Mead would
not have read, as Benedict did, Dewey's *Human Nature and Conduct* (1922). Jane Howard
(1984) reports that Mead carried the book with her, and Sullivan (1999) uses a passage
from it to articulate Mead's account of "character" in Bali. Yans-McLaughlin (1986) says
students of Boas were encouraged to read Dewey, but textual ties seem weak (although
see Niehaus, this volume, for Weltfish and Dewey). Cremin (1965) placed Dewey and
Mead on alternate pages of a work on educational theory in the United States, and Wolf
(1972) used them as twin icons of liberal reform. At a memorial for Dewey in 1952,
the philosopher John Herman Randall (1953:10) told a story about Mead reading philosophy: "A few years ago, when Russell's *Human Knowledge* had just come out, I had a
phone call. 'This is Margaret Mead. I am reading Russell's book, and I wonder whether
you could tell me briefly just what is the difference between Russell and Dewey.' We

poor professors all get calls like that. But Margaret Mead is an intelligent girl—though she puts too much faith in improved diapers for my taste—so I made the attempt to answer her." The content of his answer was likely more to Mead's liking than his gender politics: Dewey's contribution, he said, was to work out "the implications of taking 'experience' as primarily the social experience of human communities. This makes 'experience' all that the anthropologist includes as belonging to human 'culture.'"

30. On the use of "natural" categories to divide the social field in line with established power distributions, see the essays in Yanagisako and Delaney (1995).

31. Mead did write on education, but only programmatically (Reed 1993). Although her critique of education was mostly correct, she was strangely harder on schools than on the business community or the military (Mead 1958).

32. The phrasing of this question comes from Bateson by way of a story told by Birdwhistell (1977:115). Near the end of a lifetime of claiming all organisms make sense if one knows their code, Bateson was asked what question he would put to any organism if he knew its code. Bateson answered, "I'd ask that animal under what conditions, in what setting, with how many and what organization of his fellows, and what order of duration of communication would be required for him to be capable of telling the truth." If Bateson and Mead agreed that all organisms make sense according to a specific code, they likely had a point of disagreement as well. Mead thought cultures were supposed to make sense, if not now, then after some reform, whereas Bateson suffered no such illusion. In her memoir Mary Catherine Bateson (1984:61) tells the story of looking with her father at a William Blake watercolor, Satan Exalting over Eve. The daughter wanted to know why, if Satan had just had his way with Eve, he did not look happy. The father's answer is an anthropologist's version of original sin: "Because he has started the process that produced congressmen and schizophrenia and picnics and policemen on the corner, and the whole bag of tricks called culture, and it's that vision that gives him the look of agony."

33. Mead received a master's degree in psychology at Columbia before she switched to working with Boas.

34. One of Bateson's first papers was about learning to play the flute among the Iatmul and its implications in the social organization of gender (1935). After the Iatmul, Bateson turned to the problem of learning to be a body in Bali and then learning to be schizophrenic in Palo Alto. Rich essays on learning across diverse settings appear in two collections of his essays (1972, 1991); the first contains the systematics paper titled "The Logical Categories of Learning and Communication."

35. In this way, they can be aligned with the diverse influence of F. C. Bartlett (Bateson's teacher), Lev Vygotsky, Kurt Lewin, and G. H. Mead (1934).

36. Yes, but really, aren't people differentially able? Sure, but that does not mean we know how to discern those differences or how to make the most of the variation. Worse, in thinking that we know how to sort people out, we can get a great deal wrong. Johann Wolfgang von Goethe said it better: "Maybe there are people who are by nature

not up to this or that business; precipitation and prejudice are, however, dangerous de-mons, unfitting the most capable person, blocking all effectiveness and paralysing free progress. This applies to worldly affairs, particularly, too, to scholarship" (1998:53; this line is from 1823).

37. Colin McPhee (1955) showed how Balinese children are effortlessly absorbed into gamelan groups by adults who sit behind them and guide their hands until they begin to play notes that contribute to the overall musical pattern.

38. At her worst Mead wrote of Bali as a culture producing a single kind of child. Contrast Bali as a uniform entity with the multilayered, perspectival wonder in Boon (1990:ix):

> What has come to be called Balinese culture is a multiply authored invention, a historical formation, an enactment, a political construct, a shifting paradox, an ongoing transla-tion, an emblem trademark, a nonconsensual negotiation of contrastive identity, and more. Its evidence is, to employ a bookish figure, well-thumbed. To make matters still more layered, practices and ideas associated with Bali—just one complex position in the so-called Malayo-Polynesian world—cut across different historical identities and classifications. They include for the foreseeable future "Indonesian" (alias Dutch East Indies, Indian Archipelago, etc.); from the fourteenth century onward "Hindu"; and in part (the Sanskritized part) what scholars call "Indo-European."

39. For theories of school failure, see Varenne and McDermott (1998).

4. Education and Democracy in the Anthropology of Gene Weltfish

Juliet Niehaus

Gene Weltfish at work weaving a basket, Oklahoma, circa 1925. With kind permission of Ann Margetson.

Thoroughly trained in the four-field approach championed by Franz Boas, Gene Weltfish (1902–80) conducted research in archaeology, ethnology, linguistics, race, and human migration. The Origins of Art (1953), which addresses the question of how and why art originated, and The Lost Universe (1965), an ethnohistory of Pawnee culture at the end of the nineteenth century, are her best-known works. Both these ethnographically detailed studies are in the Boasian tradition of historical particularism. A student of Boas and John Dewey at Columbia University in the 1920s, and a committed activist all her life, she developed her own theory of "pragmatic anthropology," as Juliet Niehaus explains. Weltfish's outspokenness on controversial issues such as disarmament and human rights made her a focal point of congressional investigation in the 1940s and an example of the consequences of political engagement during the McCarthy era.

Born Regina Weltfish, she was the older of two daughters in a middle-class Jewish family in New York City's Lower East Side. Even at a young age she was strong-willed and defiant. Her grandmother resolved one temper tantrum by negotiating a change of name to Gene. Eventually Weltfish legally took this first name and retained her family name when she married. The early death of her father forced her to abandon full-time schooling in order to help support her family. She completed high school by attending night school and then went on to Hunter College. By her senior year she had saved enough money to transfer to Barnard College and become a full-time student there.

In 1925 Weltfish, after finishing her undergraduate work, followed the trail of Margaret Mead and other Barnard graduates across Broadway to the Columbia Anthropology Department. Because of his antiwar stance during World War I, Boas had been forbidden by the president of Columbia University to teach undergraduates at Columbia College, but he was allowed to teach at Barnard, the nearby affiliated women's college. This circumstance and Boas's desire to develop the discipline led him to recruit many female doctoral students. For them he was a patriarchal figure whom they fondly called "Papa Franz." After his retirement, the number of women anthropology graduate students at Columbia University decreased markedly.

Weltfish completed her graduate education by writing a library dissertation about Native American basketry. In 1928 she and her then husband, Alexander Lesser, also a student of Boas, traveled to Oklahoma to conduct fieldwork. Lesser gathered kinship data on the Sioux while she investigated Pawnee life. In order to get to the Pawnee reservation, Weltfish had to travel six hours by stagecoach from the nearest train station. Weltfish returned to the Pawnee several times, taking her four-year-old daughter Ann with her in 1935. In addition to The Lost Universe, she wrote a survey of Caddoan languages with Alexander Lesser (Weltfish and Lesser 1932), collected Pawnee texts in 1935 (Weltfish 1936a, 1936b), and produced a record album of Pawnee songs in 1965.[1]

After Weltfish returned from the field in 1935, Boas appointed her to a teaching post at Columbia. She taught both in the graduate program and in the division known at the time as University Extension and later as the School of General Studies, a program for nontraditional students. Weltfish was instrumental in designing its anthropology curriculum. During World War II she remained at Columbia, focusing her energies on diffusing racial conflict and active in antifascist and civil rights organizations. With Ruth Benedict, she wrote the pamphlet The Races of Mankind (1943) and In Henry's Backyard (1948), a children's book encouraging racial tolerance.

Weltfish's concerns for equality and individual autonomy carried her to other arenas of human rights, including women's rights. She was elected a vice-president of the Women's International Democratic Federation at its founding convention in Paris in 1945 and served as president of its American branch, the Congress of American Women. The federation advocated equal rights for women in economic and legal arenas, improved health and welfare for children, and disarmament. In the late 1940s both organizations, along with others to which Weltfish had belonged or lent her name, were placed on a list of "subversive" groups compiled by the FBI. Her leadership in these organizations and her authorship of books promoting racial tolerance, at a time when Congress was still dominated by the same segregationist "Dixiecrats" who had been responsible for withdrawing The Races of Mankind from distribution to the army during World War II, contributed to her being targeted by the anti-Communist fervor then sweeping the country. She was called twice to testify in Washington—first, in 1952, before Senator Pat McCarran's subcommittee on internal security, and again in 1953, by Senator Joseph McCarthy's overconfidently named Permanent Subcommittee on Investigations. During both hearings the senators questioned her closely about statements she had supposedly made about U.S. use of germ warfare in the Korean War, then winding to a close.

Just before the second hearing Columbia notified her that she would not be rehired, after seventeen years of continuous employment. Although the stated reason was a new rule that eliminated her position, the likely reason was the ongoing congressional investigation of her political affiliation and activities. She was particularly vulnerable because her appointment to the School of General Studies, technically a part-time position, placed her outside the network of collegial support of those in academic departments. Another factor was the discrimination she faced as a woman, probably the reason she did not have the security of a tenure-track appointment in the first place. In any event, neither her colleagues nor the American Anthropological Association came forward to defend academic freedom and oppose her termination.

Although Weltfish was not the only anthropologist who was called to testify (see Price 2004), the personal consequences for her were perhaps the most severe. While others kept their jobs, she lost hers, suffering for years emotionally and financially. McCarthyism also had profound consequences for the discipline. Critical voices were muted, and Cold War politics affected not only academic appointments but also research funding and publication. Even theoretical discussions of Marxist thought did not re-emerge until the 1970s (Leacock 1982; Nader 1997).

It was not until 1961 that Weltfish returned to teaching, at Fairleigh Dickinson University in Madison, New Jersey. There she ran community service projects, advocated for the elderly, and developed a continuing education program on the campus. After she retired from Fairleigh Dickinson at the age of seventy and returned to New York City, she taught at the New School and continued to organize, creating a local association of medical anthropologists. Gene Weltfish completed her life with grace and verve, sharing the excitement of anthropology until her death.

Gene Weltfish (1902–80), one of the students trained by Franz Boas at Columbia in the 1920s, is perhaps best known for her ethnography of Pawnee life, The Lost Universe (1965). Most anthropologists are not, however, extensively acquainted with her work or with the details of her life. That Weltfish was not well known beyond a certain circle of cohorts, students, and students' students is partly related to her experience of political persecution during the McCarthy years of the 1950s. Yet one could also contend that her relative anonymity is a legacy of her faithfulness to the Boasian approach during and after World War II, when few anthropologists remained focused on historicity and holism, and even fewer maintained a commitment to the inherently applied goals of Boas's anthropology.

Weltfish, though a professed Boasian, was an independent and undogmatic thinker. In her later years, she respectfully differed from "Papa Franz" in certain emphases in her work, most markedly in her unremitting application of anthropology to social problems. She was a committed Boasian, but also an avowed pragmatist. A woman of the Progressive Era, she had been greatly influenced by the philosophy of John Dewey, with whom she studied at Columbia prior to her work in anthropology.

Weltfish's pragmatism, like Dewey's, is a developed epistemology—one focused on education, understood as the primary process of human life. Her blending of Boasian anthropology with pragmatic philosophy extends and amplifies the educational emphases in the thought of Boas and highlights other shared dimensions of the work of Boas and Dewey. Weltfish's work provides a commanding demonstration of a pragmatic anthropology that draws our attention to education's centrality in cultural life, continually contextualizes educational issues within larger human and social realms, and directly contends with the reconstruction of schooling to respond to wider educational goals.

Weltfish was a personally remarkable woman, one who would allow no artificial division between life and work. This chapter first presents an overview of Weltfish's career and then discusses the specific influences of Boas and Dewey on her work. Her integration of their thinking to emphasize "culture history as education" and the role of the anthropologist as interlocutor in the dialogue between primitive and modern culture is exemplified through a discussion of her major work, The Lost Universe. Weltfish's unique community venture, the American Civilization Institute, undertaken in the 1960s in Morristown, New Jersey, is then described along with its demonstration of "holistic" education—another uniquely Weltfishian merging of anthropology with Deweyan philosophy. The perspectives on education afforded by her work for the anthropologist interested in education are considered in the conclusion.

Weltfish: Life and Works

I met Weltfish in 1977, three years before her death at the age of seventy-seven. I was then a doctoral student at the Graduate Faculty of the New School for Social Research, where she held a visiting professorship, teaching courses in the anthropology of art, of work, and of aging. Weltfish was a rather dubious figure to the "radical" New School student of the 1970s. I recall her surrounded by nurses, foreign students connected with the United Nations, homeopaths, and other cultural marginals. A brash, swift-paced old woman laden with books and bags, she would charge through the dim corridors of the New School—past clusters of bearded, seditious-looking students smoking European cigarettes and discussing Habermas, Adorno, and Marcuse. Weltfish, I came to learn, preferred such "Progressive" scholars as F. M. Cornford, Lewis Mumford, and, of course, John Dewey. The Leftist contingent at the New School was quick to derisively label her "progressive liberal" at worst and naive at best. Regularly bringing articles from the *New York Times* to provoke discussion in the classroom, assigning the works of Dewey, and insisting on the primacy of intercultural communication were not popular modes of teaching in the late 1970s.

I wondered why she was teaching at Stanley Diamond's bastion of critical anthropology. When I asked him about her presence in the department, Diamond enigmatically smiled, shook his finger at me, and said, "She studied with Boas, you know." Diamond, along with other post–World War II Columbia-trained anthropologists, had taken courses from Weltfish when she held a faculty position there from 1935 to 1953. I was to find that the esteem in which he and others of his generation held her was grounded not only in her place in the anthropological genealogy and her academic contributions, but also in the courageous stands she took as a social activist in politically difficult times. Far from a naive liberal, Weltfish had challenged some of the most powerful political forces of the twentieth century. The story of Weltfish's life reveals both the best and the worst of the professional anthropologist's experience in the academy in the years immediately before and after World War II.

Weltfish had come to Columbia in 1925. Not the typical Ivy League student, she was born in New York's Lower East Side in 1902, the older of two daughters of Jewish parents. Her father was Viennese by birth; her mother's parents had emigrated from Odessa. In 1912 her father died unexpectedly, leaving her family without means of support. She thus began work at fourteen in order to help support the family. Employed in various commercial jobs during the day, she completed her schooling at night and earned her high school degree in 1919. She continued to work and attend night school at Hunter College where she majored in journalism. She managed to save enough money to attend college full time and entered Barnard for her senior year. Here she minored in philosophy and studied with John Dewey. It was also here that she first was introduced to the anthropology of Franz Boas, who taught undergraduate anthropology to Barnard students.

While working and attending school at night, Weltfish partook of a New York in the 1920s that was flavored by immigrant concerns, the settlement house movement, women's suffrage, and the avant-garde. She came to a Columbia that was dominated by the Progressive thought of such scholars as John Dewey, who had come from the University of Chicago in 1904, Charles Beard, the historian, and Morris Raphael Cohen, the philosopher.[2] Though Weltfish had majored in journalism prior to her matriculation at Barnard, her interest seems to have receded after her exposure to the philosophers. She studied with both Dewey and Cohen, minored in philosophy at Barnard, and had an initial interest in epistemology before her course with Boas pushed her in the direction of graduate work in anthropology (Weltfish 1980:124).

In "Franz Boas: The Academic Response" she conveys her enthusiasm at the way Boas had developed for his students an appreciation for "the broad panorama of human experience" (123). She decided to pursue graduate work in anthropology and entered the program at Columbia in 1925. Boas, in his characteristically patriarchal manner, dictated that she would study art. Weltfish acquiesced, though later she was less inclined to accept the dicta of "Papa Franz." Boas, who was himself at work on the subject of art in the late 1920s (Boas 1955[1927]), assigned her the study of the technology of American Indian basketry for her dissertation topic. Because she did not have the economic resources to pursue fieldwork, she undertook an exhaustive study of museum materials. She completed and defended her dissertation "Technique and Design in American Indian Basketry" in 1929.[3]

Her dissertation, summarized in an article published in the *American Anthropologist* in 1930, identified the technique of weaving as an important factor in the artistic dimensions of basketry among North American Indians. In the absence of historical or detailed archaeological information about early Indian culture, Boas had in his years as a museum curator established the practice of classifying material objects according to tribe or geographic region. Though this was a more culturally responsive approach than the earlier museum practice of classification according to tool or object category, Weltfish felt it failed to address the active dimension of manufacturing. Her thesis identified the actual technical process of weaving inherent to basic styles of basketry and connected these styles to historical traditions. She thus developed a more culturally specific, historically valid classification. The work also added the important component of human creativity to the understanding of material objects.

After completing her thesis, Weltfish pursued at Boas's request a field study of the Pawnee language in conjunction with fieldwork on basket-making technology with American Indian groups in the Southwest. Linguistics had been an early interest, which she said she might have pursued had she been able to do fieldwork, and had Boas not pushed her in the direction of art. Her attraction to linguistics grew from her epistemological training. Language and its categories was for her an important key to understanding the workings of the human mind. In the 1930s, she authored works on Pawnee linguistic texts with her then husband, Alexander Lesser, and in 1935 Boas hired her to teach at Columbia. For the next seventeen years, she taught in the graduate anthropology program there and also held special duties in the General Studies Division, which served nontraditional adult students. There, in addition to her teaching duties, she constructed the anthropology curriculum. Weltfish's attention to the special needs of adult students served by the division contributed to her lifelong interest and commitment to nontraditional student learning.

During the war years, Weltfish joined other anthropologists contributing to the war effort. While many of her colleagues worked for the War Department, she placed her efforts on the domestic front, where she committed much time and energy to promoting peaceful relations between groups, especially to the fight against racism. She lectured throughout the country and wrote *The Races of Mankind* (Benedict and Weltfish 1943) with Ruth Benedict in the early 1940s. Originally a pamphlet, written at the request of the USO for distribution to the armed forces and used in the de-Nazification program in Germany following the war (Pathé 1988:379), it was to become quite controversial.

In 1944 a dispute arose over whether the book had depicted Northern Blacks as more intelligent than Southern Whites. In fact, what was stated was that both Northern Whites and Northern Blacks showed higher IQ scores than their Southern counterparts on World War I army intelligence tests. In the tradition of Boas, this finding was emphatically connected to differing levels of economic and educational advantage rather than to race (Benedict and Weltfish 1943:18). Nevertheless, the pamphlet was banned from armed forces libraries and later was declared subversive material. Perhaps because Benedict played a clear role in War Department anthropology and maintained a fairly nonradical image following the war, and because she died in 1948, her career did not suffer from the uproar associated with the pamphlet. The debacle was, however, to have a significant impact on Weltfish's future. The book's contents were to re-emerge as an issue for her in the 1950s during the McCarthy years, when she was called twice to testify before Senate committees.

Weltfish's political activities during and after World War II had included concern with issues facing women and children worldwide in the wake of the war. She had participated in the international women's movement in the 1940s, and at a convention in Paris in 1945, she was elected vice-president of the Women's International Democratic Federation. She was then elected president of the U.S. affiliate of this organization, the Congress of American Women, a group that was placed on the roster of subversive organizations in the late 1940s. Weltfish was brought before McCarthy's committee in spring 1953. Though she did not admit Communist involvement, she was terminated at Columbia soon afterward. Columbia never acknowledged a connection between Weltfish's termination and the publicity she was receiving due to the McCarthy hearings. The "official" rationale for the termination was a "new" ruling, which held that all part-time instructors could only remain on staff for five years. If a full-time departmental position could not be created for them in that time, their appointment would be terminated. This ruling could be waived, although in Weltfish's case it was not. Columbia administrators stated that there were no funds for a full-time anthropology position at that time (New York Times, April 1, 1953:1, 19). She may have also suffered from the same difficulties experienced by Ruth Benedict, whose promotion on the faculty at Columbia seemed to be continually hindered because she was a woman (see Pathé 1988:377 and Mintz 1981:161). Weltfish herself attributed her termination to the discrimination against women academics at the university.

After her dismissal, she was unable to find work teaching in New York. John Champe, the Nebraskan archaeologist, offered her a haven at the University of Nebraska. She accepted and for the next five years spent considerable periods of time there updating and expanding on the work she had begun among the Pawnee in the late 1920s. In 1958 she received a Bollingen Foundation grant, which allowed her to write up her Pawnee material. From this was born The

Lost Universe (1965). In addition to her Pawnee work, other publications of the 1950s included *The Origins of Art* (1953) and a number of journal articles on such topics as ethnicity, the relation between culture history and science, and the nature and social relevance of anthropological knowledge (see Weltfish 1956, 1959, 1960b). During this period her work increasingly evidenced the integration of pragmatic thinking into her Boasian perspective.

The early 1960s saw the end of Weltfish's exile from the academic world. She was hired by Fairleigh Dickinson University, where she remained teaching anthropology full-time until 1972. While at Fairleigh, she actively pursued a number of community projects in addition to her teaching load. Primary among these was a local history program she designed for the Morristown, New Jersey, community.[4] When she was seventy years old, retirement was forced on her. She then came to the New School at Stanley Diamond's invitation.

When I met Gene, I was starting my doctoral research under Diamond on German-American ethnicity. Gene was then actively involved in forming the New York Metropolitan Medical Anthropology Association. She was also (at age seventy-five) teaching anthropology at the Manhattan School of Music and actively considering, if not actively involved with, a number of community projects. Weltfish, as mentioned earlier, had written on the topic of ethnicity in the 1950s and 1960s, and when my friend and colleague Louis DuValle, who was working with her on Chinese-American medicine, mentioned my work on ethnicity, Weltfish decided that she should teach us something about the topic. We met for tutorials on ethnicity in her spare, book-lined studio apartment on West 72nd Street. And so began the snacks of apples and cheese and Norwegian biscuits, and the lunches at her seemingly favorite establishment, the American Restaurant, a classic New York Greek coffee shop. In the course of our work with Weltfish, we were instructed in the tradition of a "scientific" Boas who emphasized empiricism, holism, and historical reconstruction as a basis for studying culture. We also learned about a "humanistic" Boas who believed in the application of anthropology to the solution of contemporary social problems—a Boas who saw anthropology as itself educative of the public.

The Boasian Legacy

When Weltfish came to Columbia in 1925, Boas was well along in developing his unique American approach to anthropology. Boas's anthropology sub-

stantively differed from that of nineteenth-century European ethnology in its
concept of culture, its empiricism, and its challenge to unilinear evolutionism.[5] Boas's well-known war against the deductive evolutionism of the nineteenth century was not a battle fought against Darwinian thought per se, but
against the inaccurate and unempirical application of evolutionary theory to
the study of human culture. As the natural scientist describes, classifies, and
analyzes the phenomena of nature, Boas understood anthropology's task to
be the "analytical description of cultural forms" (Boas 1966b:267). Particular
culture history, Lesser (1981) argues, was in Boas's mind the equivalent of the
evolutionary history of particular species in the Darwinian model. Boas, however, understood culture change to be different from the process of biological evolution. In "The Aims of Anthropological Research," written in 1932, he
states:

> There is one fundamental difference between biological and cultural data which
> makes it impossible to transfer the methods of the one science to the other. Ani-
> mal forms develop in divergent directions, and an intermingling of species that
> have once become distinct is negligible in the whole developmental history. It
> is otherwise in the domain of culture. Human thoughts, institutions, activities
> may spread from one social unit to another. As soon as two groups come into
> close contact their cultural traits will be disseminated from the one to the other.
> (1966a:251)

The uniqueness of human culture within the natural world prompted Boas
to emphasize holism in its study. Holism implied not only historical data but
comparative studies as well. The entire spectrum of humanness was to be considered by Boas's science, with its domain the history of the human species
in all places and throughout time. Boas was skeptical about the discovery of
universal laws of culture similar to those that had been derived by evolutionary
science for biological forms. His anthropology was a "historical science" focusing on the study of individual phenomena rather than searching for general
laws or constructing analytical models that he felt to be too reductive of cultural process (Boas 1966a:258). Reflecting his more developed understanding
of culture, Boas states:

> Cultural phenomena are of such complexity that it seems to me doubtful

> whether valid cultural laws can be found. The causal conditions of cultural
> happenings lie always in the interaction between individual and society, and
> no classificatory study of societies will solve this problem (257).

By the time Weltfish came to Columbia, Boas, having established his basic methodology, was trying to better understand the dynamics of cultural phenomena. This later shift in focus influenced Weltfish's training at Columbia. Boas was asking new questions: Based on historical and comparative information, how do aspects of a culture impact one on the other? How does culture influence the lives of its members? How are individuals affected by, and how might they in turn affect, culture change? His fight against viewing anthropology as a social science stemmed from his wariness of the scientific reification of culture. Boas was aware not only that culture was a formative power in individual life but also that the individual, as carrier of culture, could transform or intervene in culture. Culture was always thus subject to the intervention of an important independent variable: the creative individual.

This insight into the relationship between the individual and culture, especially regarding the constraining effects of tradition, laid the basis for Boas's critique of contemporary education in its relationship to a democratic society. In the collection of papers and talks published by his son following Boas's death, Race and Democratic Society (1945), we find very clear statements on these issues. In an address to the American Association of Scientific Workers in 1939, Boas clarified his understanding of democratic society:

> If we speak of democracy we mean one in which civil liberties have been at-
> tained, where not only thought is free, but where every one has the right to
> express his opinions, where censorship is shunned, where the actions of the in-
> dividual are not restricted as long as they do not interfere with the freedom and
> welfare of his fellow citizens. We affirm that only in such a society can fullest
> intellectual freedom be attained. (1945:216)

Boas understood that intellectual freedom is more than the absence of political restrictions on thought. Intellectual freedom implies the ability to think clearly and reasonably. His anthropological studies had taught him that culture was itself an important factor in restricting freedom of thought. The unconscious phenomena of culture often unreasonably direct our habits and emotional life. He emphasizes, "Uncontrolled emotionalism is the greatest enemy of intellectual freedom. To educate people to rational ideals without destroying their emotional life is one of the great and difficult tasks of our times" (17).

Where does Boas find antidotes to this "uncontrolled emotionalism"? He looks first to education as the institution through which free thinkers should be created. Rational, nonemotional, and nonhabitual thinking should be the target of education. Only when a nation of free thinkers was produced by the educational system starting in childhood could a truly democratic society be created and fostered.

Boas was dismayed at the actual nature of American education. He chastised its tendency to teach and reinforce patriotic and emotionally laden ideals rather than to foster rational, critical thinking about self and society. Furthermore, he felt that "the very foundation of a democratic education is the requirement that every child should be given the opportunity to develop as fully as possible the powers given to him by nature" (189). This was far from achieved by our educational system, where lack of access and opportunity for the poor and discriminated against were examples of what he called "bigoted democracy."

Boas indicted teachers to the extent that they did not encourage active participation in democratic life by their students, or that in their own lives they replicated outdated, unconscious patterns of thinking. A teacher's task is not only to impart factual learning, in Boas's mind, but to educate personalities through fostering the development of will power, control of emotions, and active participation in the society (186–190).

Anthropology, the science itself, also could play an important role in educating the public about culture and providing rational, scientific countering to the habitual thinking of the past. Boas's social activism, which primarily took the form of press releases and acerbic letters to newspapers and magazines, reflected his belief in the role anthropology should play in cultural critique and change. Much of his early activism was, as is well known, linked to his antiwar efforts and his fight against racism. Less publicized were his efforts to fight the proliferation of "bigoted democracy." This thinking seems to have had a profound effect on Weltfish and corresponds closely in many elements to that of John Dewey.

The Pragmatic Legacy

In the many sessions with Weltfish, we heard a depth of thinking about anthropology as a science and the role of the anthropologist as social change agent that are only hinted at in Boas's writing. These ideas, I believe, were stimulated by the pragmatism of John Dewey, with whom Weltfish also studied at Columbia and whose books she recommended to students throughout her lifetime as a teacher. Dewey's philosophy is complex, with epistemological, moral, aesthetic, and political dimensions.[6] This discussion highlights Dewey's basic notion of human nature as this relates to his central concepts of human experience and growth, followed by a brief discussion of the implications of these ideas for his focus on education and democracy. Those are the fundamental elements of his thinking most evident in Weltfish's work.

Human Nature

Dewey's thinking, like Boas's, was grounded in natural history. Though a philosopher, Dewey also considered his work to be part of the expansion of natural science of the nineteenth and early twentieth centuries. Philosophizing itself was to be considered as a human phenomenon and thus subject to scientific scrutiny. For Dewey, the central feature that separates humans within the natural world is the capacity to think. Thought was the "instrument" of the human species in its efforts to adapt to the world. Through thought, including its manifestations in philosophy and science, humans are able to reflect on their interactions with the external world and to consider the consequences of actions they take. They are able to learn what is effective in their problem-solving efforts and what is not. This problem-solving process characterizes all human activity.

Although Dewey emphasizes the human capacity for thought, his pragmatism rejects the classic philosophical dualisms between mind and body and between internal and external worlds. Humans think in reaction to the environment; the environment is interpreted, given meaning, and modified by the human mind. Furthermore, the internal world of humans develops through the interaction between self and environment, both social and physical. Thus a separation of the inner and outer realms is artificial and obscures the real nature of human life. For Dewey, external experience is not merely that of the physical world but also that of the social world. Dewey understood that the sociocultural realm of human life is equally, if not at times the most, challenging to our faculties.

This tenet of pragmatism, that there is no rigid division between mind and body, or self and society, laid the basis for Dewey's exploration of the interactive process in human life. This process, dubbed *experience* by Dewey, became the central focus in his inquiry into the nature of human life and growth.

Experience

Experience refers to the process whereby human thought, emergent in interaction between past experience and the present environmental challenge (physical or social), produces a solution that may or may not be successful. Each experience lays the groundwork for further tests. This indicated for Dewey that there could be no absolute Truth. What is true is what works in any given situation. Pragmatism therefore rests on inductive scientific inquiry. Practical experience, and the application of theory to concrete life, is the indispensable test of any theory.

In Dewey's concept of experience, therefore, we also find the resolution of another dualism: that between theory and practice. Experience implies the active effort to put into practice the theory that one conceives. Theorizing without active application is not meaningful to the pragmatist. The human mind seeks to solve problems and through these solutions to adapt more successfully to our environmental challenges. In continued efforts to find new and better solutions, we grow and develop as individuals, as societies, and as a species. Problem solving, the essential process of human experience, is basic to all human endeavor.

Growth

Dewey saw the world in its totality as a realm of emergent, growing things. Evolution, which Dewey speaks of most often as simply *growth*, is inherent to human nature as part of the natural world. Social evolution is emergent in the experiential moments of human life, in which new challenges pose new opportunities for learning.[7] This growth through experience is the very "stuff" of human life and history. Dewey saw strong implications of his theory for our understandings of both education and democracy.

Education

The notion that the primary process of human life is learning through experience inevitably led to Dewey's interest in education. For Dewey, *education* is a lifelong process of passive undergoing in conjunction with active experimentation. Experiential learning is basic to all human activity, whether reflected in the everyday problem solving of the individual, in the inductive work of the scientist, or in social interaction and political life.

Dewey was dismayed by the reduction of education to the passive acquisition of knowledge. In a number of works, including *My Pedagogic Creed* (1897), *The School and Society* (1899), *Democracy and Education* (1916), *Art as Experience* (1934), and *Experience and Education* (1938), he emphasizes the active dimension of learning and the need to implement a type of schooling in which active experimentation would allow students to engage in truly meaningful learning in the classroom. His own "laboratory school," founded while he was at the University of Chicago from 1894 to 1904, sought to create this type of institution. Students were taught in the context of learning occupations. For example, in cooking classes, students learned weights and measures. They learned about the economics of production and distribution through engaging in the manufacture of items and then following their movement throughout the economic system through visits to actual factories and distributing sites. Such an education created students who understood in depth the process of living in their society and who could transfer their problem-solving capacities to any number of activities in life. This type of individual could be a real participant in the community. Schools were, in fact, for Dewey primarily social institutions—places where the important social learning took place. Therefore, they should always be in articulation with community and home life. For Dewey, education and democracy were tightly connected.

Democracy

Dewey is perhaps best known as the prophet of Progressive democracy. He defined *democracy* as not merely a political form, but as "a mode of associated

living, of conjoint communicated experience" (1944[1916]:87). A democratic
society was, Dewey felt, most conducive to human growth. The experiential
learning so basic to human nature would be maximized in a society where
freedom of thought and speech combined with the active interchange of ideas.
Coercive political structures, racism, and bigotry deadened the interaction of
talent, energy, and ideas.

A democracy was, in a way, a special kind of community: one where diverse
peoples came together and could share and exchange the solutions each had
generated to life's challenges. Dewey was especially impressed by the opportunities for social growth that immigrant communities could provide the American democratic community. Other cultural ways, borne by the immigrant, provided important external challenges to the existing social order and provided
access to alternate solutions should Americans be open to dialogue.

In his continued effort to override the dualistic separation between individual and society, Dewey stresses that this kind of democracy implies not only a
characteristic type of social interaction but also an individual state of mind. For
Dewey, democratic life rests on voluntarily cooperative action with individuals
readily participating in the maintenance of their way of life. Dewey clarifies:
"Instead of thinking of our own dispositions and habits as accommodated
to certain institutions, we have to learn to think of the latter as expression,
projections, and extensions of habitually dominant personal attitudes in individual human beings" (1944 [1916]:222–223). Individuals, open to interaction
and exchange, and educated in the processes of experiencing and learning, are
both the beginning and end of a democratic life.

Dewey was far from convinced that the brand of democracy in the United
States fulfilled his ideal. Like Boas, Dewey spent much of his life as a social
activist, lecturing and contributing his energies to social reform movements
in an attempt to increase communication between groups and to right injus-
tices. He often called attention to the ways in which his ideal was not realized.
For example, in his article "Creative Democracy—The Task before Us," written
when he was eighty years old, he states,

> Intolerance, abuse, calling of names because of differences of opinion about
> religion or politics or business, as well as because of differences of race, color,
> wealth, or degree of culture, are treason to the democratic way of life. Merely

legal guarantees of the civil liberties of free belief, free expression, free assembly are of little avail if in daily life freedom of communication, the give and take of ideas, facts, experiences, is choked by mutual suspicion, by abuse, by fear and hatred. These things destroy the essential conditions of the democratic way of living more effectually than open coercion. (1968:225)

Central to Dewey's concern is that citizens recognize the importance of other viewpoints, other lifestyles and cultures, to the future of American society. Communication between groups toward the end of sharing solutions and developing in new directions is critical to the continued life of a democratic society.

Syntheses

This overview of some essential aspects of Dewey's work indicates that there were significant convergences in his views and those of Boas. Both saw their disciplines as rooted in the natural sciences. Dewey's efforts to resolve the dualism between mind and matter, individual and society, leads him to ask questions similar to those of Boas, who, in tackling the relationship between the individual and culture, also explores the ambiguity of cultural process. The notion of growth through interaction, experimentation, problem solving, and "using what works" in Dewey's pragmatism is similar to the interpretations Boas applies to understanding the process of culture history: groups come into contact, share ideas and technology, and select those that are meaningful in their own lives. And as Boas hoped that anthropological knowledge could teach us something about our own problems, Dewey finds in immigrant cultures new ideas that would contribute to a developing American society. Boas and Dewey both critique present life in the United States as a bogus democracy and spend much of their time actively in pursuit of social justice. Finally, both see education as central to rectifying the lapses in American democracy, focusing on its role in producing rational and creative citizens. It is these similarities between the two scholars that Weltfish integrates into her "pragmatic anthropology."

Weltfish emphasizes culture history as representative of a particular group's problem-solving experiences when faced with its own particular environmental challenges. She understands anthropology itself to be a "tool" for use to the end of continued better adaptation of the human species. Anthropological science has as its goal facilitating communication between past and present, between primitive and modern cultures as the basis for implementing change. In all her anthropological efforts, she maintains a holistic viewpoint, understanding this to mean more than a utilization of the four-field approach toward understanding human phenomena. Weltfish elaborates holism to incorporate Dewey's resolution of the dichotomies between individual and society, mind and body, theory and practice. In all dimensions of her work, as with Dewey's, education and learning take on a central place in understanding the processes of human life.

Culture History as Experiential Learning

Boasian anthropology was built around the central understanding that cultural differences are not born of any inherent mental differences but are a function of our varied histories. The phenomena of culture would be primarily accessible in culture history. Reconstructing the history of various cultures had revealed the complexity and particularity of human cultural process—a dynamic of diffusion and invention in the midst of the continuous articulation between individual and culture. This appreciation of particular culture histories as unique phenomena was central to Weltfish's work.

Weltfish was dismayed by the theorist's tendency to lose contact with the on-the-ground reality of human history. History was grounded in the dilemmas real people face daily. Her distaste for professional jargon and reductive thinking made her, as Morton Fried states, "positively famous for her remarkably low tolerance of academic nonsense" (Fried 1980:263). As neophyte graduate students easily seduced by the glitz of metatheory, we would often provoke her chagrin. Weltfish would ridicule us when we lapsed into rhetoric, insisting we should talk about the real world, real people, and real history. This meant no easy globalizations: No "They constrain us . . . ," no "the State compels us . . ." Rather, she emphasized: What do people do? How have they constructed their social lives? How do they experience their lives and their worlds?

In the Boasian tradition, she maintained that there is no static culture in the sense that the culture pattern theorists had described. She states, "A single pattern of culture is an unjustifiable fiction with relation to any group—an administrative hope, perhaps, but not a social reality" (1956:215). The nature of culture history was, in Weltfish's thinking, however, strongly colored by the Deweyan notion of growth through problem-solving and intercultural communication. As she states in *The Origins of Art*, "In different places and in different times, each civilization has worked out its own way of coping with its problems" (1953:227). Culture change emerges from the results of new solutions to problems posed (invention) and from diffusion that is, in her thinking, precisely the communication and sharing of solutions to basic life problems. The result is a continual modification of group life as newer and better solutions to the problems of living posed by the physical and social environment are learned and exchanged.[8] Culture history is essentially a process of experiential education, wherein Dewey's learning through exchange and active experimentation occurs in the realm of social life and results in cultural change and growth.

The Anthropologist as Interlocutor: Learning from the Pawnee

To Weltfish, like Boas, anthropology was less a social science than a natural science (Weltfish 1980). Social science was developing an overly reductive picture of the human world—the human experience could not be broken down into isolatable analytic units. In her own work, she often sought to define more clearly the nature of the anthropological epistemology as one that highlighted the complexity of cultural phenomena as natural ones in their own right. For example, in her article "The Anthropologist and the Question of the Fifth Dimension" (1960a) she argues that the even the material dimensions of objects in the physical world are filtered, interpreted, and understood through the medium of culture itself. Culture, she maintains, has itself become a significant dimension of objective reality.

Weltfish's aversion to the elaboration of scientific models in anthropology grew, like Boas's, from an awareness of the depth of culture's effect on our thinking. She was convinced that anthropologists must always be self-critical of their scientific thinking. Western science was, she wanted us to remember, our own creation—one of any number of human epistemologies. It was epistemology itself, the human process of thinking and creating symbols for interpreting the world, that was an important focus of anthropology study. Thus she had us read such arcane works as E. A. Burtt's *The Metaphysical Foundations of Modern Physical Science* and Fung Yu-Lan's *Chinese Philosophy* in the hope that we would appreciate the sources of our own worldview and the nature of other worldviews.

For Weltfish, then, our goal as anthropologists in the Boasian tradition is not to analyze and derive cultural laws, but neither is our task limited to reconstruction of the history of cultures. As Boas had stated in *Anthropology and Modern Life*, "a clear understanding of the principles of anthropology illuminates the social processes of our times and may show us, if we are ready to listen to its teachings, what to do and what to avoid" (1962:11). For Weltfish, this applied goal of anthropology, restated by Boas in numerous writings and, one assumes, at numerous times to his students, became central to her own vision of anthropology. What can we learn from others and how can our lives be different because of our science?

Weltfish was less cautious than Boas in believing that anthropology could play a central role in constructing our future society. In her 1956 article "The Perspective for Fundamental Research in Anthropology," she discusses the shift in emphasis in anthropological research from "culture history—culture philosophy" to "social engineering"—the latter a Progressive Era concept if ever there was one (1956:63). She documents the blending of these two approaches in post–World War II anthropology and advocates the continued refinement of the applied dimension of the field. By the blending of social engineering with culture history, Weltfish is referring to using our knowledge of other cultures to build our future world in a more humane manner. This was an exciting and important venture for Weltfish. She often spoke of "our work," or "our science," engaging her colleagues and students in what was clearly for her an exhilarating task, the anthropological reconstruction of society.

Weltfish's "science" was more adventurous than Boas intended; its roots lie in the influence of John Dewey and his pragmatic thinking. In a 1945 article, "Science and Prejudice," she notes that science is "an instrumentality or tool" (1945:210). Anthropological science certainly focuses on the study of other cultures to the end of building "a long view of the common human community." However, for Weltfish, "we have derived from the study of other cultures an unforeseen 'fringe benefit' in the social contrast they afforded us, the better to assess our own ways of life" (1968b:306). This assessment of our own culture based on ethnographic knowledge was central to Weltfish's work. The anthropologist was, in a sense, the interlocutor between cultures in the Deweyan process of communication and exchange of ideas.

Her ethnography of Pawnee life, *The Lost Universe*, reveals the parameters of such a role. Weltfish began her work with the Pawnee in 1929. She was then primarily concerned with recording the Pawnee language and using the field opportunity to continue her research on the artistic dimensions of basketry.[9] Over thirty years later her ethnography of the Pawnee was published. What transpired in her life in those three decades conditioned the definitive perspective we find in *The Lost Universe*. This ethnography was not written by the young, idealistic student of "Papa Franz," but by a woman who had experienced a brief, unhappy marriage, had raised a daughter as a single parent, and had experienced profound social betrayal. In his preface to her festschrift, *Theory and Practice*, Stanley Diamond states that she had "fought a solitary losing battle to maintain the position that Boas had originally bequeathed to her at Columbia, only to find that students and colleagues alike (almost without exception) found ways to avoid supporting her" (Diamond 1980:ix).

The events of the McCarthy years might have left many people much more pessimistic about their abilities to change their social worlds. Weltfish, however, seems to have only solidified her insistence on this task as central to her science. She begins *The Lost Universe* with the question "How do we find our way into tomorrow?" She answers: "The Pawnee way of life is very different from our own and bears very little resemblance to ours even in its fundamentals, and by that very token it opens up a new world of human possibilities that we need to ponder before we can come back to our own problems with a fresh outlook" (1965:1–2). She continues: "The future American dream must grasp realities that are not yet here. . . . Whoever of us has knowledge of science must bring it to bear on [those problems] with which we are so urgently confronted at this time" (11).

This is, of course, reminiscent of Boas's description of the aim of anthropology. And indeed, in *The Lost Universe* there is much of Boasian culture history. Weltfish renders tanning practices and other concrete details of Pawnee technology in all their minuteness. Her presentation of the Pawnee as a group defined by its history and her incorporation of archaeological and linguistic data reflect Boas's historicity and holism. But though Weltfish's ethnographic sensibility is rooted in Boas, the idiom of *The Lost Universe* is all John Dewey's.

The Pawnee, Weltfish tells us, interested her from the onset of her work with them for two major reasons. First, they were matrilineal and lived in extended family lodges and thus exemplified a dramatically different style of home and family existence—a family life from which our society could learn (Weltfish 1965:5–9). She states, however:

> Even more startling to me than the contrast in home life was the question of political control among the Pawnees. They were a well-disciplined people, maintaining public order under many trying circumstances. And yet they had none of the power mechanisms that we consider essential to a well-ordered life. No orders were ever issued. No assignments for work were ever made nor were overall plans discussed. There was no code or rules of conduct nor punishment for infraction. There were no commandments nor moralizing proverbs. The only instigator of actions was the consenting person. (1965:5)

She continues with the point that, "in all his work, both public and private, the Pawnee moved on a totally voluntary basis. Whatever social forms existed were carried within the consciousness of the people, not by others who were in a position to make demands" (1965:5). And further on she states: "Time after time, I tried to find a case of orders given, and there was none. Gradually, I began to realize that democracy is a very personal thing which like charity, begins at home. Basically it means not being coerced and having no need to coerce anyone else" (6). Dewey's concerns with the individual as the source of social life and with voluntarism versus coercion as the central feature of democratic living are central themes in her thinking.

We can, according to Weltfish, thus learn something very essential from the Pawnee in our own efforts to implement democracy. In *The Lost Universe*, Weltfish looks for the source of the Pawnee democratic attitude. She notes that the Pawnee outlook on reality is in its very essence the opposite of our own. For Americans, the material, concrete realm is primary in our determination of empirical reality. The realm of ideas is the furthest removed from those things we consider "real." However, in estimating the world around him—in setting future goals for himself—the primary level of reality the Pawnee takes into account is, in fact, thought. For the Pawnee, she says, "the thinking man was the essential human being. The universe continued its seasonal round only when man willed it through his thought of Heaven and its creative power. In creating man, Heaven had also created the moving force of the universe. In this order of things, events were an adjunct of human ongoing" (1965:12). This perception of the effectiveness of the individual in relation to the world was founded on an origin myth that depicts the creator as actually initiating the process of creation with thoughts. The Pawnee, modeled in his image, were guided to conduct their affairs in like manner.

For Weltfish, the connection is important—the Pawnee are democratic: they have the ultimate belief in themselves as efficient creators. In the vocabulary of Dewey, she sums up her perspective: "The Amerindian . . . preserved an understanding of the individual personality as the keystone of society rather than as a function of it" (1965:60).

This inherent belief in their creative potential as individuals was learned by the Pawnee in the context of cultural life and supported by and within family and social structures. The Pawnee, Weltfish tells us, were also deliberately taught by their parents and fellow Pawnee from childhood to have concern for all; this concern was modeled for them in daily interaction in their camps and supported and reinforced by a family and household structure, extended family lodges, which were based on mutual dependence and mutual concern.

The family lodge was of particular interest to Weltfish, whose holistic anthropological eye saw the connection between enculturation, family life, and democratic consciousness. The extended family allows for a sharing of the emotional and physical responsibilities of child rearing and sets the stage for a continuation of this sharing of responsibilities in all arenas of life. She says:

> It gave personal satisfaction to its members and within itself produced the whole material and social base for an ongoing community . . . this is what we wish our family life would do. . . . Sibling rivalries, partial or total rejection of child by parent or smothering attention, demands on the child for the unfulfilled ambitions of the parents, or overprotection because of the resented parental hardships, heavy-handed control of parent over child in a severely restricted social environment—these are ills that are intimately linked with the very physical arrangements of our present family living. There are things about Pawnee life that suggest that an enlarged home environment for our children would improve our lives. (1965:5)

So Weltfish, once she understood what underlay democratic life among the Pawnee, attempted to bring this home to solve our own family and social problems. With the help of an architect, she designed a housing project, based on the Pawnee roundhouse. This building was a response to her concern that single-parent families and older people were often isolated in large apartment buildings. In her design, a central area, closely accessible to all apartments, would allow for communal childcare and socialization for the elderly. It would structurally encourage social interaction among all residents and reinforce in American life the types of democratic social interactions and attitudes she had observed among the Pawnee.

With *The Lost Universe*, the approach of her pragmatic anthropology is set. At any number of points in Weltfish's work in the 1960s and beyond, the same themes predominate: current social problems are posed; alternative solutions offered by the examples of other cultures are presented. And from this learning from others' solutions to similar problems constructs for a new social existence for ourselves are offered. For example, in "The Anthropology of Work" (1979) she presents the problem of alienated labor in our own society and juxtaposes this with the conditions of work in other cultures as a means toward offering directions for the reclamation of authentic labor in our own life. Her community program in Morristown was similarly concerned with issues of work and exemplifies another important dimension of Weltfish's pragmatic anthropology.

Holistic Education in Morristown

Weltfish's anthropological perspective is primarily a holistic one. Like Boas, Weltfish maintained we are simultaneously biological, cultural, historical, and symbolic beings. She consistently held that all aspects of our humanness should be brought to bear on our discussion of cultural issues. Her 1979 article "The Anthropology of Work," in which she presents primate studies and evolutionary materials as well as ethnographic information, is a masterpiece of the four-field approach—an approach that she saw to be definitive of the uniqueness of American anthropology (Weltfish 1962:171; 1968a:306). Her book *The Origins of Art* (1953) likewise includes archaeological, ethnological, and linguistic materials as the basis for her argument. There were few discussions on topics of present social concern that took place in her small apartment that did not include reference to the evolutionary or archaeological knowledge that would inform us on the subject. This holistic approach of Boasian anthropology is, however, supplemented by the added emphasis on Dewey's own insights into holism. Dewey's bow to the complexity of human life highlighted the dynamic relationship between mind and body, individual and society, and theory and practice. Weltfish's educational project developed with the Morristown community brings together Boasian and Deweyan concepts of holism in a unique effort to address the holistic nature of learning.

The Morristown project engaged local high school students and teachers, students at Fairleigh Dickinson, and other interested area professionals in a local community history project focused on the archaeological excavation and restoration of a pre-revolutionary home in Morristown. The program, initially entitled "New Vistas on Work and Leisure" and incorporated as the American Civilization Institute of Morristown (ACIM), was devised by Weltfish in conjunction with local educators in the mid-1960s to address the contemporary problem of unemployment and changing work demands and patterns in the United States. In her summary booklet (1967) of the project, subtitled "An Innovative Program for Relevant Education of School and Community," Weltfish notes that the changing technological scene of American work necessitates that educational goals undergo significant change. First, as the need for applied skills for work in more highly specialized occupations grows, traditional education's schooling in abstract ideas fails to prepare students for the world of work. Skill training should be addressed more centrally in the curriculum. Weltfish states, "The program of ACIM moves toward establishing one world of theory and practice in order to meet this contingency" (1967:1). The project curriculum was not unlike that of Dewey's laboratory school and reflected his model for the integration of theory and practice in education.

However, Weltfish does not advocate occupational preparation as the only goal of education. Education should prepare students to live a "fulfilled life"—one that will be longer due to greater life expectancy and one in which the individual will have more time for leisure activities. Following Sebastian de Grazia, she makes a distinction between recreation and leisure central to the theoretical underpinnings of ACIM: "Leisure is a cultivated art; recreation is a relief from work" (Weltfish and Wenner 1970:12). The ACIM project was intended to "offer our youth a pathway into the future through a new combination of study and humanistic work as a combined venture to promote both personal education and at the same time equip the student with new occupational skills" (1968b:1).

The processes of excavation and restoration involved students in internships in a wide variety of areas. Excavation taught students not only archaeological technique but also engaged them in chemical analysis of finds, botanical studies, and geological and ecological appraisals. Ethnohistorical materials supplemented archaeology as students did oral history and worked with primary documents in the local historical society and library. In the course of their work, they achieved mastery of skills in science and technology, geography, research, indexing, photography, mapping, and a multitude of other related areas, "opening the way for a combination of study and occupational training sufficiently flexible for the individual need of the student and taking into account the indefiniteness of the delineation of occupational categories that can be expected in the near future" (1968b:3).

ACIM was Weltfish's clearest effort to educate for democracy. She not only hoped to prepare students for fulfilled lives but also to engage teachers in voluntary, committed involvement in the project as a way of cultivating the very human art of leisure in their own lives. Through involvement in ACIM, students and teachers were actively creating community in the present and, through their archaeological work, experiencing a historical depth in that sense of shared community. This project in pragmatic anthropology was grounded in a realization of the connection between education and social change and acknowledged the fact that education is a process central to communal life—not merely what goes on in schools. Education about one's own culture or community, in the active context of communal life, Weltfish hoped, would subtly serve as the basis for reconstructing our present society.

Conclusion: The Pragmatic Anthropology of Education

The pragmatic anthropology developed by Weltfish is especially significant in its provision of a qualitative model for a renewed depth of perspective in the study of education by contemporary anthropologists. Drawing on the work of two comprehensive scholars, Franz Boas and John Dewey, Weltfish's thinking about education reflects a wide-ranging understanding of learning as a basically human and social activity. In the tradition of Boas, Weltfish approaches education from a position of theoretical complexity that highlights education as a cultural process analyzed within a comparative and holistic framework. In the tradition of both Boas and Dewey, she elaborates an understanding of education as both a process of learning and a social institution. These dimensions of her thinking have much to offer in grounding present-day scholars in the salient issues relating to education.

The comparative and holistic perspective so central to Weltfish's work is basic to the American anthropological tradition. Weltfish's holistic evaluation of education is ever aware of the way in which the educational institution is responsive to basic human needs. Informed by lifeways in other cultures, she keeps an eye to the nature of the communal and social purpose of education. By considering modern American education within this wider framework, Weltfish is not distracted by culture-bound questions about problems and goals. Education for the anthropologist in the Boasian tradition is the process of learning to be a fulfilled human being who can successfully participate in the cultural life of the group in question. Stated in the tradition of Dewey, education is not coterminous with schooling; it is the central process of human life, the lifelong, problem-solving processes that individuals engage in as members of society.

Weltfish did no direct study of "education" as a particular aspect of culture. What was of interest to her, again in the Boasian tradition, was to understand the manner in which education is integrated with other domains of cultural life. To separate education from other domains of culture would have been an artificial abstraction for her—a reduction of the very complex process of human cultural life and a failure to see the multidimensionality of what is involved in the process of becoming a participating member of any social group. As she demonstrated among the Pawnee, education involves not only skills and knowledge, but also attitudes. To study what was learned involves also the understanding of how it is learned and how the many other aspects of cultural life reinforce the learning.

Such a perspective on studying education is not one that is easily formulated in quantitative terms. Weltfish's anthropology was not a social science geared toward reducing educational phenomena to analytic models. Most central to her work is the consistent attitude that all learning has application as its goal, and that all knowledge must be put to the test of application before it has any meaning. As in Dewey's epistemology, the learning by undergoing must become active—and this results in not an endpoint but another jumping off to a new set of questions. Education cannot be separated from life itself.

Weltfish's pragmatic anthropology sought to override the anthropologist's own dualism between scholar and change agent through integration of theory and practice. She practiced in her own life the basic understanding of democracy as a personal way of living—a perspective found in the work of both Dewey and Boas. She shared with Dewey an attempt in her own teaching to integrate the particular individual experience of students with the theoretical material to be learned—in the understanding that outside the context of personal involvement, learning could not truly take place. She encouraged students to study topics of immediate relevance to their own personal and social struggles. In this she fulfilled Boas's call for teachers who modeled citizenship for their students.

Though Weltfish never achieved stardom within professional circles in anthropology, her impact on her students and colleagues was far-reaching. Weltfish led a life committed to, in Boas's words, moving in "an opposite direction"(Boas 1962:246). She, in effect, became a Pawnee—one who saw herself as creating her world, and who insisted that the world did not exist except through our efforts to implement it. This is her primary legacy to her students. For Weltfish insisted that anyone she dealt with must also become Pawnee in their own fashion. And thus our world is more democratic, she taught, for we have become more so.

Notes

I would like to thank Richard Blot and Ray McDermott for both their encouragement and their valuable editorial suggestions. Thanks also go to Ruth Boettker for her help with access to the Gene Weltfish Papers at Fairleigh Dickinson University and to Richard White.

1. The songs were recorded in 1936. The 1965 album, Smithsonian Folkways Recordings #04334, was titled Music of the Pawnee—Mark Evarts.

2. See Dearborn (1988) for a lively social history of New York in the early twentieth century presented in the context of a reconstruction of the romance between John Dewey and novelist Anzia Yezierska. Columbia's Teachers College for immigrants and

Extension Division courses for adult workers were characteristic of the university's active response to the social climate of the time. Political and social actions were the very heart of theory for the resident masters there.

3. Weltfish did not formally receive her degree until 1950. She was unable to afford the high cost of publication of her thesis—in 1929 a requirement for official degree status. This requirement was waived, and mimeographed theses were deemed acceptable in 1950. For all fellowship and academic qualification purposes, however, her degree was effectively granted in 1929.

4. See Pathé (1988) and Diamond (1980:351–362) for further discussion of Weltfish's various "applied" endeavors.

5. As his student Alexander Lesser (1981) and colleague Marian Smith (1959) have argued, the source of these signature facets of Boasian anthropology lie in Boas's basic natural history perspective. Lesser states that Boas "came to the study of man as a naturalist, as a student of natural history, and tried to understand man and peoples as part of the natural phenomena of the world" (Lesser 1981:8).

6. The summary of Dewey's theory presented here reflects information strewn throughout his books and articles cited in the bibliography. The reader might wish to also consult two recent works on Dewey for clarification of his theory: Rockefeller (1991) and Westbrook (1991).

7. Stephen Rockefeller (1991:401–402), in his recent critical biography of Dewey, points to the centrality of the concept of growth to Dewey's thinking.

8. This insight rebounds dramatically on Weltfish's notion of the depiction of any culture's identity. I was slightly perplexed when, in considering the appropriate title for my doctoral study of the processes of German-American ethnicity, she off-handedly suggested "something along the lines of continuity and change." This sounded vaguely dated to me at the time. I came to understand, however, that for Weltfish ethnic group identity is a complex meshing of both its present and its past. She explains that, "historically every group is a composite as the general trend of world history, even in its earliest stages, has been from smaller to larger social groupings, each of which has come about by an alliance of at least more than one family. The identity of the several groups that have been combined does not entirely disappear" (1956:210). Any valid discussion of American cultural identity, therefore, should include its various sources as well as its present character. The Pawnee were, for her, a case in point. Though the Pawnee have lost much of their cultural distinctiveness, their way of life represents as much a part of the picture of American culture history as "our Old World roots." She states, "There seems to me no reason why the anthropologist should not give to our American tradition an account of what the Pawnees or any other of our ethnic groups has done to survive over time in a common mode, so that our history will have a genuine ethnic as well as political dimension" (1959:334).

9. See Weltfish (1980) for personal commentary on her early experience under Boas.

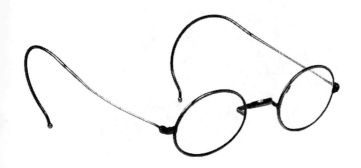

5. The Social Anthropology of Hortense Powdermaker

Jill B. R. Cherneff

Hortense Powdermaker in 1930, published July 15, 1930, in the *Evening Journal*. Courtesy of the Harry Ransom Humanities Research Center, University of Texas at Austin.

Hortense Powdermaker (1896–1970) is well known in anthropology for her introspective memoir of her fieldwork experiences, Stranger and Friend (1966), one of the first in what has become a substantial genre. She is also remembered for the remarkable diversity of her field sites and innovative topics of study: her early ethnography of Melanesians, her observations on race, her study of social change and popular culture in Northern Rhodesia (now Zambia), and her analysis of the Hollywood film industry. A contemporary of Margaret Mead and Ruth Benedict and, like them, interested in psychological anthropology, she created a blend of psychological and cultural perspectives different from that of the mainstream American anthropology of her era. She brought this approach to her examination of race relations and education in the United States, Jill Cherneff's subject.

Powdermaker was born in Philadelphia in 1896. When she was young, her family moved first to Reading, Pennsylvania, and then to Baltimore. She remained in Baltimore through graduation from Goucher College in 1920. During college she was active in trade unionism, organizing Baltimore's textile workers. After graduation she moved to New York City, where she worked for the Amalgamated Clothing Workers of America, one of whose senior executives was Joseph Schlossberg, father of Ruth Landes. Although there is no indication that Powdermaker and Landes were associates, or even that they knew each other, they did have somewhat overlapping lives. Both broke new ground in the study of race relations and spent time in the 1930s at Fisk University in Nashville, Tennessee.

In 1925, after a few years of emotionally and physically draining work as a union organizer, Powdermaker went to England. She spent the next three years at the London School of Economics as one of the first three students of Bronislaw Malinowski (1884–1942). As she later wrote, Malinowski, one of the founders of British social anthropology, was the first to make anthropology an observational science, to pitch his camp in a native village, and to be a participant-observer (Powdermaker 1967). He also is known for his functionalist approach to social analysis and for his testing the tenets of Freudian psychology in the laboratory of so-called primitive societies.

Powdermaker completed her PhD on the topic of leadership in primitive societies in 1928. She then went to Melanesia for fieldwork on the island of New Ireland, off the coast of New Guinea. A. R. Radcliffe-Brown (1881–1955) became her adviser, and Gregory Bateson one of her pidgin tutors. A year later her return was heralded in newspapers across the country. Headlines reporting Powdermaker's travels included such phrases as "Divorce Easy—Just Isn't Any on Sea Isle" and "Expert Explorer." The caption of a photograph of Powdermaker working at her desk accompanying a story in a New York newspaper reads, "Dr. Hortense Powdermaker, anthropologist, of Brooklyn, has just returned from the wilds *of New Ireland inhabited entirely by cannibals. She is the only woman to risk her life for so long a time—ten months—among cannibal Melanesians."*

Her fieldwork complete, Powdermaker searched for a place in New York in which to evaluate and write up her data. Clark Wissler at the American Museum of Natural History became her sponsor and supported her appointment to the new Institute of Human Relations (*IHR*) at Yale University. Edward Sapir became her next mentor and supervisor. Awarded funding from the National Research Council, she completed and published her first book, based on her Melanesian fieldwork, Life in Lesu (1933).

It is a traditional ethnography showing the influence of both Malinowski and Radcliffe-Brown, each of whom was associated with different aspects of functionalist theory. In contrast to the historical particularism of Boas and his students, functionalism was ahistorical, focusing on the interdependent social mechanisms that maintained a society. Malinowski became identified with "psychological functionalism." He focused on how the needs of individuals shaped social institutions. Radcliffe-Brown and his followers, "structural-functionalists," analyzed social institutions, particularly kinship. Powdermaker treated the village of Lesu as a bounded and isolated society, describing its social organization in its entirety through categories such as childhood, initiation rites, marriage, work, magic, and religion.

For her next project Powdermaker chose the American South. To prepare, she went first to the Social Science Institute at Fisk University, then one of the most important intellectual centers in the United States for academic discussions about race. After a few months there, she went alone to Indianola, Mississippi, in the fall of 1932, beginning fieldwork that would lead to her ethnographic account of American race relations. When she returned to collect additional data during the summer of 1934, she took along a young psychology student named John Dollard, an *IHR* colleague. After introducing him to the community and mentoring him that entire summer, she was enormously disappointed when Yale University Press decided to publish Dollard's study, Caste and Class in a Southern Town (1937), and declined to publish hers, After Freedom (1939). Disheartened and discouraged, she departed Yale to help create the Anthropology Department at the newly built Queens College in Queens, New York. She returned during World War II to Yale's campus two days each week to share her expertise with the Army Specialized Training Program focused on the war effort in the southwest Pacific.

Powdermaker's research in Indianola was the catalyst for her next projects. She wrote a series of papers for conferences and journals on the psychological aspects of race, including her widely used textbook for high school students, Probing Our Prejudices (1944b), intended as a tool to combat racial prejudice. The book was used for years in New York City high schools, among others, to facilitate discussions of what today is called cultural diversity or sensitivity training. Her time spent in the strictly segregated South also inspired her research on the Hollywood film industry. In Mississippi she had examined the impact of movies on segregated audiences; now she turned her attention to their production. Stretching the possibilities of anthropological methodology once again, during a sabbatical year in 1946–47 she went to Los Angeles to conduct a study of the social organization of the feature film industry, Hollywood, the Dream Factory (1950). The same interest in mass media was evident in her fieldwork in Northern Rhodesia, her last, which resulted in her landmark ethnographic study of popular culture in a mining community, Copper Town: Changing Africa (1962).

Throughout her forty-year career Powdermaker's own interests dictated her research agenda. She was very attuned to "the extension of the areas of self awareness, of perception, of action, and of the range of identifications" (Wolf 1971:784) in herself and in her informants, which she described in Stranger and Friend (1966). Although in this book, as in all her research, she anticipated future anthropological currents, she remained somewhat outside the mainstream of American anthropology, for several reasons. She was a woman; she was trained outside the United States; and her interest in perception and self-awareness was quite different from the attention to national character and child socialization that dominated the American culture-and-personality school.

Powdermaker spent the longest part of her career teaching undergraduate anthropology at Queens College. She taught no graduate courses there, but her undergraduate teaching inspired many students to pursue anthropology as a career. The vision of anthropology she shared with them is summed up in her conclusion to Stranger and Friend, in which she described anthropology as an art and a science. If this dual nature is accepted, she wrote, "there is no reason why each cannot be expanded. The inherent ambiguities of this approach are only a reflection of those which exist in life itself" (1966:306).

Hortense Powdermaker (1896–1970), an American anthropologist trained by Bronislaw Malinowski in the 1920s, was an observer of modern American culture.[1] She took an unusual step when, in the 1930s and 1940s, she chose to direct her studies toward uncovering and describing the adaptive strategies of African Americans living in a multiracial setting. An early anthropological researcher in the field of race relations, Powdermaker was interested in the impact of education, in a general sense, on the acquisition of culture. Until then it had not been a particularly common topic of research in her discipline. Focusing primarily on issues surrounding relations between Black and White Americans, she believed that an understanding of education in its broadest sense as an enculturation process was critical to an overall appreciation of the complexities of a multiracial society. During much of her life her words and work were a public stance against prejudice and racism in the United States.

There is curiously little written about Hortense Powdermaker and almost no citation of her work by others who, after her, resumed research in areas that she had previously investigated.[2] She was not as prolific a published writer as some other anthropologists. Yet the monographs she did contribute to the body of anthropological knowledge were always innovative for the time in which she wrote each of them (Cherneff 1991b; Hier and Kemp 2002). This is no less true of the publications that concerned her observations on the educational process. While Powdermaker's name does not come readily to mind in this area of anthropology, her writings and research were often concerned with education and its cultural ramifications. She published a textbook on racial prejudice for use in the New York City school system (1944b); she was involved in conferences and seminars concerning education and the cultural process (1943a, 1944a); and she studied the impact of mass media on culture and education (1950, 1953). Hortense Powdermaker's professional life was a blend of political activism, of functionalist training under Bronislaw Malinowski, and later of psychological insights garnered from Edward Sapir and others in the field of psychoanalytic studies. She believed that education included learning to play certain roles that are advantageous to the individual in adapting to a particular culture. As such, she also believed that education could not be studied as isolated from other aspects of life, especially in culturally heterogeneous situations.

Powdermaker's interest in what later became the subfield of anthropology and education covered three basic precepts: that for the individual, the dichotomy of rational thought and emotional feeling is artificial; that the adaptation to one's surrounding social environment is subtle and continuous over a lifetime; and that the crucial problems of modern society are those centering around power in the economic and political areas of life.

After completing fieldwork on the South Pacific island of Lesu in 1929 and publishing an ethnography of her research shortly thereafter (1933), Powdermaker turned her attention to the American South and spent the year 1932–33 and the summer of 1934 in Mississippi studying race relations.[3] Her resulting book, *After Freedom: A Cultural Study in the Deep South* (1939), is a sensitive account of her research findings. All the more complex and courageous because the research was undertaken by a young unmarried White woman in a small town fraught with the racial conventions lingering from pre–Civil War cotton plantation traditions, the book was one of the early major community studies by an anthropologist of modern American race relations.[4] Still today, it continues to inform the debate (Fraser 1991; B. Williams and Woodson 1993; Adams and Gorton 2004). This fieldwork apparently had a substantial impact on Powdermaker; much of her future research touched on some continuing threads from that experience. The early to mid-1940s was a period in which many of her writings dealt with issues of race in the United States. These works included the small text used in high schools (1944b) and her various conference papers on educational and cultural processes.

Another area of interest ensuing from her year in Mississippi was the impact of Hollywood feature films on individual behavior and perceptions of culture. Because she defined education broadly as a process that occurs over an individual's lifetime in the continuous adaptation to one's culture, she became fascinated with the way in which both Black and White individuals reacted to the content of feature films. In 1946, during a sabbatical year from Queens College in New York City, she traveled to Los Angeles to study feature film production and the "social-psychological milieu in which they were made" (Powdermaker 1966:210).

Hortense Powdermaker's contributions to the subject of anthropology and education were part of a larger interest in the effects of social settings on individual personality and behavior. At a time when cultural diversity and racial tensions are flashing warning signs across both American and global landscapes, her focus on individual adaptations to one's surroundings is all the more significant.

Biographical Sketch of Hortense Powdermaker

Hortense Powdermaker was born in Philadelphia in 1896 into a German-Jewish middle-class family.[5] She moved to Baltimore as a young girl and spent the rest of her childhood and her college years there. High school introduced her to more recently arrived Jewish, working-class immigrants (she herself was a second-generation American) and through them to socialist ideology for the first time. A few years later, when she was at Goucher College, Powdermaker became active in the trade union movement. For a short time she took a job in a men's shirt factory as a seamstress. It was her "first excursion outside of [her] own environment" (1966:23), and she liked it. Even though her work experience was brief, she continued to be involved in the labor movement while in college, becoming the local representative to the Baltimore Federation of Labor of the Women's Trade Union League.

After Powdermaker graduated from Goucher College in 1920, her decided interest in the labor movement led her to move to New York, where she worked for the Amalgamated Clothing Workers of America. Much of her time during the next five years was devoted to organizing in apparel factories, first in Cleveland, Ohio, then in Rochester, New York.[6] For Powdermaker, with her middle-class and business-oriented family background, union work was similar to future anthropological experiences where, as a fieldworker, one steps into an unknown society and steps out of it again (Powdermaker 1966:32).

This social activism framed the background for her subsequent anthropological work; she often called upon her anthropological research as a source of cultural critique. Her later interest and involvement in psychological anthropology and psychoanalysis persuaded her to evaluate her beliefs from yet another vantage point. In Powdermaker's autobiographical work, *Stranger and Friend: The Way of an Anthropologist* (1966), she declared that the discomfort and frustration she experienced during her union organizing days persuaded her to adopt a style of anthropology where she "tried, as far as possible, to make no change in the society [she] studied" (1966:26). It did not prevent her, however, from continuing to write on issues about which she felt political commitment and to use her anthropological training and her career in college teaching to educate others in what she felt were vital issues in her own society.

After five years of intensive political activism and her resulting exhaustion, she desperately wanted a change of environment and decided to travel abroad. When Powdermaker left New York for London in 1925, she could not have envisioned that journey as the first of many subsequent travels far distant from the American East Coast. Hers was a serendipitous entrance into anthropology when she became, while in London, one of Bronislaw Malinowski's first students in a new anthropology program at the London School of Economics. Much of her subsequent research was influenced by his functionalist theories and his quarrels with the psychoanalytic studies of Sigmund Freud.

The social anthropology associated with Malinowski in the 1920s, generally known as functionalism, was based on a synchronic approach to culture; that is, a society was studied as it existed at the time that research was conducted, without considering the impact of either past history or outside influences. In this way, the focus was on the manner in which different domains within the culture were interconnected since aspects of culture needed to be understood not in isolation but in the context of their use (Kuper 1973:44). Defining social institutions by their functions and looking at how the various parts of a culture perform together as a whole served as a basis for Malinowski later to develop his theories of "basic needs" as the shaping forces of a society. Further, he felt one must study environmental influences and cultural relationships at the same time. As with Powdermaker's writing, much of Malinowski's emphasis was on the individual and the individual's goals. Individual beliefs served psychological functions even as they contained a utilitarian core. Malinowski's focus on how social organization functions to make a sensible culture possessed of an internal feeling of coherence, as well as his focus on the individual's emotional, intellectual, and biological needs both greatly shaped Powdermaker's work.[7]

It was during this time that Malinowski challenged Sigmund Freud's notions of the universality of the Oedipus complex and his assumptions concerning infant sexuality and racial conscience in a book entitled *Sex and Repression in Savage Society* (1927). It appeared in print while Powdermaker was still studying with him in London. Using materials from his field research in the Trobriand Islands, Malinowski was able to show that relations between father and son in a matrilineal and avunculocal descent system were quite different from those in the patriarchal Viennese society of Freud. In London, Powdermaker became acquainted with these theories and Malinowski's criticism of them. Additionally she knew of Malinowski's rejection of Freud's concepts concerning social origins and the arrested evolutionary development of non-Western cultures. When she later began her own research in psychoanalytic studies, she too continued to shy away from the more traditional Freudian theory, favoring Henry Stack Sullivan's emerging psychoanalytic theory of interpersonal relations.[8] After earning her PhD in 1928, Powdermaker left for a year's field study in the South Pacific.[9]

She arrived in New York in 1930 to settle on the East Coast once again. Soon after her return she moved to New Haven, Connecticut, where her next seven years were spent in affiliation with Yale University. Her residency as a postdoctoral fellow at the Yale Institute of Human Relations and her relationship with Edward Sapir and others such as Harry Stack Sullivan affected the future direction of her work by bridging the gap between anthropological and psychoanalytical thinking.[10]

Research at Yale: Powdermaker's *After Freedom*

The Yale Institute of Human Relations (IHR) was established in 1929 with a grant from one division of the Rockefeller Foundation. When the idea for an institute was first conceived by Milton Winternitz, the dean of the medical school, and Edgar Furniss, the dean of graduate studies, it was to be an interdisciplinary research center dedicated to the study of the human body, the human mind, and the "relations of man to others and to his environment" (Morawski 1986:228). Yet ultimately it was the psychologists who became leading figures in the institute and directed its emphasis and focus. The basic goal was to create an orderly methodology to substantiate knowledge of the human psyche and behavior as an alternative to the emerging image of the mind as nonrational and inseparable from its environment and past experiences. This goal and its philosophy led to quantitative methods of research (Morawski 1986).[11]

Edward Sapir was one of the academics outside of psychology recruited to expand the institute's breadth, a mandate of the Rockefeller money. An anthropologist and linguist with a strong interest in psychology, he came to Yale in 1931 from the University of Chicago and worked there until his death in 1939. A pioneer in advocating the collaboration among anthropology, sociology, and psychoanalysis, Sapir was actively interested in the relationship of personality and culture. Like Malinowski, he stressed a nonquantitative emphasis on the cultural world as structured by individuals. Sapir's interest in "the meaning of culture, its relativity and its bearing on personality" (Darnell 1990:337), is reflected in the title of his major course at Yale: The Impact of Culture on Personality.

Hortense Powdermaker moved to New Haven, Connecticut, in the fall of 1930, shortly before Sapir's arrival. Through a letter of introduction provided by Radcliffe-Brown, whom she had met in London and again in Australia, Powdermaker was invited by anthropologist Clark Wissler to occupy a research post as a postdoctoral student and assistant professor at the new institute, an arrangement that made it possible for her, with a grant from the National Research Council, to write up her new fieldwork data.[12]

At Yale, Sapir exerted a major influence on Powdermaker's work. She became one of his early protégées while she was affiliated with the Institute from 1930 until 1937 (at which time she joined the faculty of Queens College in New York City). After *Life in Lesu* (1933) was completed and a publisher found, Powdermaker decided to undertake a second major field research project—in Mississippi. Here she planned to study issues of acculturation and race relations in a rural community. Sapir encouraged her to pursue her Southern studies and backed her proposal for fieldwork funding by the Social Science Research Council (SSRC). His involvement in the SSRC and its culture and personality committee brought her to her psychological interest in and approach to community studies. Unlike others in anthropology, Sapir believed it possible to study modern societies using traditional anthropological research methods rather than sociological surveys and the statistical methods of psychology. Furthermore, he believed that interdisciplinary work between psychology and anthropology had much to offer in the "understanding of the individual's process of adjustment" (Darnell 1990:306) to his or her culture. Powdermaker's proposal to study a small, self-contained Southern town fit well with his own theoretical vision as well as with the SSRC's interest in interdisciplinary studies.

Before her departure for Mississippi, Powdermaker had occasion to meet with Sapir's good friend, psychoanalyst Harry Stack Sullivan. She first encountered Sullivan during the summer of 1932, when she vacationed with the Sapir family at their holiday residence in New Hampshire, and Sullivan joined them as a guest. At Sapir's request, Sullivan had read Powdermaker's proposal for her Southern study and agreed that it had merit (Perry 1982:357). Soon thereafter, both Sapir and Sullivan helped Powdermaker arrange her orientation to this Mississippi fieldwork at Fisk University (Perry 1982:358; Powdermaker 1966:134–135). Charles S. Johnson, head of the Social Sciences Department, and E. Franklin Frazier, professor of sociology, were her hosts.[13]

The outcome of this research, her book *After Freedom* (1939), presents a rich description of the individuals who lived in the town of "Cottonville," Mississippi, and the processes that either worked to maintain the traditional culture or caused it to change.[14] Ultimately, Powdermaker concluded that there were great psychological costs to all individuals, both African Americans and Whites, in adapting to the race/caste system of the South. The emphasis of the study was on African Americans, but to understand them she knew that "there must be an understanding of the Whites who form so large a part of [the community]" (1939:x).[15]

After Freedom presents a combination of Powdermaker's initial functionalist training with Malinowski and her subsequent interest in culture and personality inspired by Sapir. Her mentoring by these two men, both of whom were interested in individuals as cultural actors, promoted her increasing curiosity in this subject. Sapir, in particular, was deeply involved with the interaction of the individual and culture and the concept of personality (Sapir 1934), especially because of his special relationship with Harry Stack Sullivan. Sapir's close friendship and collaboration with Sullivan began in 1926 in Chicago. Sullivan was an American psychiatrist and psychoanalyst whose work with schizophrenic patients led him to develop theories that marked the beginning of interpersonal relations studies in the United States. Sapir's ideas on the role of culture and language in socialization and Sullivan's on individual psychology mutually influenced each other's work as they both explored the relationships of culture and personality.

It was during this time, in the late 1920s, that the study of comparative cultures once again became interesting to American-based psychoanalysts. Differing from their initial interest in anthropology as a tool to reinforce the universality of Freud's theories of the symbolism in "primitive" rites and rituals, psychoanalysts' renewed interest in other cultures evolved from their realization of the critical importance of early childhood experiences (especially infant development and mother-infant bonding) in personality development. In general, American psychiatrists interpreted Freud's system less literally than psychiatrists in Europe (except perhaps those in Great Britain). According to Clara Thompson, a psychoanalyst of that era: "Psychiatry in America, under William A. White and Adolf Meyer, had for years been stressing the importance of environmental factors in mental illness. Therefore the men who went from America around 1920 to study psychoanalysis in Europe already had a point of view which must have in many instances modified their approach to Freud's orientation" (1950:192).

Friendships such as Sullivan's with Edward Sapir and with Clara Thompson and Karen Horney, as well as Margaret Mead's with Erich Fromm, drew psychoanalysts and anthropologists, including Ruth Benedict, Margaret Mead, Sapir, and Powdermaker, into a collection of intellectuals who began to think about the relationship of individuals to their culture in psychoanalytic ways. By 1936, this group had embarked on a neo-Freudian theory of psycho-cultural analysis, developing a model of human relations based on the study of comparative cultures.[16]

For Powdermaker, the currents of this continuing dialogue and the relationships she had formed while at Yale led to her increasing attention to the influences of culture on personality development. Her focus was the individual; the purpose of her study in Mississippi had been "to view a unit of southern American culture in terms of human beings . . . whose personalities are being constantly affected by the culture in which they live" (1939:ix). Her later theories on prejudice and publications on race, including her paper on African American personality (1943a), were prompted by the psychological climate surrounding her via her relationship with Sapir and the Institute of Human Relations while she was there.[17]

In addition to such psychological influences on her work, politics also played a significant role in the research project she undertook in Mississippi. Powdermaker's concern with race issues was rooted in an interest in social realities. Her Mississippi study was an experiment in combining anthropological research skills with her political praxis.

> There is no reason why anthropology should not be used to help make our
> civilization . . . intelligible. Its contribution on this point has been limited to
> the use of primitive societies as laboratories for comparison with our own, or

*for historical background. But the techniques of anthropology might be used
more directly. Problems of race, of minority groups, of a region like the South,
are among our most pressing issues. Anthropology could bring both knowledge
and insight to them . . . the techniques of anthropology [might] be used to help
society understand itself. (1939:ix)*

Her writings address what people believe about race and how these beliefs
motivate behavior. Throughout her life, Powdermaker continued to use anthropology as a valuable lens through which to apprise ourselves of social conflict and its complications.

Cultural and Social Influences on Personality and Behavior

Following the publication of *After Freedom*, Powdermaker continued to write on
issues of African American culture and personality. Throughout the 1930s and
1940s terms such as *cultural process, educational process,* and *socialization* appear
and reappear in social science literature (Benedict 1942b; Embree 1943; Mead
1943; Spindler 1955, 1974). Of interest was the importance of education in a
general sense (the process of transmitting culture) and the problem of how
to conceive of formal schooling within the theoretical context of socialization
studies of the time. *Cultural process,* the way in which traditions are transmitted
and their continuity maintained, was the broad field of study of which both *educational process* and *socialization* were a part. Even in the 1930s, there was awareness that in the multicultural environment of the United States the issues of
cultural process were quite complex.

In the spring of 1941, a major conference entitled Education and the Cultural
Process was organized by Charles S. Johnson and sponsored by the Department of Social Sciences at Fisk University to commemorate the seventy-fifth
anniversary of the academy.[18] John Dewey's theories of education formed the
backdrop of the symposium. In particular, *cultural process* was considered both
a method whereby a "cultural heritage is transmitted from one generation to
another" and a means through which "a society renews and perpetuates itself
as a society" (Johnson 1943:629). Understanding the situation in the United
States as that of divergent cultural and racial groups in contact with one another, the symposium addressed *education* not only as transmission but also as
transformation of societies as they come into contact with each other in gen-

eral acculturative situations. Thus, contrary to the then popular assumption that "formal education is merely a rational procedure for further carrying on and completing in the schoolroom a task begun with the child in the home" (629), Johnson's seminar explored education in contexts that were "non-rationalized" to better understand the problems encountered in attempting to weld a "workable [American] cultural and political unity"(631). Clearly, events unfolding in Europe and the horror of Fascism sensitized Americans to their own problems with racism at home.

According to Stanley Diamond (1971a), the study of formal schooling was not one that anthropologists took to willingly in the early years of the field. Because anthropology was conceived as the study of the "other" within a framework of relativism, to look at the issues of formal education affecting this "other" was to look squarely at the imperatives and policies of colonialism, something anthropology was reticent to do. This context makes the Fisk University conference all the more notable, given the large number of its participants who were anthropologists.

Powdermaker presented her paper titled "The Channeling of Negro Aggression by the Cultural Process" (1943a) at this symposium. Like other anthropologists of the 1940s, she viewed education in its broadest context including

> learning to play certain roles, roles which are advantageous to the individual in adapting himself to his particular culture. . . . Adaptation to society begins at birth and ends at death. . . . The family, church, movies, newspapers, radio programs, books, trade-unions, chambers of commerce, and all other organized and unorganized interpersonal relations are part of education. All these are part of the cultural process, which determines how behavior and attitudes are channeled. (1943a:750)

In this paper Powdermaker explains certain African American behavior patterns as reasonable adaptive responses to the surrounding cultural messages and pressures and argues that these behavior patterns change with transformations in the surrounding culture. Looking at certain specific African American personality behaviors, Powdermaker analyzes the paradox of "humble, meek, unaggressive Negro" (1943a:753) behavior as a culturally channeled adaptation to a frustrating situation of underprivileged status. Then, using Theodore Reik's model of masochism (1941) where he demonstrates that there is a certain individual sense of power and superiority in acting more virtuous than one's oppressors, she delineates the emotional compensations (as well as the more pragmatic reasons) for the refusal to resort to aggressive behavior to vent frustration. For her, the functional interplay of individual behavior and the surrounding cultural process is apparent.

> Neither the slave nor the obsequious, unaggressive Negro . . . learned to play his role in any school. They learned by observation and imitation; they were taught by their parents; they observed that role brought rewards. Since the Civil War the Negro has likewise seen the meek, humble type presented over and over again with approval in sermons, in literature, in movies, and more recently, through radio sketches. By participating in the cultural processes, the Negro has learned his role. This was education, far more powerful than anything restricted to schools; for the kind of education we are discussing is continuous during the entire life of the individual. It is subtle as well as direct. One part of the cultural process strengthens another part, and reinforcement for the role we described comes from every side. (1943a:757)

What happens when the surrounding culture changes? According to Powdermaker, when the cultural process ceases to provide incentives for the practiced behavior, "dissatisfaction with that behavior appears and there is a gradual change to another form which is more likely to bring new compensations" (758). The decline in religious faith, along with the rise in literacy, urban migration, and Black-White competition for jobs, was predictably leading toward a psychological revolution and behavioral shift.[19] Aware of the continuing powerlessness African Americans faced in the economic, political, and social arenas to attain parity in a White-ruled America, aware of their continuous frustration at this lack of parity, and with fewer compensations for maintaining the present passivity, Powdermaker predicted, "Unless some other form of adaptation takes place and unless discriminations are lessened, we may expect a trend toward greater overt aggression" (758).

Perspectives on Education and Race

The social climate of the 1930s, with the Depression, the Fascist threat, and the imminence of war in Europe, stimulated many anthropologists, including

Powdermaker, to engage in various kinds of political activism. Some anthropologists sought individual action, such as John Murra, Elman Service, and Clifton Amsbury, who went to fight in the Spanish Civil War, or Paul Kirchhoff, who served as Trotsky's bodyguard in Mexico (Ebihara 1985:112). But Powdermaker had already engaged in political action with its highs and lows when she worked to unionize the garment industry. Moreover, she was not inclined to support either socialism or communism. Instead, like many other anthropologists, she chose to express her activism through research and writing.[20]

The actual outbreak of World War II and subsequent direct American involvement in 1942 precipitated an increased and deepening awareness of other cultures in the world.[21] For American anthropologists, the war highlighted the issues of racial tensions at home. Problems associated with the American military training programs and the desegregation of the American armed services posed questions impossible to ignore in light of the war abroad.

Furthermore, the changing racial demographics in the northern United States exacerbated this festering but long-neglected problem. In 1900 there were not quite nine million African Americans in the United States, most of whom were rural Southerners, limited by "poverty, ill health, bad housing, inadequate education, scanty opportunity and an inferior position before the law" (Allen 1952:177). These conditions reinforced the predominant attitude among many Whites that Blacks were somewhat subhuman (though emancipated), incapable of profiting from education. In those many Southern areas where African Americans outnumbered Whites, it was, in part, fear that led to this disfranchisement. Such fear was not as apparent in much of the North, where their fewer numbers alleviated the White sense of alarm.

During World War I, the increased demand for unskilled labor in Northern industry and the promise of higher wages and better living conditions precipitated a dramatic rise in the northward migration of Southern Blacks. Obviously, larger industrial Northern American cities were most affected. The rearrangement of economic balance, increasing residence in White neighborhoods, and use of the public transportation system upset the previous racial equilibrium. As the Northern African American population increased, so did White anxiety; overt discrimination was proportionate to the relative size of the Black population in a community.

For those African Americans who had been drafted and fought in World War I for democracy and the rights of oppressed minorities abroad (albeit in segregated units, often placed in the front lines of the most dangerous battles), returning to racist conditions at home fostered increased resentment of their own inferior position in American society. After World War I, the South-to-North Black migration continued. Soon, the approach of World War II gave economic stimulation to a depressed U.S. economy. But although the general level of wages rose, this time there was a more fierce and intentional job discrimination. When America entered World War II, African Americans who were drafted into the military found themselves often assigned to menial duties. Thus, the racial tensions already evident in civilian life due to population mobility, industrial readjustments, and housing shortages were exacerbated.

Racial tensions also intensified with the rise in public school enrollments. American high school attendance was increasing.[22] The immense spread of secondary education and increased interaction among students and families of various racial and ethnic backgrounds brought considerable cultural education as well "in the ways of living of a variety of families in the community" (Allen 1952:222). However, this contact also produced increasing racial prejudice. Anthropologists became critically aware of racism at home as they examined the issues of the war abroad.

Sensitive to this discomfort and fiercely disapproving of racism, Powdermaker and others committed themselves to offsetting prejudice by offering scientific data to more people through the publication of general-audience popular books and articles on race. The anthropological method, whose analysis includes a broader perspective in which to understand participants' points of view, provided disciplinary expertise to policy analysis and program creation. Further, governmental support for applied anthropology projects stimulated a field of action-oriented anthropology (Schneider 2001:708). Both inspired Powdermaker to write on the subject of education and race. She published an article in the popular press on the misconceptions of racial difference (1945). Her commitment found further voice in a more academic article on the dilemma of altering racial attitudes (1944a). And she understood the potential utility of anthropology in the development of school curricula to assist the amelioration of intolerance. During this same period she wrote her book *Probing Our Prejudices* (1944b), adopted as a high school text in New York City. This book, as well as her other papers on African Americans, converged with similar writings by others in the late 1930s and early 1940s. Publications such as those by Powdermaker, Ruth Benedict (1942b), and Gene Weltfish (Benedict and Weltfish, 1943; 1948) relied on Franz Boas's *The Mind of Primitive Man* (1911; revised in 1938) to provide the core argument that physical traits of race cannot be correlated with intelligence or personality and that there exists a distinct difference between race and culture.[23]

Probing Our Prejudices reiterates Powdermaker's argument that "prejudices are not entirely due to lack of knowledge, but that they lie also in the realm of the emotions" (1944b:viii). She defines prejudice as "an attitude we have toward a specific situation that we reach without sufficient consideration of the facts about the situation" (1). This small book lays out her analysis of the origins of prejudicial thinking and of its effect upon the victim, the subject, and society itself. Powdermaker was aware that the effects of prejudice stunt both individual and societal development and that the curtailment of individual rights resulting from prejudice necessarily impedes societal development too. During this same period, she notes in her book review of *When Peoples Meet* (Locke and Stern 1942) that "the connotation of difference, either racial or cultural, with inferiority and with a status of subordination presents problems not only in the lives of minority peoples, but also limits the development of real social democracy for all peoples" (Powdermaker 1943b:476). Although *Probing Our Prejudices* provides factual evidence to dispel some of the more common prejudices most conspicuous in American society, the real purpose of the text is to sensitize students to their own emotional attitudes toward others different from themselves and thereby to the mechanisms that precipitate their own prejudicial thinking.

Powdermaker presumes that "society is no haphazard affair" (1944b:22), that it exerts its influence, however subtly, on individual thinking and behavior. In line with the reasoning of her functionalist training, she explains in the chapter entitled "How We Get Our Prejudices": "Society is a well-organized system. What we do and how we do it is not left to chance or accident. Rather does society tell us what to do, and how to do it. . . . We are seldom aware of the degree to which our behavior, important and unimportant, is regulated by the pattern of the society in which we live" (22–23).

Our misconceptions become our norm because individuals are affected unconsciously by the society in which they live. But more important for understanding the nature of prejudice is the notion that "not only is our behavior regulated by society, but so also our ideas and feelings" (24). The very existence of a work such as *Probing Our Prejudices* serves as evidence of her belief that individuals, once aware, can affect change within themselves and can alter the values held within their society. As such, it is an excellent example of a critical and self-reflexive teaching style. With teaching aids for classroom exercises at the end of each chapter and a section on the consequences of prejudice for society, the book is an appeal for a public battle against individual prejudicial behavior.

Others published similar pamphlets and books. Ruth Benedict and Gene Weltfish wrote *In Henry's Backyard* (1948), an illustrated storybook on understanding racism. The text is based on their coauthored pamphlet, *The Races of Mankind* (1943), with illustrations adapted from the animated color film *Brotherhood of Man*, produced in Hollywood by United Productions of America on the initiative of the UAW-CIO. The premise of the book is that the commonly held assumption that biological racial differences correlate with other culturally acquired qualities has no scientific basis. Powdermaker was outspoken concerning the importance of literature aimed at educating the general public to the hazards and dangers of prejudicial thinking. In her review of another of Ruth Benedict's books, *Race: Science and Politics* (1940), Powdermaker reiterates her belief that "there is an unquestionable need today for a popular book on race. . . . What Dr. Benedict does is to present a point of view and it would be well if right now this point of view could be shouted from the rooftops" (1941:474). This point of view was that "to understand race persecution, one must understand persecution as a whole and its basic economic and social causes" (474). Another paper by Powdermaker, "The Anthropological Approach to the Problem of Modifying Race Attitudes" (1944a), reiterates her belief that there were pressing needs for the popularization of books and articles on race. Along with *Probing Our Prejudices* (1944b) and "An Anthropologist Looks at the Race Question" (1945), these writings were an appeal to others to educate the public concerning the socioeconomic roots of the emotional basis of racism.

Powdermaker's Hollywood Study

Continuing her conviction that education is a process by which an individual is socialized into one's closest present cultural surroundings, Powdermaker believed mass media to be a critical influence molding the lives of people. For almost fifty years her ethnography of the Hollywood film industry was the single anthropological study of feature film production (Mahon 2000:467). Even though this publication has been subjected to criticism and critique, it was a fairly innovative venue to conduct a study. Entertainment films were a relatively new force, and she declared them exceptionally powerful. In the next twelve years after returning from her Mississippi research she continually thought about her movie theater experiences during her fieldwork in the South. She observed that a spectator's belief in honest and fair representation was culled from direct personal experience.

During a sabbatical year from Queens College (1946–47) when Powdermaker once again embarked for the field, she chose Los Angeles and went to Hollywood to study the social relations of feature film production. "All entertainment is education in some way," she stated, "many times more effective than schools because of the appeal to the emotions rather than to the intellect" (1950:14). Her study of the Hollywood film industry, *Hollywood, the Dream Factory* (1950), again stresses that the "dichotomy between thought and feeling is . . . artificial" (323). One of the more serious issues is the ability of entertainment to "manipulate the ideas, opinions and emotions of vast audiences" (322).

> Almost every movie . . . deals with some problem of human relations, and the manner in which glamorous movie stars solve these problems may affect the thinking of people about their own problems. A middle-aged woman whose husband had recently left her changed her mind three times about how to handle the situation, after seeing three movies in which she could identify her own problem. (1950:13)

Film is part of the context in which learning takes place; it influences the individual's perceptions of self and society. Her study of Hollywood film production was premised on the belief that the social relations of film production reflect societal problems centered around "power as it functions in both economic and political areas of living" (82).

The fear and anxiety of job loss in the film industry, of losing power and income, were not unlike the emotional motives causing racial prejudice in American society. Therefore, while mass communications are culturally enriching, they also have a tendency to promote conformity, both in our thinking and our emotional lives, and by so doing to affect the socialization process in perhaps a multitude of ways unintended by the films' creators. In Hollywood, Powdermaker discovered that that peculiarities in the structure of production infiltrated movie themes, moviemaking, and, therefore, audiences through movie viewing, through the exploitation of emotional desires that made for entertainment. She critiques the way in which love and violence are depicted in story lines and viewers manipulated into believing the stories, even though, as she points out, most movie characters "are passive beings to whom things happen accidentally" (1950:328). Rarely does a movie show an individual in the process of becoming either successful or undone. Rather, the cause is simply accidental. Love is expressed as an instant biological attraction to someone alluring and seductive; violence is the only way to handle difficult situations. As one watches movies, the tendency is for one's thoughts and feelings to conform to the notions of human relationships as portrayed on the screen. In this way, individuals are influenced and socialized through their absorption of values depicted.

Conclusions

Powdermaker's continued interest in the individual in culture was always framed by her functionalist approach and her involvement in psychoanalytic studies. In fact, much of Powdermaker's work evolved from her strong friendships and long conversations with anthropologists Bronislaw Malinowski and Edward Sapir and with psychoanalyst Henry Stack Sullivan. The psychoanalytic school derived from Sullivan's theories of interpersonal relations integrated well with work like that of Powdermaker and Sapir. Accepting that both organized and unorganized interpersonal relations are a part of education, Powdermaker believed that education is a continuous lifetime process and that the dynamics of learning how to adjust to certain advantageous and adaptive roles in particular cultural settings is applicable not only to children in the schools but also to all individuals in their communities.

It is problematic to reassess Powdermaker's work today, within both the frameworks of psychological studies and race relations. Powdermaker was an early proponent of culture and personality studies and taught such a course for many years at Queens College.[24] In her paper "The Channeling of Negro Aggression by the Cultural Process" (1943a), she applies a psychoanalytic and functionalist approach to explain certain aspects of African American personality. The paper is couched in the reductionist thinking that was emblematic of the time. Powdermaker uses comparisons between African Americans and the dependency state of children and refers to Theodor Reik's (1941) theories on the masochistic personality. This reductionist view in early culture and personality studies is what eventually plunged the subdiscipline into disrepute. However, if we keep in mind that such early studies were breaking new ground in the discipline and that they necessarily contained certain limitations, her work nonetheless addresses questions that remain important today. Her awareness of the significance of interpersonal relationship studies (in theories advanced by such psychoanalysts as Sullivan, Horney, and Kardiner) merits reexamination.

A second concern, that of race relations, also presents undeniable difficulties. As Gertrude Fraser (1991) has pointed out, one is aware that Powdermaker's early contributions to these issues (as exemplified by *After Freedom*), when viewed within the framework of current work, were informed by a certain racial parochialism. In order to arrive at the issues embedded in her work that have salience for our anthropological understanding of race relations today, one must confront and then move beyond her assumption that African American culture should be considered "in terms of an ascendancy to white cultural patterns" (Fraser 1991:403).

On the other hand, Powdermaker's focus on a marginalized group of people in a modern American community was an innovative project and cutting edge for the discipline of anthropology at that time. This sort of anthropological study was in the tradition of her training in social anthropology. In the United States, it was primarily sociology students and researchers out of the University of Chicago who also regularly directed their attentions to community studies (such as E. Franklin Frazier 1939; Charles Johnson 1934; and Allison Davis et al. 1941).[25] A next generation of students at Chicago met Radcliffe-Brown on American soil. He was invited to lecture at Chicago in 1926 and in so doing introduced social anthropology to students here. Shortly thereafter, William Lloyd Warner followed him to Australia, and on return Warner influenced a next generation of anthropology students both at Harvard (see the Kimball chapter in this volume) and Chicago. At the same time, in New York, the Rockefeller Fund through Columbia University enabled sociologists Robert and Helen Lynd to produce the early well-known community study *Middletown* (1929) and historian Caroline F. Ware to complete another on Greenwich Village (1935).

As a major anthropological study of this sort not focused on Native Americans, *After Freedom* was considered somewhat controversial in anthropological circles. Although Edward Sapir and Clark Wissler endorsed and reviewed it favorably, Robert Lowie voiced skepticism about this venue for anthropological research (Powdermaker 1966:133). The studies of modern American communities were, at the time, more typically the domain of sociology and social psychology than of anthropology.[26] For example, sociologist John Dollard's *Caste and Class in a Southern Town* (1937), to which Powdermaker's book is often compared, analyzed the social structure of a southern town by focusing on the psychological mechanisms that maintained the social organization of race relations there. Powdermaker had taken him with her on her second trip to Mississippi. When later Yale University chose to publish his book and refused to publish hers, it humiliated her deeply.[27]

The anthropological, qualitative methods of participant-observation and her lengthier stay in the community gave Powdermaker's study an intriguing and unexplored texture. Unlike the more objectified analyses, Powdermaker's interpretation of her data was more sensitive and empathetic. As presented both in her book and in her subsequent publications, her anthropological insights into, and keen understanding of, the complications and complexities of a multiracial American society and the impact of society on individual behavior can still be reconsidered and acknowledged.

While the field of anthropology and education has tended to narrow its focus to educational concerns as they pertain most directly to the classroom, the kinds of issues Powdermaker and others raised more than sixty years ago are still unresolved. Matters such as the social context in which learning takes place and the dialectic between the individual and his or her culture continue to be fruitful guides for current educational studies.

Similar themes arise in many of the investigations currently subsumed under the rubric of *cultural diversity* and *multicultural education*. For example, the work by Signithia Fordham (1993, 1996) on young Black female students in school and by John Ogbu (1992) on multicultural education both identify the adaptive strategies of channeling aggression. In this sense, while the current cultural milieu has evolved, these works address issues similar to the ones that Powdermaker herself addressed in the 1940s.

In a joint paper explaining some of the causes contributing to Black students' underachievement in school, Fordham and Ogbu (1986:178) suggest "low school performance is an adaptive response to the requirements of cultural imperatives within their ecological structure." This ecological structure includes a long history of substandard schooling, limited development of an academic tradition (because of the experience of slavery), and economic discrimination in the form of job ceilings and wage limitations regardless of educational accomplishment.

They point out that the collective sense of Black identity is important, and that this identity is formed, as stated in Powdermaker's paper, in opposition to dominant White culture. Black students have developed such adaptive strategies as resistance behavior to "channel their aggression." For many students, their active engagement in resistance takes the form of avoidance of the appropriated identity imposed by dominant White culture upon them. To succeed in school, to strive for success there, is to "'act white' and is negatively sanctioned" (1986:177) by the students' peer groups, leading to purposeful underachievement. In another work, Fordham (1993) considers the issues for high-achieving Black students as another form of active resistance. She claims that successful Black students are fighting to invalidate the existing norms and low expectations of school administrators by doing what Black students are not supposed to be able to do—to perform well in school and achieve academic distinction, behavior mistakenly regarded as conformity.

In contrast to the earlier works of the 1930s and 1940s, where socialization and education were sometimes interchangeable terms, later theorists distinguish between the shaping of the human mind by the two different processes of socialization and education (Cohen 1971). Broadly, socialization is defined as the learning that takes place by the individual from kin in a spontaneous and ongoing manner; education is the process of learning from non-kin in a predictable and set manner. The varying proportion of each educational mechanism in a society is an adaptive response to the cultural imperatives at a given time in a given culture (Cohen 1971:22). Issues similar to those concerning African Americans' school behavior indicate the complexities found in the intersection of education and socialization. The work by Fordham and Ogbu points out that the "adaptive responses" by Black students can be substantially different from those by Whites since the former individuals confront the surrounding culture from different vantage points. Whether constructed as the "channeling of aggression" or as "active engagement," ongoing resistant behavior culturally framed remains as rebellious a process for powerless peoples today as it was in 1943.

If, as Powdermaker believed, the social environment produces prejudice, then one must look to the sociopolitical and economic dimensions of the individual's interaction with the culture to understand the dynamics of the situation. She wrote, "Whether the contemporary community is small or large, problems have become more complex. . . . It is difficult . . . to find a situation which escapes biracial strains or hostilities between opposing power structures or ideological systems" (1966:286). The socioeconomic parameters of the cultural situation remain as emotionally charged today as they were in the 1940s. To change racial attitudes, she believed in the usefulness of anthropological knowledge and concepts for analysis and understanding.

Powdermaker emphasized specific knowledge of social contexts and historical causes to understand the nature of cultural determinants. She understood that unraveling and understanding the impact of culture on an individual would be emancipating. Powdermaker was always an advocate of human freedom. The drive for personal freedom, both for herself and for others, framed the political praxis of her work. As she notes in Stranger and Friend,

> The continuing relation between personal feelings (sensory, aesthetic, emotional) and intellectual perception is stressed—how the anthropologist feels as well as what he does, since he is part of the situation studied. In recounting my field experiences, I look inward as well as outward, with the benefit of hindsight. An anthropological voyage may tack and turn in several directions, and the effective field worker learns about himself as well as about the people he studies. (1966:14)

Examination of these fundamental issues is crucial to better understand the impact of institutional social life upon the individual. The conflict between freedom and conformity, the artificial dichotomy between thought and feeling, both remain grounded in cultural realities even as these same cultural realities may shift, evolve, and change.

Notes

This chapter draws on research conducted while the author was a research scholar at the Center for the Study of Women, University of California–Los Angeles, and a research associate at the Los Angeles County Natural History Museum. Richard Blot, Michelle Fine, Juliet Niehaus, and Roger Laverty read and commented on earlier drafts of this chapter, for which I am grateful. The editorial help of Nancy King, Leni Silverstein, and Kate Zentall was invaluable in polishing my written ideas. Reviewers for the University of Nebraska Press suggested valuable alterations and modifications.

1. When I first read Powdermaker's *Stranger and Friend: The Way of an Anthropologist* (1966) as an anthropology graduate student, I was struck by her honesty and candor in recounting her fieldwork experiences. This impression was confirmed when I read her work for the second time during my own first fieldwork in the Philippines in 1973. But it was not until many years later that my work and research led me to her other writings. Though I never had the good fortune to meet Dr. Powdermaker, I have met and talked with some of her students and colleagues from Queens College. They confirm what her writings had led me to believe—that she was an extraordinary woman, a gifted teacher, and an innovative fieldworker.

2. Interest in and citations of Powdermaker's publications are found more often outside of anthropology than within the field itself—for example, in African American and media studies.

3. The northern migration of African American populations in the East and the Midwest "explode[d] after World War I" (Baker 1998a:128) and continued in the West during World War II. These resulting changes of race and class configurations in large urban cities spurred on much new research to both identify causes of racial unrest and to establish a new notion of African American identity (139–142).

4. Earlier publications included the study by W. E. B. Du Bois on Philadelphia (1899), Alain Locke's *The New Negro* (1925), and the Chicago Commission on Race Relations report (1922).

5. Reconstructing Hortense Powdermaker's life and intellectual evolution is difficult because, at her request, all personal papers and copies of her field notes were destroyed upon her death. Her published works and two short biographical pieces (Silverman 1989; Wolf 1971) remain. For a complete bibliography of Hortense Powdermaker, see Wolf (1971).

6. For more information on her union work, see Powdermaker (1924, 1966).

7. Malinowski's methods for conducting fieldwork depended on a lengthy stay in a community to gather firsthand information on the culture. His early teaching of ethnographic methods set the standard for future ethnological research. As a result of Malinowski's tutelage, with his insistence on systematic fieldwork and rich descriptions, Powdermaker was an excellent fieldworker, and her ethnographies are insightfully written.

8. Henry Stack Sullivan described his psychoanalytic theories as interpersonal relations because he believed that activities between and among individuals were the foundation of personality characteristics and their point of discovery. For Powdermaker, this notion that personality and identity are developmental and flexible fit neatly with her studies in Malinowski's social anthropology and her training in the culture and personality views of Sapir.

9. Lesu is a village in the South Pacific island of New Ireland and the site of Powdermaker's *Life in Lesu* (1933).

10. In *Stranger and Friend* (1966:45) Powdermaker also acknowledges a debt to Clark Wissler, Ralph Linton, Alfred Kroeber, Ruth Benedict, Robert Redfield, A. I. Hallowell, Abraham Kardiner, and Erik Erikson as influences on her work.

11. Hortense Powdermaker's paper coauthored with Joseph Semper, "Education and Occupation among New Haven Negroes" (1938), is an example of this influence.

12. Wissler was respected as a generous mentor. Although his main duties were at the American Museum of Natural History at the time, he held a part-time appointment at Yale. His value as a knowledgeable psychologist turned anthropologist was increased by the interdisciplinary mandate connected to Rockefeller funding in the development of the Institute of Human Relations. That is how he was able to facilitate Powdermaker's residence there (see Freed and Freed 1983).

13. Both Johnson and Frazier were trained at the University of Chicago. Johnson studied under Robert E. Park and had left Chicago before Sapir arrived in 1925. Frazier went to Chicago in 1927 and received his degree in 1931. He presumably knew Sapir and perhaps Sullivan from those years. See also Powdermaker's account of her stay at Fisk University in *Stranger and Friend* (1966).

14. Cottonville is the fictitious name that Powdermaker gave to the town where she resided and that she used in her book. Many years later, in the writing of *Stranger and Friend* (1966), she identified the actual name of the town as Indianola.

15. For a critique of the impact of this study, see Adams and Gorton (2004).

16. For instance, from the psychoanalytic side, Karen Horney was among the first analysts to develop a description of some of the effects of cultural pressures in producing neuroses, and Sullivan presented his theory of personality development in terms of the process of acculturation (Thompson 1950).

17. For more on the interrelationships between anthropology and psychoanalysis, see Caffey (1989) and Darnell (1990).

18. The conference was held April 29–May 4, 1941.

19. In discussing migration Powdermaker states, "Between 1920 and 1930, over a million Negroes migrated from the country to the cities" (1943a:757).

20. Perhaps Powdermaker also chose to be cautious. According to May Ebihara, an unnamed anthropologist commented, "A distinction was made between one's position as an anthropologist and as a private citizen" (1985:112). A personal commitment to socialism or communism was not directly presented in classrooms or writings because, Ebihara suggests, it would have been dangerous for job security.

21. An additional impetus toward political sensitivity was the contact with intellectual refugees fleeing Europe. Even before the formal outbreak of World War II in 1939, Hitler's policies toward Jews and political dissidents in Europe had precipitated the influx into the United States of psychologists and psychiatrists escaping persecution there. As European scientists immigrated to the United States, the interaction between psychology and the social sciences increased, most notably in the fields of sociology and anthropology, resulting in evermore cross fertilization between these disciplines and psychology. This dialogue fostered increased awareness of the individual actor in culture.

22. In 1900 fewer than one in ten American students were in high school; by 1950 four out of five were being educated at this level.

23. This, along with Otto Klineberg's (1935) and Melville Herskovits's (1927) denunciations of intelligence testing, forms the core argument against the racial inferiority of Blacks. The postulate is that intelligence tests measure standardized individual reactions to environment and that individual performance is strongly influenced by many extraneous factors. The evidence of acculturation and cultural learning is a persuasive argument in disproving the racist myth that physical types and mental characteristics can be equated. The basic hypothesis of White superiority in general social efficiency and innate intelligence is unwarranted. For a more detailed history of the period, see Baker (1998a), Fraser (1991), and Szwed (1974).

24. See Bourguignon's memories of being a student of Powdermaker's (1991). Eric Wolf, another former student, writes, "her course on culture and personality will remain especially memorable to her many students" (1971:748).

25. From its start, the Chicago sociology department created by Albion Small in 1892 and then later directed by Robert Park was a collective enterprise with no single seminal figure such as was Boas at Columbia. In a rapidly changing city, the department was intent on observing what modernization had wrought, rather than recording details of the bourgeois Victorian world before it disappeared. The department believed in description as the proper way to determine social reality. Robert Park joined the faculty in 1914 after earning a PhD in Germany and having traveled through the American South with Booker T. Washington. In his Southern travels he found himself a participant-observer among African Americans and returned to the North with a strong commitment to improving the social good with his research. Thanks to the encouragement of Park,

the University of Chicago became an early training ground for African American sociologists and their publications. Many were published in the Chicago Sociology Series, the chief conduit of classic Chicago studies begun in 1923 by Park and Ernest Burgess. When anthropologists Edward Sapir and Ralph Linton joined the faculty in the 1920s, they corroborated the importance of empirical evidence and fit in with the existing mavericks and individuals there whose approaches were interdisciplinary and holistic (Kurent 1982).

26. It was, though, within the tradition of the British social anthropology in which Powdermaker had been trained. Most mature American-trained anthropologists at the time had studied at schools influenced by Boasian methodology, not at the University of Chicago.

27. Dollard, a fellow research assistant at the Yale Institute of Human Relations, accompanied Powdermaker when she returned to her Mississippi field site during the summer of 1934. She provided his introduction to the community from which he collected the data for his book (Darnell 1990:358). The reasons for Yale choosing Dollard's study for publication are complicated. Certainly gender and departmental politics played a part. The details are beyond the scope of this chapter.

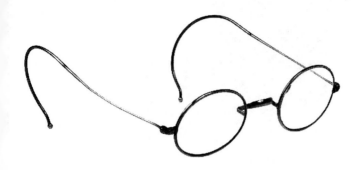

6. Culture and Race in the Classroom

Jules Henry and Ruth Landes on American Education

Richard Handler

Ruth Landes in Potawatomi cloak, circa 1935. Courtesy of National Anthropological Archives, Smithsonian Institution (91-4_732).

Jules Henry (on horseback, *left*) with Mescalero Apaches on their reservation in the 1930s. Courtesy of the National Anthropological Archives, Smithsonian Institution (91-4_731).

When Jules Henry (1904–69), born Jules Henry Blumensohn in New York City, entered Columbia University as a graduate student in the late 1920s, the Anthropology Department had already granted doctoral degrees to two generations of Boasian students. The program was under the stewardship of Franz Boas, though Ruth Benedict was becoming the day-to-day interlocutor of the students. Henry enrolled in Margaret Mead's field methods course. He also worked with Boas, whose comprehensive approach to gathering descriptive data he adopted, and whose interest in anthropological linguistics he shared. His attentive adviser Benedict inspired his commitment to viewing a culture as a holistic and integrated unit, and like her, he was to frame much of his research in terms of culture and personality. Boas, Benedict, and Freud were the major influences on his work.

As a graduate student he traveled to the Southwest to study the Mescalero Apaches under the supervision of Benedict. His subsequent fieldwork with the Kaingang in southwestern Brazil, also under her supervision, was the basis for his dissertation, completed in 1935, and for Jungle People (1941), the first psychoanalytical ethnography. In 1936–37 he and his wife, Zunia Henry, carried out fieldwork among the Pilagá of northern Argentina, concentrating on the then little studied topic of childhood psychological development. In 1944 this resulted in their Doll Play of Pilagá Indian Children.

Between 1939 and 1941, Henry traveled to Mexico to record Indian languages and develop a plan for extending literacy to outlying areas. He had been invited by the progressive administration of President Lázaro Cárdenas, which was attempting to implement the reforms promised by the 1910 Mexican Revolution. There Henry began to see the possibilities of using his anthropological skills to encourage socialist solutions to dilemmas of poverty and the plight of the poor. The work was interrupted by the entry of the United States into World War II. Like Mead, Benedict, and many others, he refocused on American needs and volunteered for governmental work. At the conclusion of the war, he continued his research on issues of learning, invigorated by a new interest in modern American culture and a commitment to social justice.

Part of Henry's talent was developing new research techniques that he and his students used in intensive detailed observation and fieldwork in schools. Henry focused on the methods used by schools to enculturate children to think and behave as Americans, to conform to national values. He was already a recognized authority on anthropology and education by the time of the landmark 1954 Stanford Conference, where he presented a paper presenting dichotomies derived from observations he made while among the Pilagá and from his and his students' observations in American classrooms (Henry 1955). Among his conclusions was that while some types of education like additive, target seeking, and diffuse are universal, others like spiraling, typified by the Socratic method and often employed in the United States, are not. His paper "A Cross-Cultural Outline of Education" (1960) is a guide for educational data organization in either preliterate or industrial cultures.

Henry's approach to culture was dialectical. He thought that behavior creates the framework of the beliefs and activities in which it resides, and also that this cultural environment determines behavior. Cultural units are not constant. In his acclaimed Culture against Man (1963), which he described as an essay in culture and personality (1973:66), he characterized American culture as "driven" by the cultural creations of "drives" and "values." Henry believed in the value of anthropology as a lens through which he could view the impact of American culture on marginal individuals, championing a social commitment anthropology could provide by making the results of research available to the general public.

He focused on the areas of mental health and education. When he looked at the interstices between competing adjacent cultures such as poor students of color learning in White middle-class school curricula, he found loci to enlarge the scope of social action. His ethnographic studies of schools and classrooms begun in the early 1950s and subsequently published in Culture against Man (1963), and, posthumously, in On Education (1972) and On Sham, Vulnerability and Other Forms of Self-Destruction (1973), along with his major work on mental illness, Pathways to Madness (1971), all reached popular audiences. Through them Henry accomplished his goal of demonstrating that anthropology had the capacity and could exercise the responsibility to adapt to the study and critique of complex cultures.

Ruth Landes (1908–91), born Ruth Schlossberg in New York City, was a classmate and friend of Jules Henry. The two remained in touch throughout their lives. Like him, she studied under Boas and became a protégée of Benedict, earning her PhD in the same year, 1935. Landes had begun graduate work at the New York School of Social Work, a part of Columbia University, following the completion of her college degree from New York University. Her master's thesis grew out of research within the Black Jewish community of Harlem.

She met Boas through Alexander Goldenweiser, a favorite early student of his and also a friend of her father. Boas encouraged her to publish her findings and persuaded her to enter his graduate program, which she did in 1931. An early short marriage and consequent divorce before beginning her anthropological studies influenced her fieldwork among the Ojibwa and her resulting book on gender relations, The Ojibwa Woman (1938). Praised for her insight into women's lives and for examining the vitality of the culture as it seemingly was being diluted, Landes was also criticized for her lack of historical perspective, particularly as the long-standing loss of autonomy and erosion of traditional culture had severely altered economic and gender roles (see Leacock 1978:251–252; Visweswaran 1997:608).

After Landes received her PhD in 1935, her next field experiences took her first to the Potawatomi in Kansas for seven months that year and then to Brazil in 1938–39 under the continued mentoring of Benedict. Her fieldwork among Black women in Bahia led to her discovery that the same women who performed spiritual roles in the practice of candomblé, a syncretic Afro-Brazilian spirit possession religion, were also community leaders of informal social and economic networks in impoverished neighborhoods. Thus, these religious enclaves also served as reciprocal support societies supplying a network of female solidarity (see S. Cole 2003). In 1947 Landes's Brazilian work was published as the landmark The City of Women, in which she explored issues of gender, race, and class while including herself as one of the main characters in the book. Criticism of her behavior and personal conduct while in Brazil prevented her professional advance, and she found herself marginalized and continually struggling to find work to support herself.

An unexpected but fortunate outcome of this period of transient employment occurred while she lived in California, from 1956 to 1965. She turned her creative thinking to teaching teachers how to take best advantage of the multicultural classrooms in which they worked. From this experience she wrote Culture in American Education (1965), which speaks to the need to sensitize teachers to the various worldviews of their culturally diverse students. Both Henry's Culture against Man and Landes's Culture in American Education were published at the end of a tranquil postwar era, just before the social protest movements of the 1960s. They both believed in the power of anthropology to explain and correct social inequality. Henry proposed intellectual insight and assessments as a solution. Landes chose a hands-on activist approach instead.

In the following chapter, Richard Handler contrasts the differing research positions Jules Henry and Ruth Landes held in their studies of American education during the 1950s and 1960s. Both wrote about the disjuncture between normative White middle-class values presented by schools as "American" and students of other cultures struggling to learn this new set of cultural norms, and both looked to cultural explanations to account for school failures rather than blaming the marginalized. While Henry's tone is that of an eyewitness and outside consultant, Landes writes as a participating insider who is not so much an onlooker as a problem solver. Their common dedication to use insights from anthropology to address social issues and contest ethnocentric biases gives their work continued relevance.

Jules Henry (1904–69) was born in New York City, the son of a "well-to-do family"; his father was a "highly successful physician" (Gould 1971:793). Henry
took his undergraduate degree (1928) at the City College of New York, where
he was deeply influenced by the philosopher Morris Raphael Cohen.[1] He began graduate studies in anthropology at Columbia University in the late 1920s,
where he studied with Ruth Benedict, Margaret Mead, and Franz Boas. During
the summer of 1931 he worked among the Mescalero Apaches, under the direction of Benedict (Modell 1983:179; Caffrey 1989:261), and then completed
fourteen months (1932-34) of fieldwork with the Kaingangs of Brazil (Henry
1941:xxii), followed by twelve months (1936–37) of research among the Pilagá
of Argentina. These research stints resulted in his well-known monograph,
Jungle People (1941), and a later study, coauthored with his wife, Zunia Henry
(Henry and Henry 1944). During World War II he worked as a social scientist
for the Mexican and American governments and went to Japan in 1945 with the
U.S. Strategic Bombing Survey.

   Ruth Landes (1908–91) was born in New York City, the daughter of Russian
Jewish immigrants; her father was a cofounder of the Amalgamated Clothing Workers of America. Landes took her undergraduate degree at New York
University, completed a master's degree in social work, and then went into the
graduate anthropology program at Columbia in 1932, where she studied with
Boas and Benedict and received her PhD in 1935. Benedict sent Landes into
the field during her first summer in graduate school, when she went to Mani-
tou Rapids, Ontario, to work among Ojibwa people. With continuing support
from Benedict, she returned to the Ojibwa (Chippewa) people at Red Lake,
Minnesota, in 1933. In 1935–36, she undertook a third season of fieldwork.
Benedict sent her to study the Potawatomies of Kansas, but en route Landes
spent several weeks with Frances Densmore studying Siouan-language speak-
ers near Red Wing, Minnesota (Landes 1937: unpaginated acknowledgments
and preface; S. Cole 2003:61–62, 71–72, 107–46). No fewer than five monographs resulted from this work, although three of them were only belatedly

published (Landes 1937, 1938, 1968a, 1968b, 1970a). Returned from Kansas, Landes hoped to continue her Potawatomie work, but Benedict enlisted her for a Columbia University research team in Brazil (S. Cole 2003:145). She did fieldwork among urban Afro-Brazilians in 1938–39, resulting in the publication of *The City of Women* (1947), the work she considered "the high point of her career" (S. Cole 2003:203; cf. Landes 1970b, S. Cole 1994).

Henry and Landes were classmates at Columbia. They were on good enough terms to exchange letters from the field (S. Cole 2003:113, 134). Both found it difficult to secure academic positions during the Depression and World War II. During that time, Henry did a great deal of government and applied work, but after the war he landed a tenured position at Washington University, St. Louis, where he stayed until his death. There is evidence, nonetheless, that he felt himself to be marginalized with respect to the prestigious centers of American anthropology. Far more highly marginalized than Henry, Landes depended on applied contract work and various temporary government and teaching positions, and did not find a permanent position until 1965, when she went to McMaster University in Hamilton, Ontario (Landes 1965:1–8; Mahony 1996; S. Cole 2003:227–46). Henry, by then well established, wrote a letter of reference to McMaster on Landes's behalf, describing her as "among the top people in the new field of cultural factors in education" (quoted in S. Cole 2003:238). Landes could enjoy her tenured position only until 1973, when she reached sixty-five, the age of mandatory retirement in Ontario (S. Cole 2003:243).

Within the context of these similar yet differing career trajectories, both Henry and Landes did significant research on American public school education in the 1950s and 1960s. In this both were well ahead of trends in the larger discipline, although, of course, their Columbia University mentors set examples for them with respect to anthropological commentary on American culture, examples that still inspire us all. It is difficult to comment extensively on the motivations, beyond the circumstantial and institutional, that prompted either anthropologist to move in this direction (there is no biography of Henry, and Cole's excellent study of Landes says little about her research on education). Nonetheless, in this chapter I compare their projects in terms of one key issue, which we might call the *subject position* of each scholar.

First, to focus on commonality: like most Boasian anthropologists, Henry and Landes shared a basic "cosmographic" (Boas 1887b) understanding of "culture" and its importance. On the other hand, like many third- and fourth-generation Boasians, their cosmographic orientation was leavened with strains of postwar scientism (Henry's psychoanalytic framework, Landes's Benedictian culture-as-laboratory model [1965:284]). Like most anthropologists (of their time and since) who have studied American education, they understood that public schools served students from many backgrounds, that the normative culture of the schools was White and middle class, and that many pupils came from families who were otherwise cultured. Anthropologists of education often understood the educational difficulties of non-"mainstream" students in terms of culture conflict or cultural miscommunications, and many knew as well that such conflicts could have dire consequences for pupils and were anchored in the socioeconomic inequalities of the wider society. Thus, though Boasian anthropologists who studied American public education might talk about the ways in which various "minority" cultures did not match the normative expectations of the schools, very few of them subscribed to a simplistic culture-of-poverty theory that blamed the "failures" of subordinated people on the "pathologies" of their own cultures (see the chapter by Hochwald in this volume). There is a fine line here between talking about what Benedict once called "a genuinely disoriented culture" (1934b:226), on the one hand, and about a culture (or social group) subjected to harassment or oppression, on the other.[2] Landes and Henry skirted that line in somewhat different ways.

Jules Henry's angry and funny *Culture against Man* (1963), in which the main lines of his education research are reported, is above all a critique of mainstream American culture. Its author writes as a citizen of that culture, and the people about whom he writes are for the most part its White male "everymen." (To be more precise, he writes about those men at their various life stages, and he devotes considerable attention as well to schoolgirls and wives, but mainly as people confined within rather traditional roles, which he seems to critique either for not being traditional enough or for being sexist and degrading to women.) As he put it, discussing his own book: "I set myself to construct an anthropological theory of American culture that would help me explain the contemporary character of our people. . . . [To] be more candid . . . there are many qualities I dislike in myself and many I lament in my fellows, and I wished to account for them" (1966:91). Thus *Culture against Man* reads in some respects like a classic 1950s diatribe against conformity and "the organization society." As the historian Philip Gleason notes, these analyses of conformity preceded the rise in popularity of the concept of *identity*, an idea whose influence waxed while that of *conformity* waned (Gleason 1983). Henry was indeed concerned with children's identity yearnings, but his main arguments showed the way such yearnings were at once aroused and stifled by those features of American culture that bred conformity.

Culture against Man pulled together research that Henry had conducted since the mid-1930s, when he first began anthropological observations of contemporary American life at a psychiatric hospital in New York City. In the late 1940s, he studied case histories as cultural documents at the Washington University Child Guidance Clinic (Henry 1949, 1951). In 1951–52 he did fieldwork on a "psychiatric unit" of "a private general hospital" (1954a), where he studied, among other things, the social hierarchy of the hospital and "laughter in psychiatric staff conferences" (1954b). At that time he also studied a maternity ward, probably in the same hospital (Henry 1952). In 1953–54, he conducted research at the Sonia Shankman Orthogenic School, Chicago, "on the invitation of Dr. Bruno Bettelheim, Director of the School" (Henry 1957:725).[3] From 1953 onward, he conducted studies of public school classrooms (Henry 1965:7), including elementary and high schools and lower-, middle-, and upper-middle-class White children and lower-class Black children. That Henry's subject position, as an ethnographer of American education, was in some respects normative should not lead us to think that he was not clear-sighted about racial and ethnic differences in the United States. Consider the following remarks, from an essay on "Sham":

> An outstanding example of social sham on a large scale in our society is the condition of the Negro, who lives like a rat, being told he lives in a democracy and that everything is being done to improve his lot; and the Ghetto riots are the expression, on a social scale, of the underlying schizophrenic dialectic. The hostility of the Negro erupts in shooting in the presence of sham, while the clinical schizophrenic, having learned that he dare not erupt, goes mad, and may shoot himself. (1967:7)

We might quarrel with some of the terms Henry uses here—and certainly the psychoanalytic rhetoric is currently out of fashion—but it seems to me that

at least he is appalled by the situation of racialized minorities in the United
States and sees their plight as a function of oppression rather than their own
failures.

Although most of his public school ethnography was carried out in White
middle-class schools, Henry's work in a St. Louis housing project "inhabited
by very poor Negroes" led to a published analysis of the correlation between
"problems of motivation" among Black children and the socioeconomic oppression of their families (Henry 1965:7–8). Henry argued that the housing
project was a "City of Women" (he quoted the phrase, but there is no reference
to Landes), in which many families are without resident fathers, "employment
is precarious and poorly paid, and resources are scarce" (11). He placed blame
for this situation on White society, which had "cast out" Blacks (12). In that
situation of extreme deprivation, it was no wonder, Henry thought, that Black
elementary school students could not perform well in an institutional culture
oriented to middle-class notions of achievement: "the households of the project have no hope relative to middle-class orientations and . . . their behavior
therefore appears random (i.e., unorganized) to a middle-class observer" (9).
In one classroom that he and his students observed, a White middle-class
woman teacher struggled to distance herself from the disorganized behavior
of most of the Black children, so that she could focus on "the three who were
able to resist the general *strain toward disorder* and do their work" (13). But in
classrooms of thirty to fifty children and one teacher, these were losing battles
(14). Henry concluded with recommendations for the sorts of early interventions that were soon to become popular in the Head Start program. The entire
analysis flirts with culture-of-poverty notions, but Henry did not overlook the
racist oppression that was the root cause of poverty.

Moreover, Henry was as critical of the destructive effects of middle-class
culture on middle-class children as he was of its effects on impoverished Black
pupils (hence the title of his best-known work, *Culture against Man*). In his analyses of middle-class public school classrooms, Henry focused on the "sham"
of a culture that proclaims individual development as a valued goal yet in its institutional routines crushes individuality and trains students to be docile. Consider Henry's discussion of a music lesson. In this lesson, the teacher stimu-
lates her pupils to suggest which songs will be chosen to be sung in unison;
Henry argues that in such practices, the real teaching and learning concern not

music but a particular self-discipline, as each child competes for the teacher's attention. The "songfest" is thus converted into "an exercise in Self-realization," although the self realized is a "company" self: "the kind of individuality that was recognized . . . was mechanical, without a creative dimension, and under the strict control of the teacher. Let us conclude this discussion by saying that *school metamorphoses the child, giving it the kind of Self the school can manage, and then proceeds to minister to the Self it has made*" (Henry 1963:290–94).

Henry's discussion of the American "Self" does not extend into a discussion of the way people in different racial categories are assigned different sorts of selves. But it is just this topic that is central to Landes's 1965 book, *Culture in American Education*. In the late 1950s, Landes was teaching graduate students at the University of Southern California's School of Social Work, which led to an engagement (1959–62) "to conduct the Anthropology and Education program for training teachers" at Claremont Graduate School (Landes 1965:8, S. Cole 2003:236). Working with teachers, she began with their notions of normal selfhood, precisely those that Henry exposes in *Culture against Man*. But Landes's goal was to use anthropology to teach teachers to challenge their normative notions; thus she tried to make them self-conscious of their values and to show them how to engage, rather than dismiss, the values of other groups.

The backdrop for Landes's study is the booming postwar Southern California economy, an economy that was creating, as Landes depicts it, a mass society of the future. "With spiraling incomes and hopes," Landes writes,

> people acquire numerous goods and services. But it is widely observed and deplored that they fail to create personal ties with a local community because they move elsewhere, . . . lured by job opportunities . . . by the chance to get a new "tract house" in real estate developments that wipe out the vernal countryside and the vast fragrant citrus groves, by the sheer love of moving on wheels, by the conviction that better things lie beyond. California's burgeoning opportunities do not ease people's acute awareness of personal isolation and drift.

Indeed, she concludes, in a passage as bleak as anything from *Culture against Man*, Southern California had become a "jungle of anonymous faces" (1965:14).

If "future shock" at that time and place meant the growth of an anonymous mass society, it meant as well renewed tensions between racial and ethnic groups—specifically, increasing populations, or increasingly visible and vocal populations, of those categorized as "Negro, Mexican-American, Nisei, American Indian, and Anglo-American 'poor white' or 'Okies and Arkies'" (1965:22–23). Landes's specific task was to work with teachers in schools whose "ethnic and racial composition" was rapidly changing due both to postwar social mobility and to school desegregation and anti-discrimination legislation.

Landes directed her anthropological perspective not only at public school students but also at the teachers themselves. In other words, although the teachers faced the "problems" of "under-achieving" students from "minority" groups, Landes conceptualized the problem as one of intercultural communication. Thus, from her perspective, a starting point for analysis was both the students' and teachers' cultural backgrounds, especially the teachers' professional assumptions and feelings of "frustration," competence or incompetence, and status anxiety.

Some of Landes's teachers were aware that their work required them to impose middle-class values on students of other cultural backgrounds, but even the most liberal in this regard had little understanding of the ways in which professional-pedagogical categories of persons were underpinned by racial categories. According to Landes:

> Educators assemble a typology of pupils which purports to describe ability but also carries along certain obscure and confusing interests. These interests should be singled out and examined. . . . Then it appears that professional concern with tutelary programs is embedded in prejudicial stereotypes which are barely masked by pretentious labels. The labels group certain pupils by their "deficient motivation," others as the "slow learner," . . . others as evidencing "bilingualism," a supposed handicap which is noticed predominantly among "underachieving" Mexican-Americans. Individualities are blanketed under easy generalizations about "problem children" and "transients," racial or "ethnic" differences, "remedials" or R, mentally retarded or MR and "exceptionals," low IQs or Specials, the unsuccessful in academic high school or Generals, the hostile or apathetic. (1965:21–22)

All such classifications, Landes concludes, "supposedly imply a related reading ability, keyed to over-all assumptions that whites read better than Negroes

. . . [and] Mexicans" (21–22). To Landes, with her extensive research and life experience among African diaspora peoples, not to mention her experience of professional marginalization, it was obvious that such labels and classifications did not discriminate randomly among a mass population but reflected and reinforced racial and class hierarchies.

Landes brought to her project of teaching teachers a sophisticated understanding of the ways racial hierarchies shape conceptions of self and rules of social interaction among such racially defined selves. As she puts it, "few men can live despising themselves, as minorities are often expected to do. The Negro taught to defer to whites, the Jew taught to defer to Christians, the Catholic taught to defer to Protestants, does not wholly accept the mandates but incorporates them along with fears and rebellions" (1965:44). Such minorities are at once expected to live up to normative standards of behavior and communication, hindered from doing so, and punished (in different ways by different interlocutors) when they succeed in doing so. The result, as Landes understood, was that social interactions between stigmatized selves and normative officials, such as those occurring between minority pupils and teachers, are fraught with contradiction and misunderstanding. "Minorities . . . consciously struggle," she tells us, "to meet requirements and persons of the dominant society across cultural gaps and blocks. There is a constant exchange of cues—in words, voice tones, body bearing, dress, silences. On both sides, these are often misunderstood, some are penalized, some go lost" (45–46).

To help teachers overcome such "cultural gaps and blocks," Landes devised successively more sophisticated "projects" for her students to carry out over the semester- or year-long courses in which they were enrolled with her. "The first project assigned to the students was to observe strangers in some public place without speaking to them, and then to record the details of appearance, action, and speech, and describe what these conveyed" (1965:68). At first uncomfortable with making inferences from cultural cues rather than from verbal answers to questions—the kind of answers they had been taught to define as "facts"—the students gradually learned to become fascinated by cultural details and to trust themselves, and each other, as interpreters of such details. Landes's second project sent her students out "to collect meanings of seven words commonly used, listening to them orally in free interviews." The words chosen were *delinquent, crisis, diagnosis, interaction, prevention, role,* and *deviation* (69). Without making use of textual communication—in particular, without communicating normative spellings to their test subjects—students were startled to discover how widely meanings varied across context and social domain. Landes comments:

> Each respondent projected his own interests: a bookkeeper spoke of delinquent accounts, a mother referred to delinquent boys, an engineer spoke of a delinquent angle; only one informant made "prevention" synonymous with "contraception"; and one informant made "deviation" synonymous with "homosexuality." At times these identifications coincided with the questioner's definitions and at times differed drastically from them. (1965:69–70)

Moving beyond these initial exercises with what we might call narrowly contextualized data, the later projects Landes devised for her students took them into more complicated cultural analyses. The third project, designed "to show that social 'facts' are not self-evident," required the students "to interview several persons . . . about intermarriage" (71). Landes directed her students to prepare for their interviews by learning about gender roles in the cultures of their subjects. But that was only the beginning. Intermarriage "is an explosive complex . . . involving American ideas of racial and religious separateness, ideas of individual rights to happiness and self-determination, the primacy of romantic love, and the trend toward [racial] integration generally" (71). Looking at intermarriage, the students learned not only about cross-cultural differences in family ideologies but about their own prejudices and those of their colleagues—prejudices that, some of Landes's students thought, "handicapped" teachers in the performance of their jobs (73).

The fourth project (the most interesting for our purposes) pushed the students further along the path to critical cultural self-awareness. Landes asked "each student . . . to reconstruct the cultural ways of his family in three immediate generations" (1965:74). This project makes perfect sense when we remember that Landes had focused her study not on "deviant" cultures and cultural deviants, but on the interactions between so-called deviants and representatives of normal or mainstream society. She began with teachers' "frustrations," and she traced those to interactional gaps and blockages. To train teachers to overcome such blocks, she needed to make them culturally self-conscious (as Benedict would have put it), and such self-consciousness meant knowledge not merely of self but of self in relation to other, where both *self* and *other* are culturally defined, in the American case, in terms (among others) of racial and ethnic categories. "The yearning for personal identity," Landes noted, "was expressed in urgent terms by all teachers" (1965:76). Indeed, they had "fretfully debated their 'identity' and that of minorities." The project helped them, Landes thought, "to conceptualize the boundaries of [their] own inherited culture" (75). Such knowledge in turn helped the teachers "weigh afresh" the cues and actions of their pupils and led them to challenge their "school's practice of imposing middle-class traits on pupils of other origins" (76–77).[4]

Returning, now, to the question of the differing subject positions of Jules Henry and Ruth Landes, as expressed in their studies of American education: although the critical cultural insights of the two anthropologists, borne of the same Boasian milieu, are similar enough, Landes was practicing an "applied" anthropology in which she could not, or chose not to, adopt the critical rage and detachment that Jules Henry displays in *Culture against Man*. Henry portrays himself in his published work as a consultant, an outside expert. Like Landes, he worked with teams of students, research assistants, whom he sent into schools to conduct observations. Henry's written reports frequently acknowledge that quoted data derive from an "observer" other than himself; but it seems clear that Henry is the guiding figure in the research, the "principal investigator," as we might say today, who dealt on an equal plane only with the authority figures of the subject institutions. The point here is that for the most part Henry talked to his informants, probably quite empathetically, in one way and to institutional gatekeepers in another, relying less (one would guess) on empathy and more on expertise.[5] And although he occasionally included policy recommendations in his work (for example, in the paper on "low-achieving" Black pupils [1965:15–16]), his voice was that of the detached critic or, alternatively, the engaged cynic.

In Landes's work on education, by contrast, the subjects of her research were also her students: she was teaching teachers how to analyze their relationships to their pupils, and she did that, in the projects described above, by turning her students into ethnographers. Unlike Henry (in his published work, at least), Landes often presented her student-ethnographers' analyses of their materials, not just the "raw" data. Indeed, reading *Culture in American Education*, one is often hard-pressed to know whether "the informants" are Landes's students (professional teachers) or the informants of Landes's students. To put this another way, there are passages where it is not obvious if Landes is speaking to her readers about her own observations or about the observations and analyses of her students. It is sometimes even difficult to know whether the subjects of Landes's observations are her students or their pupils. This confusion (if it is confusion) makes sense, given that Landes's goal was to teach her students that they, too, possessed an "inherited culture" (1965:75). Landes's teachers were, in other words, both her students and her "natives."

Landes wanted her teachers to "respect other cultures," but she recognized as well that such respect did not mean they would "alter [their] own best values or professional goals." Rather, cultural awareness would enable teachers to communicate those goals more effectively than they could if their knowledge of minority cultures continued to be grounded solely in normative stereotypes (51–52). "It became possible," Landes tells us, for her teachers to learn "to rephrase 'frustrations' in teaching as semantic blocks traceable to confusions of social origin" (73). She urged that such cultural training would succeed only if "entire school systems" were to adopt the perspective of cultural anthropologists, helping teachers, administrators, and even parents and pupils to develop "a reliable sense for cultural phenomena." That such education was necessary, she did not doubt, as "folk and great traditions will yield to our mechanized age and universal literacy." But, she expected, "principles of cultural existence will persist," and thus it was worthwhile work to apply anthropology to public life (288).

Lacking fuller biographical materials (especially for Henry), at this point we can only speculate on the motivations and influences that shaped these differing subject positions. Institutional resources might well have played a role. Henry was secure in a tenured position, at a wealthy private university; he could afford to be a critic. Landes moved from one temporary post to another; until very late in her career, she had to deliver educational services to the agencies that sponsored her. Gender might also be relevant. Landes seems to have adopted some of the social-engineering orientation of Benedict and Mead; Henry, apparently, was more influenced by the authoritative critical voices of psychoanalytic and anthropological philosophers. I have spelled out such a contrast elsewhere, in a paper comparing Benedict and Edward Sapir (Handler

1986). Boas's women students, Benedict and Mead, were perhaps more "marginal" to the American academic mainstream than were Jewish men like Sapir; in any case, these women used a rhetoric of science and social engineering to make their way in the academy, whereas Sapir certainly established himself with his scientific (linguistic) virtuosity but then retreated to the position of cultural critic. A similar gendered contrast seems applicable to the anthropology of education of Landes and Henry. Indeed, one might ask whether the anthropology of education is itself a "gendered" field, with far more women practitioners than men, and focusing on grade school teaching, which is mostly done by women, and primary socialization, which is mostly done by mothers. And this subfield exists within a field, anthropology, which is itself becoming increasing "feminized," at least with respect to the sex ratio of its practitioners (Wilson 2003), and perhaps also with the increasing salience of feminist theory. What remains to be seen is whether anthropologists can play a role (as critics, as social engineers, or as both) in the policy debates about public education that will become increasingly heated in the next decade.

Notes

1. Henry described himself as an elementary school pupil who had "declare[d] war on all teachers, having come to look upon them as enemies. By the time I hit the fourth grade, I was often kept after school and made to write thousands of repetitions of meaningless sentences and words in order to 'discipline' me." At City College, he found Cohen's "intellectual brilliance" to be "a transforming light" (1961:541–42).

2. Comparing what she saw as the rich and integrated culture of the American Northwest Coast to that of the "tribes" of the British Columbian interior, Benedict wrote of the latter: "their culture gives an impression of extreme poverty. Nothing is carried far enough to give body to the culture" (1934b:224). Here is a notion of a "culture of poverty" not unrelated to those that became popular in the 1950s and 1960s, although Benedict did not conflate economic and "spiritual" culture, as later discussions of the concept did.

3. Three recent biographies of Bettelheim (N. Sutton 1995; Pollak 1997; Raines 2002) scarcely mention Henry. Sutton devotes a few pages (251–256) to Henry's observations of the Shankman School but does not evaluate them other than to say that Henry was generally supportive of Bettelheim's work.

4. The fifth and sixth projects, which I do not review here in detail, had students study culturally differing notions of health and sickness, and of authority—two topics that, obviously, had relevance to teachers' dealings with their pupils.

5. It would be useful to know more about Henry's relationship to Bettelheim. The paper on laughter in psychiatric staff conferences affords a glimpse of Henry's research modus operandi. "The participants," Henry says, "were a psychiatrist, an anthropologist, and an observer who wished to discover . . . what situations psychiatric personnel found amusing." At twenty-three weekly staff conferences of about seventy-five psychiatrists, social workers, nurses and medical students, the observer "seat[ed] herself in the center of the group, . . . the most strategic position to note interactional subtleties." It was apparently this observer's job to take notes ("transcrib[e]"); then she, the anthropologist, and the psychiatrist analyzed the data (1954b:176).

Henry is rumored to have been personally difficult. Harold Gould writes that when he was Henry's student in the mid-1950s, "I discovered the gentle, civilized man who languished behind the often abrasive facade he presented to the exterior world in his need to lash out against the misuse and destruction of human potentialities" (1971:791). David Schneider portrayed Henry as an abrasive but constructively critical mentor (1995:61–62), but also remembered (personal communication) observing Henry in empathetic interaction with the denizens of the institutions he studied.

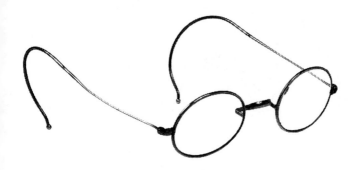

7. Human Activity and a Theory of Schooling

An Assessment of Solon Kimball's Anthropology of Education

Alexander Moore

Solon T. Kimball at Anthropology Department party, University of Florida, 1974. With kind permission of Allan F. Burns.

Solon Toothaker Kimball (1909–82) was among the first American anthropologists to do research in a contemporary Western society. Family and Community in Ireland, first published in 1940, an ethnographic classic, broke new ground in field methodology and community studies. These research areas continued to engage him in his extensive research in the United States. Throughout his career Kimball believed that the field of anthropology was essential to the success of public policy programs. Never one to contest the social order, nonetheless he advocated what seemed to be radical remedies, based as they were on "unsuspected social realities" (Moore 1984:389).

Little is known of Kimball's early life because he rarely talked about it. He grew up in Manhattan, Kansas. He began graduate study in anthropology at Harvard in 1930, under the supervision of W. Lloyd Warner, who was then directing his famous Yankee City (Newburyport, Massachusetts) study, a collaborative project that described the American class system and expanded anthropological fieldwork to modern industrial communities. Kimball collected data on schooling for that project. Warner then took him to Ireland to work with Conrad Arensberg as part of a larger research project known as the Harvard Irish Study. Warner encouraged Kimball to continue his interest in research methods for whole communities, to seek out the relationships between individuals and then the relationships between these groups of individuals with one another and so on to render the social system of a community.

From this experience, which he later compared to a classic rite of passage (Kimball 1972), he wrote his 1936 PhD dissertation, "The Tradesman and His Family in the Economic Structure of an Irish Town." Family and Community in Ireland, written with Conrad Arensberg, was social anthropology descended from Durkheimian theory, and as such it was an examination of the nature of social behavior. Envisioning "society as an integrated system of mutually interrelated and functionally interdependent parts" (Arensberg and Kimball 1968: xxx), the authors described the small farm economy of rural County Clare, Ireland. Set in a Western European community rather than among an "exotic other," it was an approach to anthropology different from that at Columbia University, where Boas's students were engaged in the historical reconstruction of culture, primarily among Native Americans.

After graduate school, Kimball found work doing community studies. He was employed by the Bureau of Indian Affairs to carry out socioeconomic surveys on Navajo reservations (Kimball and Provinse 1942). With the outbreak of World War II Kimball was recruited by the War Relocation Authority to do community analysis within the Japanese relocation centers (Kimball and Provinse 1946). In 1944 he was one of the founders of the Society of Applied Anthropology.

After the war, he held academic teaching positions and continued to research American communities, advocating selecting representative communities as microcosms for study. The community, he said, was the crucial hub for cultural transmission, and community study a tool as well as a subject of social science. He claimed that anthropological methods—particularly "'event analysis,' in which the factors of time, space, activity, persons, and conditions are all . . . taken into consideration in analysis" (1955b:1140) could be applied effectively to American society. At the same time he recognized that there had been no anthropological analysis of the "larger integrative organizations of American society" (1139), a challenge he was to take up later in his career, when he became involved with the new subfield of anthropology and education.

Similarly, when he introduced the newly translated 1909 work Les rites de passage by the Belgian ethnologist Arnold van Gennep to an American audience, Kimball argued that van Gennep's analysis of ritual behavior and the dynamics of group life in traditional societies was relevant to urban industrial society. According to Kimball, the absence of ceremonies that focus on the individual supported within a community group during "life crises" contributes to the problems of the "alienated" and the "unclaimed" of modern societies (1960a:xi). Furthermore, this deficiency may contribute to mental illness because an increasing number of individuals are forced to accomplish their transitions alone and with private symbols (xvii).

In 1953 he joined the faculty of Columbia University's Teachers College. The next year Kimball took part in the 1954 Stanford Conference that became the founding event of the subfield of anthropology and education, in which he discussed the applicability of the "natural history" method to educational research. He was the main presenter in a session about the implications of the Supreme Court decision in Brown v. Board of Education of Topeka, which just had declared "separate but equal" segregated education to be unconstitutional. Kimball analyzed the immediate impact of the Brown decision on regional institutions and African American communal life (1955c).

At Teachers College Kimball was general editor for the Anthropology and Education Series published by Teachers College Press in the 1960s and 1970s, one of the earliest expressions of the then-emerging subfield of anthropology and education. The nine books then in the series exemplified the collaborative possibilities between anthropologists and educators to enrich and improve educative practices in the United States and internationally. Even after Kimball left Teachers College in 1966 for the University of Florida, he continued as the general editor.

In the next chapter Kimball's colleague Alexander Moore discusses Kimball's commitment to the "natural history" approach to ethnographic work. Kimball was a firm believer in the importance of direct observation as an essential research tool, in the role of the fieldworker as a neutral observer, and in the importance of applying research findings to social policy. In the areas of applied anthropology, community studies, and field methodology, Kimball was a respected authority, a meticulous researcher, and a fine teacher. Two of his colleagues dedicated an edited volume to him this way: "To Solon T. Kimball who teaches that the study of human behavior should be of service to people" (Eddy and Partridge 1978:iv).

Solon T. Kimball (1908–82) came to Teachers College, Columbia University, in 1953 as a full professor. He joined that faculty as a highly successful social anthropologist, ready to bring the tools of his trade to bear upon the study of schooling. Kimball left behind the chairmanship of the Department of Sociology and Anthropology at the University of Alabama. His postdoctoral career had been geographically and socially mobile, starting with applied work in government settings, followed by a move to academia (Michigan State University) after World War II. In the career paths then current in American academia (Caplow and McGee 1958) such a move, from the "Siberia" of Alabama to a tenured full professorship at a major research university, was nothing short of a triumph.[1] Kimball was later to better that triumph by being recruited to the University of Florida as Graduate Research Professor of Anthropology as part of their effort to build an academic reputation by recruiting "stars." He gave that new doctoral program in social anthropology immense credibility.

Kimball's induction into anthropology and education at this stage in his life meant that he was not to do firsthand, face-to-face ethnography of schools. Rather, his role was that of teacher of anthropology to educationists, including future classroom teachers; consultant to foreign-aid missions for educational development; publicist of articles expressing his ethnographic view of education; intellectual collaborator with a philosopher of education (James McClellan); and supervisor of ethnographic doctoral studies of schooling, both at Teachers College and at the University of Florida. Thus he came to anthropology and education at the top and did not have to earn his credentials as did his own doctoral students, such as Jaquetta Hill Burnett, Mark Atwood, Ruth Harwood, Reba Anderson, and Donald Wyatt, to name a few, from the ground up by nitty-gritty observation in the schools.

Intellectually Kimball's career move to Teachers College was the beginning of his effort to introduce his particular brand of anthropology to the study of schooling. Together with Conrad M. Arensberg, Kimball was committed to the ethnographic practice they called "the community-study method" or "culture and community." Although community studies were widely embraced at the time, the approach of Arensberg and Kimball was significantly different from such influential scholars as Julian Steward or Robert Redfield.[2] Kimball's previous fieldwork among Irish countrymen, the Navajo, and in an Alabama town (Talladega) had convinced him that in each and every case community study must reveal social patterns of behavior that are not apparent to the casual observer and that are seldom brought to consciousness by the members of the community itself. He also believed that cultural values are an expression of social relations, of behavior patterns that link individuals to each other.

Moreover, his work with the Federal Indian Service among the Navajo and the War Relocation Authority with Japanese internees had given him a well-founded suspicion and distrust of colonialism and bureaucracy (and of paternalism in general). Likewise he believed that applied and development programs work best with the consent, and hopefully the control, of the community at hand, when informed with detailed ethnographic information about community social patterns. However, the central hypothesis underlying all these intellectual tools was "that the chief determinant factor in human society may well be human activity itself" (Arensberg and Kimball 1940:xxvii). This key phrase is in the preface of *Family and Community in Ireland* and dates from the first edition of 1940. This chapter focuses on the relation of this central hypothesis to Kimball's work on education.

Human Activity: "The Chief Determinant Factor"

Kimball's fascination with human activity stems from a "creative cluster" at Harvard during his years of graduate study there. W. Lloyd Warner influenced Kimball and his friends Conrad Arensberg, Eliot Chapple, Elton Mayo, and William Foote Whyte, among others. However, it was biochemist Lawrence

Henderson (chair of the Society of Fellows, where both Whyte and Arensberg were junior fellows) who stimulated their interest in human activity and operationalism in science.[3] These young social scientists were rising to the personal challenge to make human relations a science. They came to view the essence of science as measurement of functional interrelations among phenomena, measurements that could be repeated by other observers and hence rendered "operational." The method, as they refined it, was inductive "natural history," as opposed to deductive experimentalism. The phenomena to be observed, measured, and classified were human activities.

I have delineated the method, refined into four steps, as I learned them from Arensberg in graduate school: 1) isolating a field for study, that is, defining initial boundaries and human subjects in a natural setting; 2) charting the interrelationships of phenomena observed within the field; 3) reformulating and validating the observations according to the operations of description; and 4) making statements of theory regarding such points as order, probability, limits, patterns, law (Moore 1998:63–66).[4]

The focus on human activity meant giving priority to ethnographic observation over the interview, for recording what people actually did, rather than what they said they did. In any given field setting, human interaction was assumed to be in functional dependence with all other human interaction within the field. This reflected the concept of homeostasis as expounded by physiologist Walter Cannon. They simply assumed human activity to be tending toward equilibrium with other human activity. This helps to explain why—in spite of their interest in empirically grounded pure research—Arensberg, Chapple, and Kimball were among the founders of the Society for Applied Anthropology in 1942, and why Whyte had a distinguished career in "participatory action research," that is, applied sociology. They saw their interest in interaction leading naturally to intervening action that would help to bring about a new dynamic equilibrium.

Among this group, Eliot D. Chapple worked hardest to build anthropology on the base of rigorous observations and quantified measurements of human interactions in time (1940, 1970, 1979, 1980; Chapple and Coon 1942, 1978). Indeed, Chapple made *interaction theory* the centerpiece of his long, maverick, and resolutely single-minded career. He was not alone in this endeavor, having worked out his initial precise formulation with Arensberg (1940). Interaction theory holds that one must start an "operational" social science by observing human beings interact in pair events and in events of three or more actors ("set events"). The object is to measure frequency and direction of interaction over time and classify all actors by these criteria as A (who initiates interaction more frequently than not), B (who receives interactions more frequently than initiating them), and C (to whom interaction terminates more frequently than it is relayed or than C initiates it). These *operations of description* measure—a mark of science—but also redefine and validate the taxonomy, which thus goes beyond the initial observations.

The Harvard human relations school's natural history method reaches its most codified form with Chapple, who treats interactional pairs and sets as the building blocks of human societies. His classifications resemble dominance hierarchies in primate ethology, but they can also provide for egalitarian analysis, if members of pairs or sets initiate interaction with each other in equal frequencies. (In that case they are all A's.) Chapple's thinking has much in common with contemporary network theory, but it insists that members of any network are conditioned to interact with each other in ways that can be specified through observations. In his later work he sees pairs and set events as tending toward synchrony or asynchrony. In the latter case they become dysfunctional. Successful institutions are led by "pacemaker" individuals who set the rhythm of motions of their followers.[5]

Kimball was a party to the discussions from which interaction theory emerged. As he recalls,

> By the late spring of 1936 Eliot Chapple and Conrad Arensberg had already begun the intellectual exchange which would eventually lead them to the formulation of what has now come to be know as 'interaction theory.' . . . On sunny days the two of them would gather for an hour or so on the grass outside of Harvard's Peabody Museum and there talk about the uses of scientific method in the study of behavior. On several occasions I joined them in these informal discussions. In retrospect some aspects of what was later precisely stated in Measuring Human Relations had begun to emerge . . . in the early months of 1938, Arensberg wrote to me on the Navajo Reservation that he and Chapple had perfected the method of interaction analysis, the essential segments of which he then described. (1974:189–190)

However, for all their familiarity with the quantifiable model for interaction theory, neither Kimball nor Arensberg were to use it specifically as such in their subsequent ethnographic investigations. They had already used an approximation of the model for rural Ireland, generalizing a "map" of five human relations systems (step 4, above) (Arensberg and Kimball 1940:299-306). But these relational systems or patterns were not presented to the reader with an actual count of interactions resulting in classifying individuals as A's, B's, and C's. It would not have taken much to have converted their description into those terms, however. After all, they had done the research before Chapple and Arensberg hit on precise methods of measurement. Moreover, Kimball's students were to use it explicitly in a study of high schools in Gainesville, Florida, and Arensberg used the model in reformulations of other people's ethnographies (see esp. Arensberg 1972). Even though they did not quantify the frequency and direction of interaction, both, however, always sought to describe routine behavior as it builds into events, and as these events in turn give pattern to institutions.

Thus both Kimball and Arensberg held as an article of faith (that is, a premise or an axiom, rather than a hypothesis) that social structure is derived directly from interaction in pairs and sets. Indeed, this is the whole thrust of Kimball's critique (1975) of Orvis Collins and June M. Collins's *Interaction and Social Structure*. He vehemently disagrees with their conceptualization of social structure, derived from Radcliffe-Brown, as a set of abstract normative rules guiding social interaction. For Kimball, the rules, and values (1966, reprinted 1974), are always to be derived from ongoing activity. It is the activity, not the rules, that make the structure, the rules coming after the fact.

Induction into Teachers College: Getting a Grip on Education

I am not privy to the documents surrounding Kimball's recruitment to Teachers College, but Elizabeth M. Eddy asserts (personal communication 1993) that Margaret Mead, who was adjunct professor of anthropology at Columbia, was instrumental to the process. There was very little applied or practical interest in the Columbia Anthropology Department, located in the Faculty of Political Science across 118th Street from Teachers College.[6] Mead, on the other hand, deplored academic ivory towers in general and was always convinced anthropology had much to say to the professions. She remained in communication with Kimball during his tenure at Teachers College, the two sometimes vigorously debating issues such as the relation of child-rearing patterns to the rest of culture.

Arensberg alludes to Kimball's having studied the schools in Yankee City at Warner's behest (Arensberg 1983:8).[7] Yet Kimball never seemed to have thought of that research as his induction into anthropology and education, for I can find no other mention of it. Rather, his induction started at Teachers College. At age forty-four and a full professor, he was in his vigorous prime and enjoying his prominence as the anthropologist in a premier institution. He taught anthropology to Teachers College students—indeed he enthusiastically embraced a very heavy teaching load—and began to think about studying schooling. He did not get around to doing so immediately, but by the time he left Teachers College thirteen years later in 1966, he had established himself squarely in the field.

He approached the new field as in any prospective ethnographic situation, by "natural history." It is important to realize that Kimball, with Arensberg, had written a widely recognized masterpiece of social science in *Family and Community in Ireland* (Arensberg and Kimball 1940). The final statement of that book was in a chapter entitled "The Framework of Relationship." Patterns or "maps" of relationships were the statement of theory here. Significantly the second of the five classes of relationships delineated was *the relationship of age grading, or generation* (1940:302). Schooling as such did not figure as important in the life of the countrymen, but town apprenticeships to shopkeepers were very important to the life histories of many people. (That part of the story had to wait until the second edition, in 1968.) Bear in mind that *patterns of behavior* can constitute scientific findings, the fourth and final step of their natural history method. Indeed the book bears much in common with another masterpiece of natural history observation, Jane Goodall's *The Chimpanzees of Gombe: Patterns of Behavior* (1986).[8]

As Kimball explained natural history to his peers at the 1954 Stanford Conference on anthropology and education, a natural history study is properly holistic.[9] Within that holism comes taxonomy, classifying what is there at first sight "on the basis of observable differences and similarities." (In conversation with me, Kimball regularly decried "mere taxonomy" as the one and only methodological step of Boasian American anthropology. One had to go beyond superficial similarities.) Next is *functionalism*, to "search for the meaningful relationships that explicate the process which [one] observes" (1955a:83). This is, of course, the step I have termed *operational* above, one that is measurable, or at least replicable by others. In this step one also *redefines* the initial taxonomies according to the observations of activities. Here Kimball recommended that "we focus upon the child in his total habitat. His activities must be viewed in the context of sequential events accompanied by testing devices which measure change. The results should give us the base from which we may modify the environmental situation, if need be, to facilitate cultural transmission" (84). In other words, the measurement of activity as it fits into "human relational systems" is the fourth and most important task for any field worker.

Kimball was approaching "the child" much as he had earlier approached the Navajo, as the object of an eventual intervention in applied anthropology. In the late 1930s Kimball and anthropologist John Provinse researched ways to implement a stock reduction program for the Indian Service, a conservationist policy conceived and implemented from above without any consultation with the subjects. Kimball and Provinse tried to change that. First they conducted a natural history ethnography, starting with family relations within the household and then going on to identify the "outfit" or matrilineal extended household under the command of a senior male, who had married into the group in the previous generation. Next they identified the "land-use community": a number of outfits occupying a given area with the potential for cooperative action under the joint leadership of outfit elders.

Then came what Henry F. Dobyns (personal communication 1981) calls a "briefly carried out experiment/demonstration in anthropologically guided local grass-roots decision-making/administration by Navajos. . . . [Kimball] did so several years in advance of any other applied anthropologist." The two anthropologists turned one land-use community into a pilot project, co-opting local leaders to implement general conservation measures, including dam building. The Indian Service staff rejected a plan to extend this pilot to the entire tribe, since the bureaucracy preferred to implement stock reduction by coercive methods (Kimball and Provinse 1942).

At Teachers College, Kimball, however, was to take his time before studying

schooling. He wrote a proposal for an ethnographic study of higher education for the Social Science Research Council (SSRC). It is surprising how overwhelmingly taxonomic the proposal is, although it is integrated by a tempo-
ral and processual strategy to consider college years as a rite of passage. The
proposal was never funded; indeed, it may not have been intended for funding
but rather was to serve as a document setting priorities for SSRC funding. In
any case, Kimball never translated it into a full-fledged research proposal with
specified research sites, field workers, calendar, and budget.

In 1958–59 Kimball served for a year as a resident consultant for UNESCO on
community organization and education at the Brazilian Center for Educational
Research of the Ministry of Education in Rio de Janeiro.[10] Once again his reports from this experience (1960b, reprinted and revised 1974) are disconcert-
ingly preliminary and necessarily only taxonomic. Actual ethnographic observations of the sequential activities of the child have not taken place. (Kimball,
almost certainly, was not hired to make such observations.) From statistical
and library sources Kimball writes a holistic, global assessment of Brazilian
primary education and assesses it as a stunning failure when judged against
its own goal of compulsory universal education. He further posits community
control as a desirable future goal. However, in 1974 he confesses that such
was "pure fantasy," given the social realities of Brazil. Insofar as his analysis
is functional, he discerns that the exclusion of the masses from secondary and
higher education may have fit the needs of a traditional agrarian society divided into two classes: elites and masses. But, he asserts, it does not meet the
needs of an urban, corporate, and industrializing society. The goal of applied
research for Kimball, then, is to bring formal institutions into accord with
each other and the "needs" of the kind of society at hand. However, this study
remained only a background portrait, something one might draw up prior to
plunging into a natural history ethnography of Brazilian schools, which neither Kimball nor his students ever attempted to do.

Kimball was able to achieve at least the beginning of the ethnographic study
of sequential activities in his involvement in a later international education
project. From April 1963 to September 1964 he was campus coordinator for
the Teachers College–Agency for International Development (TC/AID) Educational Development in Peru Project, which he had organized.[11] Although Kimball remained in residence at Teachers College, anthropologist Ruth Harwood

did do ethnographic observations in schools all over Peru under his direction.[12]

In Peru, Kimball came to grips with an agrarian country that was not modernizing at the same pace or scale as Brazil. He encountered a Ministry of Education (that probably reminded him of the U.S. Indian Service) that spent an inordinate amount of time planning but that made little or no effort to put plans into effect. Kimball quotes extensively from the several mimeographed reports of Ruth Harwood (1965a, 1965b) in his own article on the project, which did not appear in print until his 1974 volume of his collected writings.[13] From Harwood's observations and a study of the literature (and surely from meetings of the project team), he came to realize that the aim of Peruvian education was moral. *Formación* was the key word. The student had to be formed from the outside in and had to submit to authority. The ethnography of the classroom disclosed that all lessons at all levels were conducted by the rote recitation of questions and answers, both transmitted from higher authority.

Pondering it all, Kimball calls for similar ethnographic observations for everyone connected with the educational system, not just teachers and pupils, but parents, organized into associations of *Padres de familia*, and ministry bureaucrats. Relevant civil and religious associations must be examined. This ideal "ethnography of the schools" has an applied purpose:

> It is from such a base line of knowledge of structure and process that the preparation of new national goals in education can be projected. From this base it then becomes possible to prepare a plan for educational development that might not otherwise be possible. It is this type of research that all developing nations must engage in if they are going to utilize education as a major instrument in the reconstruction of their societies. (1974:230)

To summarize Kimball's thinking about studying education at this point, then, he always intended to apply his version of the natural history method. One first defined a field holistically—in this case a school system as in Brazil or Peru. Second, one made an initial taxonomy of human relations within that field, based on preliminary observations. Third, after intense study of the sequential activity of the human beings within the field, one then redefined and reclassified their relations according to the way their activities cohered. Kimball termed this coherence *functional interdependence*. This third step was "operational"; that is, it included measurements of frequency of interaction and modeling of their directions and was ideally replicable by other observers. Fourth came some generalizing or summary statement, usually of social patterns, or statements of systems of human relations. These patterns might well be quite unknown to both native and outsider. Once one was aware of them, then, one had the means for a fifth step, *planned intervention* in human behavior, with the participation of the subjects, in order to bring about change.

Kimball had, in addition, come to see schooling as a specialized institution arising alongside the ordinary process of education going on within community and family. In one's analysis one must look for congruence among the various institutions of a society, including schooling or formal education. A fully informed rational planning process, however, might redesign any institution, either to bring it into better fit with the other institutions of society or to move them all along together through catalytic action toward humane development.

Throughout, Kimball remained preoccupied with community study. Schooling was distinctly a secondary institution within the primary one of community. Thus one engaging piece he wrote as a byproduct of a lectureship in a teacher-training institute for Aramco, Saudi Arabia, is titled "American Culture in Saudi Arabia" (1956). Based on a three-weeks visit, it is a thumbnail taxonomic ethnography of a community spawned by American corporate culture. In the final analysis Kimball discerned that something was missing there, but he was hard-pressed to define what it was. This brush with corporate culture and community was to carry over when he began his collaboration with James McClellan at Teachers College.

At every stage in his career Kimball wrote at least one major study with a coauthor. He enjoyed face-to-face give-and-take with peers or with juniors (the works were never with his hierarchical seniors). Moreover, collaboration was probably an enjoyable shortcut to getting a grip on a subject. In each case, of course, he brought personal and intellectual strengths to the relationship.[14] McClellan was Kimball's peer on the teaching faculty at Teachers College when they struck up their friendship. In 1961–62 when Kimball had an SSRC Faculty Research Fellowship, McClellan had a sabbatical. The two got together and wrote a trade book, *Education and the New America* (Kimball and McClellan 1962), for educationists and interested laypeople, writing simply in the text while putting its immense wealth of intellectual references into voluminous footnotes.

It is interesting that Kimball's collaborator at Teachers College was not an educationist, but a philosopher of pragmatism. Of all the branches of philosophy, American pragmatism shares the most with functionalism; indeed, the two are convergent cultural movements. Both intellectual traditions were preoccupied with how things work. Pragmatism is remembered today, certainly far too simply, by the slogan "That which works is good." Together the two academicians set out, most excitedly I am sure, to bring John Dewey's philosophy of education (summarized by another slogan, "learning by doing") up-to-date to the "New America"—urban, industrial, and corporate—that Dewey had scarcely known. "We had to discover the categories that account for these new forms [of human association], or where we couldn't discover them, *try to forge them for ourselves*" (Kimball and McClellan 1962:vii–ix, emphasis added).

The book bears Kimball's imprint most recognizably in the chapters discussing community and values: its sections on the Midwest Main Street Town and on valuing in Irish familism and Navajo "reality and symbolism." The book's treatment of the modern metropolis and of corporate life is drawn from a wide variety of sources. The two men were extremely well read and erudite. But the facts, the detailed information, of the social sciences in this case were meant to serve moral questions: how could schooling instill a sense of self and moral commitment in the youth of a New America?[15]

The book echoes Kimball's concerns from Brazil and Peru. How does an educational system fit the needs of a changing society? The schools were serving neither agrarian America nor the early industrializing country. The New America is mobile, corporate, tenuous, and self-transforming. The family has likewise become mobile and poised for change. (Kimball meant the process whereby middle-class children are launched into a future free of their parents and kin, but the observation is even more germane today after the explosion in the divorce rate.) The question then was, how could corporate America become congruent with American family form, and by extension, how could family and corporation become congruent with schooling? (The old concern for social congruence reasserts itself.) The answer is the *task force or production team.*

Such task forces as the Manhattan Project had captured Kimball's imagination. "The well-designed production team" seemed at once the cure for the outmoded rigidities of old bureaucratic hierarchies and the bridge to make schooling congruent with the freewheeling nuclear family. The sequential activities of such a team were those of a company of peers. In Chapple's terms they were all A's, but all A's who could be B's for each other. They would trade around the initiation of action. In this social setting were to be found "the elements of commitment and the sense of self" (the title for chapter 12). They were, of course, referring to the social self, citing George Herbert Mead but not discussing his thought at length. Specifically, a sense of self can arise only from firm social anchoring in the mirror of significant others. A sense of commitment can arise only from the undertaking of shared activities or tasks. Hence the well-designed production team provides "these four features of group association":

1. Task-orientation;
2. Responding to wide ranges of personality in others and expressing wide ranges of one's own personality in groups;
3. Every group association is conditioned by the imminence of disruption; and,
4. The meaning of any group association is conditioned by its relation to the total social system (Kimball 1974:271–276).

The activities then, are of a group of self-directing and self-regulating peers. Leadership is informal and traded around. The task is the goal; schedules and group longevity depend upon achieving the goal. Then the group dissolves, and its members go on to join another such group.

When Kimball left Teachers College in 1966 for a Graduate Research Professorship at the University of Florida, his reputation in anthropology and education was well established, most especially by this timely, lively, and erudite book written with McClellan. But it is interesting to note that Kimball's mandate to sponsor applied change in any field only after the full formulation of a baseline ethnography based on the observations of sequential activities was as yet unfulfilled for schooling. Harwood had, of course, started in this direction for Peruvian schools. Burnett (1968) likewise had engaged in such research in schools under Kimball's supervision at Teachers College, as had

Atwood (1960). These beginnings were to come to partial fruition in research in Gainesville.

Gainesville, Florida: Ethnography of Schooling at Last

In 1966 Kimball returned to a department of anthropology, leaving Teachers College and his position in a faculty of education. (Lambros Comitas later was to develop a program in anthropology at Teachers College.) At Florida, Kimball maintained his interest in anthropology and education. He set out to study desegregation. In 1972 he and Charles Wagley, an eminent student of race relations in the Americas, became co-principal investigators for a grant funded by the Office of Education's National Institute of Education.[16] A team of six anthropology graduate students conducted observations in two Gainesville high schools during the 1972–73 school year. Another six graduate students conducted family interviews during the summer of 1973. Kimball and Wagley submitted their book-length final report in 1974 but decided against trying to publish it. The report's abstract follows:

> The purpose of this research was to ascertain the consequences which ensued following the mixing of Black and White students in schools in a southern city. Intensive observations were made of classroom, extracurricular, and friendship behavior in two contrasting high schools, and families of some of the students were interviewed. Observation established that each racial group had a distinctive interactional style accompanying a near-complete voluntary separation by Black and White students in all activities except for a few task oriented or ritual occasions. This separation is paralleled in the community participation of parents where life-style, association membership, and racial residential clustering provide little opportunity for racial mixing. (Kimball and Wagley 1974:i)

The report further concluded that the local Black community had lost control of "its" high school. Only a few middle-class Black students benefited directly from integration by participating in college-track classes and associated extracurricular activities (e.g., language clubs) with college-bound White students. To the coauthors these seemed the wrong conclusions to release to the public only two short years after the rapid and radical implementation of full-scale desegregation in the local county.[17]

Rereading this report today, together with the extremely rich doctoral dissertation by Donald Wyatt that was to follow soon after (1976), I find it a great pity Kimball and Wagley did not rework and reword the piece for timely publication by the end of the 1970s. They put too much emphasis on the findings about the lack of racial social mixing (which now seem unexceptional) and failed to emphasize many other findings that today seem of greater interest. Desegregation, after all, was undertaken not to assure social mixing of the races, but equal education for all. Moreover, the study discloses that the sexes in these coeducational schools also failed to mix in the main, in exactly the same pattern as the races. That is, boys and girls interacted in terms of social familiarity only in certain ritual and extracurricular activities, the latter related to student government.[18] In all cases, the students were high-prestige participants in the academic track of classes, as was the case with racial mixing, aside from sports.

Far more interesting today is the report that African American students, for the most part, have a social, rather than an individual, learning style. A group of Black girls in a mathematics class, for example, were consistently disruptive and inattentive one semester when the teacher enforced a pattern of individual effort with one-to-one supervision by herself. The only class session in which they were observed to be cooperative and well behaved was when they had an opportunity to portray an equation, already solved, in needlework. They sat quietly at their desks absorbed in the task of embroidery, giving each other help and advice as they went along. The next semester the same group of girls in a team-teaching situation was encouraged to solve problems together as a team. They happily concentrated on the task at hand and ceased to be disruptive, reporting to the student ethnographer that they were receiving "more attention from the teacher," though in fact they were not (Kimball and Wagley 1974:28–29).

In organized sports, however, true racial mixing on the playing field and among the coaching personnel was observed. The task superseded racial difference. Once off the field, however, student athletes resumed their segregated friendships and interaction. Moreover, Wyatt's subsequent study of the desegregated high school, identified as "belonging to" the Black community, showed that informal basketball practice had very different meanings to members of the two races. For Whites it was a chance for teams to score to win, whereas for Blacks a chance for individuals to show off virtuoso performances (Wyatt 1976:118).

Wyatt's study is replete with fascinating interactional and proxemic details. Members of the two races took over different public areas at the high school and congregated in different fashions. The friendship cliques of White students were immediately apparent in their clusters in space, but not so with Blacks, who congregated in groups with high turnover. Friendship bonding among Blacks had to be elicited by questioning; it was obvious from observations of White students. Similarly, Black students sat together en masse at lunch tables in an open, highly mobile fashion, whereas Whites sat quite separately by friendship cliques. Whites lined up in orderly queues at one entrance to the school cafeteria, once again in friendship pairs or groups. If they stood alone, they did not interact with students on either side. Blacks, in contrast, milled around the other entrance to the cafeteria, and access to the entrance was by social ranking. Athletes and cheerleaders, for example, swept right to the front upon arrival. All interacted and talked as they milled at the opening (60–66).

Moreover, Kimball and Wagley classified formal schooling, not by its own "native categories" (language arts, etc.), but into three general tracks: academic (college preparatory), vocational, and general. Students in the academic track tended to come from middle-class, professional families of both races. These students tended to be the most active in extracurricular associations. In one, predominantly middle-class (and traditionally White—but no longer so), high school, extracurricular activities were left to the initiative of the students themselves, who could meet in the school after hours and on weekends. In the other, predominantly working-class high school, such activities were planned and controlled by the school administrators, who scheduled meetings during the school day. Teachers dominated these meetings, in contrast to the other school, where faculty advisers were at most facilitators, not dictators.

These are taxonomic concerns, but as in Kimball's research on Brazilian education, they are linked to evaluative ones. In general the academic program in the two high schools was a success, when judged against the graduation rate and subsequent college placement of its graduates. The vocational track was mentioned favorably in the report, but no direct statistical evaluation of its success in graduating and placing its graduates in jobs was attempted. In contrast, one gets a distinct impression that the general track was not at all successful, with many of its students dropping out before graduation, and the rest graduating ill prepared for jobs or further study.

Particularly disquieting here are the marginal ninth-grade White male students Wyatt describes. They form a social subset with three cliques. They attend school only to meet each other and to decide what to do with their day, which includes hardly any class attendance but does include wrestling and smoking as they congregate in front of the school to show off, socialize, and go off to ride motorcycles. Their clothing is worn and torn, and they do not participate in the prestige system of the other students, Black or White. The moment of truth for them comes when they reach the legal dropping-out age. If they continue on in school, and few do, they adopt a more serious attitude. These, far more than the docile Black working-class students, seem to be the casualties of schooling (Wyatt 1976:80–3).

In the last chapter of *Culture and the Educative Process*, which also appeared in 1974, Kimball pleads for anthropology as a policy science. He wants us to make policy recommendations based on ethnographic research. As an example, he slyly and rather obliquely suggests that schooling, certainly at the high school level, should make use of extracurricular associations as a "supplemental or alternative" form of schooling, pointing out how they resemble the task force. He does not mention the Gainesville research (he was probably writing before he had digested it all), but rather bases his observations on Burnett's (1968, 1969).

It seems to me that Kimball left pending one great piece of unfinished business here. The findings of this research provided at long last the potential for fulfilling the manifesto he had proclaimed for Peru. Here he really did have the opportunity to relate baseline data about student interactions to learning. An experimental curricular project might have given him the chance to try out his ideas about extracurricular associations as task force–production teams. That applied project, however, was never designed, indeed never even mentioned.

I see this as the great irony of Kimball's life. He was busy at the time, busy catching up on old business. He and Arensberg had issued a new greatly expanded edition of *Family and Community in Ireland* in 1968, which included all the material that Kimball had collected on town culture, intending to publish it in a separate volume. Wagley, in turn, was writing his retrospective ethnography of the Tapirapé, *Welcome of Tears* (1977), drawing on field notes in some case twenty or more years old. Kimball had edited the anthropology and education series for Teachers College Press;[19] the final volume was to be his compended writings on anthropology and education.

When Kimball died at age seventy-three in 1982, he was at work on a study of Southern culture. Perhaps this work would have begun to fulfill the ethnographic promise of the USOE report. At the Stanford Conference in 1954 he had made a presentation to his peers about Southern culture and the recent Supreme Court decision striking down school segregation by race (1955c). He gave a knowledgeable portrait of Southern regional culture, gained from his years of teaching in Alabama and his community study of the town of Talladega there (Kimball and Pearsall 1954).

This curiously dated document is, in his own terms, a "taxonomic" delineation of some insight. He sees the South as then dominated by an elite group, not all of whom were wealthy, but who had claims to educated, landowning ancestors and to gentility. They also all knew each other and were dominated by male elders, who made decisions behind closed doors. A cult of womanhood gave gentlewomen a great deal of informal influence, even power. He correctly saw that this group and its elders did not like open confrontation. He posited that Southern gentlewomen might find a way for accommodation leading to desegregation.[20] He also saw, based on his Talladega study, that the White laboring class was as effectively segregated from the elite as the Blacks were.

Kimball missed two essential things. First, he failed to foresee that the Black middle classes were to assert the same claims to gentility that legitimated the White elites. This group, whose foremost leader was Martin Luther King, an individual born into the Black elite, spearheaded the civil rights revolution. We can forgive Kimball the lack of a crystal ball here, since no one else foresaw it either, but he also missed the political manipulation of the White agrarian and laboring masses by the elites, even though that was clearly pointed out by Wilbur J. Cash in his landmark *The Mind of the South* (1941).[21] Racism was essentially a bill of goods sold to the poor White voters by the elites to keep the latter in power, even at the expense of poor Whites' own material interests.

How would Kimball have put his knowledge of Southern culture together with ethnographic detail about Gainesville schools? It is reasonable to suppose that he might indeed have juxtaposed his 1954 portrait of Southern culture against the Gainesville ethnography. He was interested in Celtic culture as a stream in the South and thus would most likely have taken a hard look at the poor Whites so ill-served by schooling as reported.[22]

An Activity-Based Theory of Schooling?

In conclusion I maintain that the weight of Kimball's work on anthropology and education does indeed contain a viable activity-based theory of schooling. The theory came to fruition in the Gainesville study, although useful applications were never derived from the work, nor was it ever published. Now, with hindsight, I regret the lack of a book on the desegregated schools of Gainesville, let alone an action project based upon it.

Although it is possible that Kimball, had he lived, might have returned to the Gainesville school ethnography in his projected study of Southern culture, it is equally possible that he did not realize its importance in the corpus of his life's work. He was so convinced of the interactional base to culture, and so persuasive in his rhetoric about it, that he might not have felt the need to demonstrate it conclusively. Moreover, he may have lost interest in schooling by that time. His thinking about culture and community in his later years was in terms of "roots" and symbolic forms.[23]

As a concluding observation, I want to add that Kimball's work over his career was cumulative. He remained true to his intellectual roots and grew from them. In a discipline that is only haltingly cumulative and certainly never as a whole consensual, that is in itself extraordinary. He sought to tame culture and personality studies by assimilating the Mead and Bateson child-rearing model of Balinese socialization to his own social patterns model (1963, reprinted 1974). That is, Kimball saw Balinese flat, affectless behavior as reflecting a basic social plan of hierarchy seen in the family but also in all other social relations.[24] Kimball was never sidetracked by structuralism, as were so many doctoral students in the late 1950s or 1960s. When he turned to philosophy, it was to pragmatism, which he simply adapted to a metaphysically informed social science guided by a moral imperative.

The Arensberg and Kimball culture and community approach could and did contribute much to cultural ecology, but Kimball was uninterested in anything like a cultural materialism that maintains, a priori, that a subsistence base dictates the form of the rest of culture. Moreover, the starting point of activity sequences as a "platform" for anthropology obviates arguments about tripartite divisions into infrastructure, structure, and superstructure and which is prior. Activities, structure, symbols, and ritual are there from the start. Thus he was very much interested in rites of passage; he had van Gennep's seminal work (1960) translated and published in English and wrote about van Gennep (1968). He was also enthusiastic about the work of Victor Turner in symbolic anthropology.

However, sympathetic as he was to humanism and the human quest in anthropology, he was not taken with Clifford Geertz's "interpretationist" stance on ethnography (Geertz 1973). For Kimball, "thick description" started always with sequential activities. The guiding principal for undertaking an ethnography might be a moral imperative for Kimball, but it was never the aesthetics of the ethnographer's development as an artist, nor as avant-garde rebel. I am sure that Kimball would have found some of the latter-day expressions of postmodernism in anthropology quite repugnant.

Finally, one major gap in Kimball's thinking about applied anthropology has been filled in by advances in conceptualizing the "policy process" (Chambers 1986; Eddy and Partridge 1987; Van Willigen 1986; Moore 1991, 1998). When one conceives of the policy process as a phase model of sequential activities in an "event chain," then the anthropologist's role becomes clearer at the beginning of the process. As I have rendered these phases:

1. Awareness of need.
2. Formulation and evaluation of policy choices.
3. Implementation of one policy choice.
4. Evaluation of that policy (Moore 1998:528).

Kimball was very good at phase two, but he was quite poor at phase one: publicizing a need and marshaling support for the subsequent phases. His brilliant land-use project for the Navajo, for example, was a success as a pilot project but was sabotaged by bureaucrats of the Indian Service (Kimball and Provinse 1942). His stance was that of the brilliant social scientist and publicist, whose own authority as senior professor and expert ought to be enough to set wheels in motion. Least of all should the expert engage in partisan politics. This stance was not sufficient for problems of schooling in Brazil, Peru, or Gainesville, Florida. The phase model can be a tool for sophisticated timing of the injection of scholarly influence and authority into public debate about "needs."

Yet, when one rereads the reports on schooling in Gainesville, one is convinced by overwhelming evidence that an activity-based ethnography, with rigorous observation of interactions and measurements of their direction, *works*. It is ironic that, when the end was within his means, Kimball did not reach out and use this ethnography to fulfill the applied mandate he had proclaimed a decade earlier for Peru. There is one great book, a potential masterpiece, missing from his bibliography, and one innovative applied schooling project missing from his life's work. However, when all is said and done, there was an artistry to the work and the life of the man. It was all of one piece, and whatever the failings, both stand together as a contribution to anthropology and to the ethnography of schooling.

Notes

My first debt is to Kimball himself, who was a stimulating colleague in my nine years on the University of Florida faculty, sharing his intellectual stance with vigor. My other debt is to Elizabeth M. Eddy, who suggested that I take on this task, and who donated her ample collection of Sol's published and unpublished materials, without which the task would have been extremely difficult. She also read and commented on an earlier draft. I wish to thank Richard Blot and Juliet Niehaus for doing the same.

1. The early 1950s were days of far-reaching institutional change for American anthropology. Until 1952, when Julian Steward took a research professorship at the University of Illinois, leaving the department chair at Columbia, the latter position had been that of the undisputed dean of American anthropology, as constructed by Boas and reinforced by Linton, until he took an endowed professorship at Yale in 1946. Linton died in harness at Yale in 1952. Steward had succeeded Linton at Columbia and rapidly asserted his role as primary theoretician and researcher in the field. Steward's, and Linton's, defection from the "number one" post to the hinterland signified the burgeoning of important research departments of anthropology. Thereafter no one department could continue to maintain hegemony, although Columbia's importance lingers in such indexes as the number of presidents of the American Anthropological Association with Columbia PhDs.

Steward was succeeded in the chair at Columbia by Charles Wagley, who continued with the preoccupation with cultural ecology as the key to community study. It would be interesting to speculate how different anthropology might have been had Solon Kimball gone to that post in 1952 rather than Teachers College.

2. To expound that difference, Redfield came to community study from Nahua-speaking Tepotzlán and Maya Chan Kom in the 1930s, the same decade that Kimball and Arensberg went to study the Irish countryside, adapting a method they had learned from W. Lloyd Warner's field study of Yankee City (Newburyport, Massachusetts). Redfield was interested in the little community as an integrated whole, as an expression of ruralness or folk culture, as the result of the interplay of several abstract, deductive variables, namely isolation, small size, and homogeneity. That is, a community becomes a town and then a city as an expression of its lack of isolation, increasing size, and increasing social heterogeneity. Chan Kom is thus simply a Yucatan village (Redfield 1941). Arensberg and Kimball were not interested in applying such global a priori deductive abstractions to the ongoing study of real life. Rather, they were interested in generalizing, inductively, from each field experience.

Julian Steward, working in the 1940s and 1950s, conceived of community as an expression of its subsistence base or cultural core. He directed the major study written up in The People of Puerto Rico (Steward et al. 1956), in which a number of doctoral students under his supervision looked at every ecologically identifiable type of community on the island, plus the prominent families of San Juan. Kimball and Arensberg never conceived of the subsistence base as the cultural core. For them, inductively identified repetitive patterns of interaction, as they tied people together in ongoing institutions, not merely subsistence, were the starting place for any investigation.

3. Whyte recalls Henderson's model, borrowed from physics, as a challenge (Whyte and Whyte 1984:263–267). Henderson dominated the weekly meetings of the Society of Fellows and decried sociologists as full of softheaded sentimentality (288). I am indebted to my student John A. Mellon for pointing this out to me (personal communication 1992). Moreover, stimulated by his young fellows, Henderson undertook to write and publish a study of Pareto (1936).

4. The reader who would like a more detailed discussion of how the method fits into contemporary fieldwork is referred to chapter 3 of my Cultural Anthropology: The Field Study of Human Beings (Moore 1998:44–69).

5. Also in his later work, influenced by advances in ethology and the discovery of the "fixed action sequence" in animals, Chapple takes up the notion of "cultural action sequences," which are stereotyped or culturally standardized ways of doing things (1970:200–220). Chapple is referring especially to work, but cultural sequences may be found in all human activities, such as ritual, play, disputing, fighting, and legal activities in general.

6. Conrad Arensberg was recruited to that department about the same time, and he did teach one course in applied anthropology. His interest was distinctly outside the department mainstream, as I can testify, having been a graduate student there during the early 1960s. The association between Arensberg and Kimball continued unabated,

however, and the two scholars published their theoretical volume *Culture and Community* in 1965.

7. Arensberg commented: "As native, 'majority group' Americans both, watching our country on the eve of unprecedented depression, Sol, I and others were all debating at the time what American culture really was. We found its social system ready to be explored by anthropology for the first time. . . . Warner looked his new students over, and assigned us our fieldwork tasks. To Kimball, Kansan Midwesterner majority-man, he said, 'Go do the schools, everybody's kids are there.' To Arensberg, Harvard senior with the perplexing German-language name, Warner posed, 'Arensberg, Arensberg, you do the minority groups. And both of you, tell one another what you find.' And we did" (1983:8).

8. *Family and Community in Ireland* (1940, 1968, 2001) has been revised twice and is still to be recommended to the student of anthropology and education. Arensberg's earlier and shorter volume, *The Irish Countryman* (1988[1937]), remains in print. The emphasis on age grading and generational process is quite clear in both books.

9. Elizabeth M. Eddy believes that this conference was a key point in the emergence of anthropology and education as a specialized field, and she has examined it at some length (1985:91–92). Note that his presentation of the natural history method was less codified than I have presented it many years later.

10. I have seen neither the correspondence nor the contract for this consulting job, only the publications resulting from it. In any case the limitations of a brief chapter, as opposed to a biographical monograph, would have prevented full utilization of such materials, if they still exist.

11. In July 1961 and May 1962, prior to the Teachers College project, Kimball was research consultant for the Teachers for East Africa Program. This had to do with the Peace Corps, but Kimball never published anything directly as a result. Once again, I do not have access to the correspondence or contract for this experience, nor for the Peru Project.

12. It is possible that Kimball visited Lima for the project, but he certainly was never in residence in Peru, as he was in Brazil.

13. It is possible that he wrote the piece earlier, but I have the impression that it was written especially (as chapter 16) for *Culture and the Educative Process* (1974).

14. For example, as a Midwestern neophyte outsider at Harvard, he was nonetheless a brilliant public speaker and conversationalist. He brought these gifts to the lifelong collaboration he struck up then with the intellectually brilliant and socially prominent Conrad Arensberg, whose conversation, while rich in substance, was handicapped by a severe stutter.

15. I see the scholarly method of this book as metaphysical. If we understand that there can be such a method in science, then the book is also social science. That is, the arbitrary principle selected for ordering abstraction from a wide sequence of diverse observations was that of a moral imperative. Other principles guiding a metaphysi-

cal method might have been simplicity, symmetry, or mathematical elegance. I am indebted to my friend physicist Arthur S. Iberall for these ideas about the metaphysical method in science (personal communication 1993).

16. Charles Wagley came to Florida as Graduate Research Professor of Latin American Studies and Anthropology in 1971. He had previously been Franz Boas Professor of Anthropology at Columbia.

17. This assertion is based on my recollection of a conversation with Wagley one evening at his home at the time; I was then Associate Professor of Anthropology at Florida.

18. Boys and girls did, of course, form "courtship pairs," but these were off campus for the most part. Very few such pairs were interracial.

19. Eddy (1983) has reviewed and assessed this series. Leemon's *Rites of Passage* (1972), for example, fulfilled the mandate of looking at college student life from the perspective of a rite of passage, called for in 1955 in Kimball's proposed ethnography of higher education. Eddy's own book on induction into teaching did the same thing for urban teachers (1969). Cazden et al.'s *Function of Language in the Classroom* (1972) brought sociolinguistics to anthropology and education and was the best-selling volume of the series. Alan Howard (1970) and I (Moore 1999 [1973]) looked at education in the holistic context of community studies. My book placed schooling in the context of traditional means of getting through life and then judged it against spontaneous literacy classes in a complex Guatemalan community of Indians and Ladinos (non-Indians of Hispanic culture). As Kimball would have appreciated, holism and taxonomy were there, and so was functionalism.

20. An interesting corroboration of this opinion is to be found in Elaine Woo's obituary of Virginia Durr (1999).

21. Cash was cited in *Education and the New America* (Kimball and McClellan 1962). Kimball would have read it during his Alabama days. It is possible, of course, that Kimball rejected Cash's interpretation as too Marxist and conflict-oriented.

22. Indeed, in the summer of 1978 Kimball led a field school to Wales to search for the "roots of American civilization" under the auspices of NEH. Griffin (1983) and Schmidt (1983) recall the field experience.

23. He must certainly have been influenced by the great success his former doctoral student Gwen Kennedy Neville was having at the time in studying the reunions and family rituals of Protestant Southerners in contrast with those of Presbyterian Scotland (1987, 1994).

24. Unfortunately, this essay is perhaps Kimball's murkiest piece of writing; not only was he challenging Margaret Mead, but he was trying to digest communication theory as well.

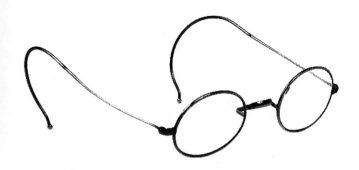

8. They Are All Our Children

Eleanor Leacock and the Anthropology of Education

Eve Hochwald

Eleanor Leacock in Labrador, circa 1951. With the kind permission of Claudia Leacock.

In nearly one hundred publications Eleanor Burke Leacock (1922–87) made major contributions to the study of band societies; the analysis of gender; Marxist anthropology; and the anthropology of education, the subject of the next chapter by Eve Hochwald. Her work always challenged biological and technological determinism. Her analyses of the conditions that introduced or perpetuated inequalities in race, class, and gender were always based on empirical research in a dialectical framework focusing on process; her activism focused on opposing these inequities.

Leacock was born in New York City and was raised there and on the family farm in New Jersey, the two places where she spent her adult life. She grew up, as she writes in a brief autobiography, "to be scornful of materialist consumerism; to value—even revere—nature; to hate deeply the injustice of exploitation and racial discrimination . . . and to be committed to the importance of doing what one could to bring about a socialist transformation of society" (Leacock 1993a:5). Her mother, Lily Batterham, had a master's degree in mathematics and had taught secondary school; her father, Kenneth Burke, was a prominent and prolific literary critic and philosopher. Her parents inhabited an intellectual, artistic, and politically radical milieu in Greenwich Village quite distinct from that of her Italian-American neighbors with whom she attended elementary school. Younger than her classmates, and never part of a social clique, she felt this part of her childhood made her "fit the picture of the psychologically 'marginal' person that we think of as common in a profession dedicated to understanding cultural differences" (1993a).

While in high school, she decided to become an anthropologist when her older sister introduced her to the subject. In 1939 she began Radcliffe College on a scholarship; while there she studied Marx and Marxist works systematically and met her first husband, the filmmaker Richard Leacock. After their marriage in 1942 she transferred to Barnard College, where she majored in anthropology. After she graduated in 1944, Leacock looked for a job in Washington to help in the war effort.[1] Ruth Benedict and Rhoda Metraux invited her to work with them at the Office of War Information analyzing "culture-at-a-distance." She was unable to accept the offer because the FBI refused her the required security clearance, presumably because of her student political activities.[2]

Instead she became a graduate student at Columbia University. Among her teachers was Gene Weltfish, who taught her phonetic transcription and introduced her to a "fully politicized anthropology" (Leacock 1993a:13). She took a leave of absence to accompany her filmmaker husband to Europe during 1948–49 and to make her own films examining families and child socialization in Italy and Switzerland. Because she was then a mother with two small children, the department assumed that her academic interest would continue to be child socialization. However, Leacock was critical of the extreme relativism of the culture-and-personality approach. Additionally she disagreed with its ahistoricism and treatment of the forces and relations of production as no more relevant than other cultural features. For example, the Pueblo, described as timeless and Apollonian in Benedict's Patterns of Culture (1934a), in reality had been affected by Spanish domination beginning in the sixteenth century. Pursuing her interest in the impact of European domination on Native peoples, she began archival research in Paris tracing the changes in social organization of the Montagnais-Naskapi (Innu) of Labrador, her dissertation topic.

In 1951 and again in 1952 she conducted fieldwork in Labrador. Only fifty-four pages long, her dissertation challenged then prevalent notions about Native American hunting territories by demonstrating that these territories were not individually owned prior to contact with the European fur trade. Even after the group had become dependent on the fur trade, it was an individual's right to trap fur-bearing animals in a particular territory that was recognized, but the individual did not have a right to other game or to the land as such; anyone could hunt, fish, or gather anywhere, as long as the object was personal use, not sale. This finding was widely cited by students of Native American and gatherer-hunter societies and has been largely accepted, despite some modifications depending on the exact area and time period under consideration (see Lee and Daly 1993:38–40).

Leacock had undertaken the research deliberately to examine the nature of "primitive communism," a term first used by Lewis Henry Morgan in his 1878 work Ancient Society (1963). However, given the Cold War and the politics of the Columbia Department of Anthropology, she did not openly declare her intent either in her dissertation or in its subsequent publication (1954). Nonetheless, as her thesis became widely accepted, it helped set the stage for an anthropology that—in spite of or perhaps in reaction to McCarthyism—"was ready to move in a much more historically informed and politically conscious direction" (Lee and Daly 1993:36). In the 1960s and 1970s, Leacock laid the groundwork for the open attribution of Marxist theory as an acknowledged scholarly source when she published her introduction, begun as a student of Weltfish, to a new edition of Frederick Engels's The Origin of the Family, Private Property, and the State (1972b). Building on Morgan's research on the Iroquois Confederacy and primitive society, Engels proposed a series of stages of human history, beginning with communal ownership, to explain the subordination of women in class society. Leacock used evidence from the anthropological record to both support and modify Engels's conclusions. The introduction was widely read and was instrumental in introducing issues of Marxism, evolutionism, and the status of women to anthropologists, feminists, and scholars.[3]

After she received her PhD in 1952, her first jobs were in applied research—housing, mental health, and education. Her first tenure-track academic appointment was in 1963, when she joined the social science faculty at Brooklyn Polytechnic Institute. In 1971 she became the first chair of the newly created Anthropology Department of the City College of New York. She remained there until her untimely death in 1987 in Samoa, where she was analyzing problems of youth, education, and the labor market (Leacock 1993b). She also wrote about the Margaret Mead–Derek Freeman controversy, arguing against the biological determinism and ignorance of history manifest in Freeman's attack on Mead (Leacock 1992). Her own work in Samoa continued her long-term interest in education, a subject she had previously investigated in Canada, the United States, and Africa.

Leacock was not a dogmatic Marxist; rather, she believed that Marxist theory must be applied to meet the challenges of new knowledge. Arguing for an expansion of Marxist scholarship, she wrote:

> There is no substitute for Marx's method of detailed analysis in specific cases, based on a dialectical and materialist theory of relationships that must constantly be tested, elaborated upon, and refined, both through theory and action. Rather than seeking comparabilities . . . among what are too often superficial features of different situations, comparabilities must be sought at the level of determinate mechanisms, at the level of processes that are generally hidden from view. . . . Hypotheses about social laws or processes are ultimately to be found in the laboratory of historical experience. (1972b:61)

Nor did she suggest that the connection between theory and practice was simple. Theory depended on sound research and hard work to inform action, and advocacy, in turn, was the "key for the outsider to the 'inside' view that is essential to the fully rounded understanding of the culture" (Leacock 1992:25). She made no distinction between applied and theoretical anthropology (Leacock 1987). To charges that advocacy and objectivity were incompatible, she replied that "scientific" understanding—not objectivity—was the goal. Similarly, she answered critics who accused her of projecting a too rosy, mythical, egalitarian past on pre–class societies by referring them to the scientific evidence presented by the ethnohistorical record.

Leacock used an anecdote from her ethnohistorical research to illustrate the clash between the patriarchal and authoritarian assumptions of the Jesuits—the first European educational emissaries—and the Innu egalitarian society they encountered. As recorded in *the seventeenth-century Jesuit Relations, the Jesuits were disturbed by the Montagnais custom of sexual freedom for men and women.*[4] *"How will you know if your wife's children are really yours?" one asked. In a rejoinder Leacock enjoyed retelling, to illustrate what had been lost in centuries of European and capitalist domination, one of the Montagnais men replied, "You French people love only your own children, but we love all the children of our tribe" (see Leacock and Goodman 1976:82). Leacock, also concerned with the well-being of all the children, saw this example of a less competitive past as indicative of our potential to create a more cooperative future.*

Eleanor (Happy) Burke Leacock (1922–87) remains one of the most influential anthropologists of her generation. Her research in anthropology and education, in common with all her work, demonstrates a concern with levels of integration and processes of socialization; with institutionalized inequality—whether based on gender, race, ethnicity, or social class—and its origins; and with the role of anthropology in the struggle against psychological and biological reductionism and ideologies of domination.[5] As a practitioner, she believed in "advocacy anthropology," and she was instrumental in designing two courses of study, one to instruct science and engineering majors in the social sciences (Leacock 1968) and the other to educate applied anthropologists (Leacock et al. 1975). Wherever she was, she was an involved observer who combined theory and practice.[6]

Her approximately thirty publications concerning aspects of education cover topics such as the socialization of children and adolescents, classroom processes in urban schools, community control of local schools, language use in the classroom, the unwarranted acceptance of the culture of poverty concept in educational circles, the impact of missionary (mis)education of Native peoples, and the effect of "modernization" on African education.[7] She chose education as a subject because "as the reproduction of social relations and ideology, [it] affords an excellent way to study contemporary society" (1993a:27).

Her research in education was integral to her opposition to racism, to the culture of poverty concept, and to neocolonialism. It coincided with the cen-

tral role schools were playing in the struggle for equality worldwide and with
the social turbulence of the times, when radical scholarship in anthropology
and the social sciences was gaining new prominence. Her classic *Teaching and
Learning in City Schools* (1969) is based on fieldwork in New York City. She also
conducted research on education and related topics in Canada, Zambia, and
Samoa. In addition to its theoretical importance, her work in anthropology
and education is an important example of the relevance of anthropology to
understanding and resolving contemporary educational and social issues.

Activism and Anthropology in Leacock's Career

One of Leacock's first jobs after she received her PhD from Columbia University in 1952 was at the Bank Street College of Education. There in 1958 she
began the classroom-processes study that would become the basis for *Teaching
and Learning in City Schools*. She found Bank Street—friendly, nonhierarchical,
and seriously intellectual—a congenial place to work. Having four children
was an asset rather than a liability, and the collegial environment supported
her during a turbulent period in her personal life, the end of her first marriage
to Richard Leacock and the beginning of her relationship with the man who
would become her second husband, James Haughton. Haughton was a labor
activist and founder of Harlem Fight Back, an organization fighting for minority jobs in the construction trades (1993a:24). Leacock's 14th Street office was
close to her Greenwich Village home and her children's school, and research
team members remember her children often stopping by the office.

In 1963 Leacock accepted a full-time tenure-track appointment at Brooklyn
Polytechnic Institute. There she headed a project to develop an undergraduate
interdisciplinary theory and methods course, which produced eight readers for
a series titled *Social Science Theory and Method: An Integrated Historical Introduction*
(Leacock 1968).[8] Each volume and most of the selections contained an introduction, nearly all written by Leacock herself. The purpose of the readers was
to present sources for seminar discussion. They include some of the primary
sources of the dialectical, evolutionary, and scientifically grounded modes of
analysis that she drew upon in her own work. In each volume's preface, Leacock argues forcefully for a historical perspective and an integrated view of human behavior in all social sciences.[9] Both of these goals characterize her own

work on the issues of racism, innate aggression, gender bias, sociobiology, and levels of social integration.

Always politically active, throughout the 1960s Leacock demonstrated and circulated petitions for civil rights and against the war in Vietnam. In the battle for community control of the New York City public schools, she marched on parents' picket lines and for a time taught two days a week in an alternative Freedom School set up for the Harlem school children boycotting their assigned schools in order to protest their exclusion from the academically competitive high schools. While writing *Teaching and Learning in City Schools* (1969) and editing *The Culture of Poverty: A Critique* (1971a), she produced a community newsletter, *Facts for School Action*, and participated in a citywide council that coordinated activities and formulated strategies to help parents play effective roles in school reform.

She was a prime mover behind the American Anthropological Association's 1969 resolution condemning U.S. involvement in the Vietnam War. In 1971 she played a central role in creating the Anthropologists for Radical Political Action network, whose chapters proposed resolutions, organized symposia and sit-ins, and raised political issues at professional meetings.

In the 1970s, the same decade in which she published her introduction to Engels (1972b) and wrote the much discussed article "Women's Status in Egalitarian Society" (1978), Leacock introduced feminist resolutions at the annual American Anthropology Association meetings and founded the New York Women's Anthropology Caucus, an organization that examined the theoretical and substantive content of anthropology from the newly emerging women's perspectives. She always spoke against the assumption of the universality of women's subordination, pointing out the ideology embedded in anthropological notions such as the *exchange of women* and in the presumed opposition between "nature" and "culture" and "public" and "private" domains (Leacock 1981; Rapp 1993). In the 1980s she was a founder of the International Women's Anthropology Conference, a network of women anthropologists, and the Genes and Gender Collective, a group of scientists and activists who challenge genetic determinism in such guises as sociobiology, innate aggression, and racism based on IQ.

Nine years after her first academic appointment at Brooklyn Polytechnic Institute, in 1972, Leacock went to the City College of New York as a full professor and the chair of the newly formed Anthropology Department. She credited the women's movement for her City College appointment, because it had opened up senior academic jobs to women candidates, and because the great interest in her work on Engels—a cornerstone of the new feminist scholarship—had enhanced her reputation. Since the impact of feminism on scholarship occurred more than a decade after she completed *Teaching and Learning in City Schools*, that book takes little note of gender. However, the women's movement influenced Leacock's subsequent scholarship and activism, always linked.

Accompanying her belief in anthropology's mission to understand and remedy social problems was her interest in training anthropologists as practitioners. One of her first acts as chair was to plan a course of study for a master's degree in applied anthropology, the first in New York City, based on the four-field approach. Leacock argued that three distinct areas were to be mastered: (1) a cross-cultural perspective derived from the study of cultural anthropology and linguistics; (2) a holistic and historical perspective derived from the study of cultural anthropology, archaeology, and physical anthropology; and (3) the awareness that behavior is in great part the enactment of culturally defined roles that are appropriate to various social statuses and the concomitant recognition of the need to interpret one's own role behavior in terms of the expectations of others as well as of oneself. In addition, she expected the program to foster skills in interviewing; observing and recording behavior and interaction; and collating, processing, and evaluating data (Leacock 1975).

Leacock remained a professor at City College, teaching as well at the Graduate Center of the City University of New York, where I was her student, until her untimely death in 1987. Among the projects she left unfinished was a book about levels of integration that she had planned to write with her longtime friend and colleague Ethel Tobach, a comparative psychologist and cofounder of the Genes and Gender Collective. The concept of levels of integration is pivotal because it is a synthesis of evolutionary and dialectical theory. In an unpublished, undated one-page statement of the problem to be addressed, Leacock writes,

> The human individual is social in a profound and specifically human sense that has not yet been clearly formulated. . . . One thing is clear, the erroneousness of the assumption implicit in most educational and psychological re-

search: that a single individual (typically a child) functions at an "individual
level" at the point of direct group interaction. As an individual, the human
being always is functioning at a social level. *The principle is simple enough,*
yet its implications for a reassessment of existing material on learning, under-
standing, and education are enormous.

She distinguishes various levels: "This, that we have agreed to call the 'psycho-
social' level is of course interdependent with, although different from, what
we have agreed to call the 'societal' level on the one hand, and what we have
agreed to call the 'physiological' level on the other (with the bio-physical and
bio-chemical level below it in turn."[10]

Social Levels of Integration in Urban Schools

The ways in which the social—and not the individual—level of the interactions
between teachers and students in the New York City schools affect educational
outcomes is the point of *Teaching and Learning in City Schools* (1969). Addressing the question of what children actually learn in school, the book is a careful record of the ways the well-intentioned behavior of well-meaning teachers
undermines children's mastery of stated educational goals. The study compared classrooms of African American and White children, at the second- and
fifth-grade levels in four schools, in middle-class and working-class neighborhoods, creating a sample of eight classes. When the teaching processes
were observed, and the teachers interviewed, significant differences became
apparent. Educational goals for working-class children of both races and for
middle-class Black children were lower than for middle-class White children,
who were encouraged to take charge and share their ideas in a way that the
others were not.

Children in the Black working-class classrooms were allowed little self-ex-
pression or room to explore the curriculum and were not expected to make
serious efforts. The Black middle-class children were exposed most to discipline, negative criticism, and constant reevaluation of their achievements. In
one telling contrast, the researchers found that in the White middle-income
fifth-grade classroom the teacher favored children with high IQ test scores
whereas in the Black middle-class fifth grade, the teacher was more likely to
criticize the high scorers. In other words, the teacher's expectations of the

students, the quality of the curriculum taught, the social organization of the classroom, and the respect and affection shown for the children were variables whose combined effect determined what the children learned, both from the curriculum and about themselves as individuals.

As Leacock notes, the negativism expressed was not simple racism, for the teacher was hard working, well meaning, and African American. Rather, it must be "understood as part of the overall pattern whereby the double-track structure of schools, in keeping with the employment structure of the society, exerts its influence on teachers by lowering their goals for working-class black children" (1969:51). She concludes that "the teachers' differential behavior towards children of different backgrounds . . . reflects, not the individual incompetence of a minority, but an institutional system of race and class bias that patterns the practices of the vast majority" (49).

Teaching and Learning in City Schools appeared at a time when education was—then as now—the subject of national scrutiny. It was written in the dual context of the national debates about achieving equal educational opportunity, as called for by the 1954 Supreme Court desegregation ruling, and on improving American schools in the post-Sputnik era. In the September 1969 Special Education Supplement of the *New York Times Book Review*, the sociologist Edgar Friedenberg, a school critic himself, reviewed *Teaching and Learning in City Schools* along with other 1960s books critical of the American educational system, among them the classic first-person accounts of George Dennison's *The Lives of Children*, James Herndon's *The Way It Spozed to Be*, John Holt's *How Children Learn* and *How Children Fail*, and Elwyn Richardson's *In the Early World*.

Following the conventions of the time, Friedenberg refers to "Mrs. Leacock" throughout his essay. He correctly points out that what distinguishes her book is its method. As he notes, her study is an example of the careful application of scientific method, including a carefully constructed sample, objective classroom observation, structured interviews with teachers before and after the observation and with each child in the study's classrooms, use of the comparative method, and quantitative and qualitative analysis of the data collected to reveal both formal (overt) and informal (covert) aspects of teachers' behaviors and attitudes.

Another part of Leacock's method, not mentioned by Friedenberg, is the balance and diversity in the team of collaborators she assembled. She formed a group, mostly graduate students, who represented the disciplines of anthropology, psychology, and education, and who had disparate backgrounds as well. As she describes her intention,

> Whatever the precise method being used, the final outcome can go no further than the understanding of the researchers. Therefore, one consideration in bringing together the research team was that it should, insofar as possible, contribute different points of view from varied experiences—the viewpoint of the teacher as well as the researcher, the more individual orientation of the psychologist as well as the group orientation of the anthropologist, the empathy and understanding of the Negro, white, man, and woman. (1969:14)

From Leacock's perspective, however, the distinguishing attribute of her research, more than method, is its dialectical approach, which focuses on change itself: "A dialectical view assumes matter to be in constant motion, with opposing or conflicting forces inherent in all phenomena leading to a series of 'quantitative changes' until the point is reached when the opposition resolves itself through a 'qualitative leap,' a transformation into something new" (Leacock 1968, vol. 3:1). Applying this view begins with a formulation of the problem being addressed. As she writes in the opening chapter of *Teaching and Learning in City Schools*:

> The initial problem to be resolved in a study of teaching and learning as broad cultural processes is how to deal with the complexity of individual growth and development within a social context. One is tempted either to emphasize the content, and think of it as basically a mold into which individuals are pressed, or to emphasize the individual and see the social system as essentially a sum total of psycho-biologically motivated entities. Clearly, neither is adequate. (1969:15)

Complicating this problem is the need to deal with given institutional settings as arbitrary cutoff points in a historical or developmental process, while recognizing that social institutions shape people at the same time as people are shaping social institutions. One must, Leacock writes,

> conceptualize the way in which institutions achieve and maintain their functional relation to the total society through building and reinforcing habitual

actions and attendant attitudes of the very people, who, as they operate within
them, are changing the institutions by expressing in their actions and thoughts
unresolved problems with the institutions themselves or conflicts between them
and other parts of society. (1969:16)

Leacock's solution is to make *cultural process* her focus and to emphasize the socially patterned responses of individuals, depending on their social roles and status. In *Teaching and Learning in City Schools*, as in all her work, Leacock argues against reductionist thinking and against a "unitary concept of cultural patterning and cultural norms" (1969:16). Thus, she sees the classroom as defining patterned behavioral and attitudinal alternatives for children, with some of the alternatives transmitted covertly, to both the children and their parents. One alternative is resistance, as in the case of those who had been active in achieving community control of the schools (Leacock 1970; see also Berube and Gittell 1969 and Rubinstein 1970). In fact, as Leacock observes, the post–World War II protest of the African American community in the United States concerning segregated and unequal schooling was the catalyst for focusing national attention on schooling as a means of obtaining equal opportunity (1982:49).

Friedenberg's review misses another important implication of Leacock's findings, which she later pointed out in "Abstract versus Concrete Speech: A False Dichotomy" (1985 [1972]). There Leacock argues against the premise that a linguistic basis exists for presumed cognitive deficiencies among lower-class children. She writes that "even so careful and sensitive an observer as Edgar Friedenberg can write blandly, without qualification or explanation, that there are 'systematic differences in cognitive ability' and that they follow from 'differences in the way symbols are used in the homes of the very poor and of the middle class [which] are so great as to be almost ineradicable'" (112). All too often, she continues, "white middle-class members of Western culture are seen as abstract, rational, and logical in their patterns of thought, as opposed to members of simpler societies and lower-class people, who are said to be concrete, nonrational, and nonlogical" (114–115).

Through a series of well-chosen examples, she illustrates how both Western and non-Western peoples make use of both abstract *and* concrete thought, depending on the situation and context. The article is at once an explication of Benjamin Whorf's hypothesis that language exerts influence on thought, correcting the oversimplified position derived from it that "primitive" peoples function at a conceptually lower level than "civilized" ones; a demonstration of the situational context in which all peoples use abstract *and* concrete speech; and a rebuttal of the widespread belief that the use of nonstandard English in everyday speech is the cause of Black students' failure in school.

Refuting the Culture-of-Poverty Thesis

Teaching and Learning in City Schools was intended to affect public policy. Leacock's target audience is the "reformers and policy makers and designers of teacher education" who think that "cultural barriers between the schools and the home for children in lower-income neighborhoods—styles of language and experience which are in conflict with styles met and valued at school—are responsible for their lower school performance" (1969:5). This idea had become known as the "culture-of-poverty" hypothesis. The concept that the poor have a universal culture of poverty comes from the anthropologist Oscar Lewis, who, at various times, identified it with varying numbers of individual attributes, ranging from thirty-six to eighty (Rigdon 1988:113). Static, nondialectical, and reductionist, its premise is that the poor have a bundle of traits—inability to save and plan, lack of future orientation, a sense of fatalism, passivity, psychopathology, among others—that characterize a way of life inherited from generation to generation, and that are linked to low educational and occupational motivation. The culture of poverty is seen as more pervasive and more damaging than poverty itself.

Critics of the culture-of-poverty hypothesis pointed out that to the extent that such traits could be identified as characteristic of some poor people, they were individually *adaptive* and not inherited. In collapsing values, attitudes, and behavior into "culture," they argued, adherents to the culture-of-poverty theory confused culture with the state of poverty itself. Leacock's edited collection *The Culture of Poverty: A Critique* (1971a) is a definitive rebuttal of this theory—if theory it was. As she argues persuasively, not only did the culture-of-poverty adherents misrepresent the life of the poor, but they also exaggerated the motivation of the middle class.

Looking for differences in the school experiences of low and middle income, black and white children, that would explain differences in their scholastic performance, . . . we were expecting to find that a clash in values between teachers who represented "white middle class" or "mainstream" views and pupils from working class and or black homes was alienating these children. However, we found . . . systematic differences in teacher attitudes and practices [which] startled us to the extent to which they were undermining already disadvantaged children. The primary "middle class value" we observed was hardly the motivation for success stressed in the literature, but a basic lack of respect for people who are poor and nonwhite coupled with the expectation that their children would not succeed. (1982:50)

Nor were middle-class children necessarily well served: schools were failing all children, not only the poor and disadvantaged. In a criticism that continues to ring true, she writes,

Our "well-educated" children . . . are not that well-educated, they are trained for test-taking—for the performance of set tasks quickly and ably and not for humanistic understanding or for innovative exploration. How can they be when they are so largely taught a myth—a myth for lower class and middle-income children alike? Not only is the existence of this country's majority [i.e. the working class] virtually denied in the classroom, but any "controversial" issue is avoided. The bland version of the world presented in the classroom contradicts reality. . . . The basic myth of the elementary school classroom leads, not only to the denial of their existence for many school children, but to a denial of the truth for all. (1969:214)

The Myth of Modernization

While on sabbatical from Brooklyn Polytechnic Institute in 1970, Leacock went to Zambia to continue comparative research on schooling. Interested in political developments in Africa, she wanted to experience cultures that contrasted markedly with the Native American societies she knew. Again she examined the social levels of integration and the dialectical cultural processes, this time at work in the transfer of Western educational models to newly independent African countries. Her specific research topics were the role school played in preparing children for adult life, the relationship between the school curriculum and children's out-of-school experiences, and the impact of Western influences on teaching styles and curriculum content (1977). She found that assumptions about "traditional" societies and processes of modernization paralleled those that characterized the culture-of-poverty concept. Western schooling was idealized, and the scientific and intellectual content of African life and culture was underrated or derogated. "Tribal" was equated with "poor" and "nonwhite," and failure at school was attributed to "cultural" differences.

Such stereotypes were found in supposedly objective studies of how poorly African children were prepared for "modern" education by their home backgrounds. These studies were written by Western, middle-class observers who used the modern-traditional framework, which "by transmuting political and economic problems into ideological ones, helps maintain the illusion of scientific neutrality and detachment" (1980:171). Leacock explains:

> Like the culture-of-poverty concept, the "modernization" concept allows theoretical confusions, and sociocentric and racist biases, to intersect with political influences in discussions of oppressed peoples. Both concepts freely use "culture" as an ill-defined term that focuses heavily on the social-psychological ideological dimensions of social-historical process, and glosses over structural realities of political power and economic control. (173)

Throughout the social "scientific" literature on Africa, Leacock finds references to the disruption caused by urban life to traditional forms of education such as apprenticeships, story telling, and riddles. Although increasing access to formal schooling, urban life was said to have impaired children's motivations and ability to learn through the effects of poverty, malnutrition, and social disorganization. In other words, rather than counteracting the supposedly adverse effects of "traditionalism," urbanization had compounded children's learning problems by adding deficiencies along culture-of-poverty lines (1980:169). She writes:

> The resulting mystification encourages and reinforces a series of assumptions about education that are not only taken for granted by most Western social scientists, but are all too widely accepted, with but minor modifications, by

> Third World people themselves. The traditional-modern framework, by mask-
> ing neo-colonial realities, fosters the assumption that what is needed to "mod-
> ernize" a nation or to achieve a standard of living commensurate with the West
> is to attain a level of education presumed necessary for technological advance-
> ment. The stumbling block is seen not as structural, but as "cultural." "Tradi-
> tionalism" affects children's cognitive style and motivation, and hinders their
> readiness for scientific and technological training. (171)

The inherent bias, and the prevalence of the modern-traditional framework that Western observers imposed on African children, were even evident in the title of Leacock's article, "At Play in African Villages" (1972a). Chosen by an editor at *Natural History* magazine, it contradicted the clearly stated fact that the research on which the article was based had been conducted in a working-class suburb of Lusaka, the capital city of Zambia (63). With characteristic verve, Leacock demolishes the stereotypes of backward African children, attributing the problems of African schooling instead to the poor fit between the Western model and African circumstances and to flaws inherent in the model itself. First, there is the issue of culture-bound testing that supposedly measured the students' cognitive "deficiencies." Next, there is the decidedly mixed influence of the European-style mission schools. Although often staffed by gifted and dedicated teachers who introduced literacy, mission schools emphasized dis-cipline and rote learning, with a curriculum based on European materials that often was nonsensical in the African context. Nonetheless, because success at mission schools led to jobs in the colonial and neocolonial economic struc-ture, parents sought to enroll their children in them, and educators continued to emulate their authoritarian and unimaginative educational style.

For these reasons, Leacock looks elsewhere for evidence of the potential and accomplishments of African children. Observing children at play in Lusaka, she describes their enormous creativity, thought, and ingenuity, which most other Western observers had missed:

> Technical skills, linguistic skills, and numerical skills, were all constantly be-
> ing developed and exercised as children made model houses, pottery, wagons,
> and all manner of other toys; played nsoro, the Zambian version of the Afri-
> can checker-like game that involves calculation . . . ; interacted with children
> speaking other languages than their own; made musical instruments and com-

posed songs; formed ball-playing and other clubs and took on odd jobs to buy equipment and club shirts; helped their parents or relatives shopping, sewing, cooking, making bricks or whatever it might be; and so on. Most impressive, perhaps, were the wire models of trucks and automobiles that were cleverly constructed from wires scrounged from dump heaps or filched from fences. Indeed, the Zambian children I observed were engaged in precisely the kinds of activities recommended in new Western curricula for developing cognitive skills. (1980:172)

Her research in Zambia confirmed the existence of a worldwide pattern of discrepancy between the ideal of education for equal opportunity and the structural reality whereby schooling keeps all but a handful of children within the socioeconomic category into which they are born. As for the study of children in school, she concludes: "the role education has played historically in socializing each new generation is ignored, and the myth of schooling as the inevitable road to progress continues to prevail. Yet it is clear that something is wrong. The ideology embodied in the culture of poverty, and the modern-traditional concepts would argue that it must be the children" (1980:178).

Educational Remedies

What remedies does Leacock suggest? Her ideal school, she writes, would give children competence in technical skills as well as an understanding of the world as a composite of social and natural processes that invite individual and collective adaptation and intervention. Children would grow up with an understanding of themselves as being basically similar to others, but with a feeling and respect for the nature and importance of individual and group differences. Schools should provide the basis for such understanding through their curriculum, as well as through furnishing an atmosphere for reinforcing this understanding (1969:18).

She upheld this standard in her own teaching. The series of seminar readings she edited are historical, multicultural, and inclusive. For example, her discussion of early historical sources credits West African court historians, Polynesian royal genealogists, Egyptian scribes, the scholarly tradition of Chinese historiography, and myth and oral history. These versions of history are not so different from our own:

> The earliest sources of a critical or analytical view of society do not lie in his-
> torical writings. The function of semi-historical myths in the primitive world
> is to explain and rationalize the existing order, and formal history apparently
> arises with the need to validate the power of ruling families. . . . Indeed, this
> function of history is very much alive in the modern world, and we are famil-
> iar with this use (or abuse) of history to validate various claims to power by
> corporate states or vested interests within them. The "good guys versus the bad
> guys" version of our own history which is taught in elementary school is a sad
> reminder of that fact. (Leacock 1968, vol. 5:1)

Then, discussing the earliest sources of actual social analysis, she writes:

> Although great wisdom is shown in the writings of the ancient civilizations,
> they are not directly critical or analytical in a self-conscious "scientific" sense.
> Probably the critical attitude was carried in the oral tradition of popular po-
> ems and tales. . . . The wisdom embodied in the folktales of the African slave,
> Aesop, is of an analytic order. . . . Ashanti proverbs crystallize a critical view of
> the political and social order. (2)

Another remedy is the improvement of teacher education programs by clarifying the bias inherent in the culture-of-poverty concept, offering clearer insight into "middle-class" values, and recognizing that some of the "new" ideas urged to improve the education of low-income children are actually a rediscovery of Dewey and traditional progressive education. Their application would improve the education of all children (1969:208). Also, teachers must be supplied with models of innovative teaching, particularly examples of lessons geared to everyday life. In New York City there should be material relevant to working-class life; in Zambia, books that reflect the realities of African history, geography, and politics. The curriculum content needs to relate to, and respect, children's life experiences and interests, and to incorporate elements of play, such as observation, experimentation, and problem solving.

At the same time, Leacock saw teachers as the too-easy focus of intervention, because they are captive audiences. Teachers' efforts are negated, she said, if they are not backed by changes made at the administrative levels (John-Steiner and Leacock 1979:78), and if they are not coupled with ongoing community programs that affect the health, nutrition, and employment of adults as well as the literacy of children. Rejecting the traditional belief in schools as the primary institutions of socialization, and in the school building as the setting where shared values, beliefs, tastes, and habits are transmitted (88), she recommends that schools become community buildings, with teachers but one group of adults working with parents and others to help children learn.

Emphasizing that the institution of schooling is failing, and not teachers or children, she advocates its transformation through the joint efforts of scholars and educators. Urging that meaningful research in schools be comparative and holistic in both method and conceptual framework, she advises researchers to avoid the narrow empiricism endemic in the search for short-term and largely illusory solutions, and not to become defensive about the use of traditional field methods. Contrary to prevailing trends, she writes, quantification is not synonymous with scientific method. Counting traits, or making checklists, is an important aspect of description, but not analysis. She warns against the "fetishism of the chi-square" (1971b:170), which may result in the loss of highly significant—but infrequent—incidents or episodes.

Significance—both academic and political—depends on the questions being asked, which in turn follow from recognizing the connections and interactions between families, schools, and communities. For example, research in support of administrative reforms should consider the structure of the entire school district, not of a single school. If their students have no decent intermediate or high school to attend, it is pointless to recommend teachers prepare them for one. Research that describes and analyzes links between groups and community struggles also can be useful in campaigns to improve schools, since the better informed participants are, the more effective such struggles can be.

Anthropologists play a crucial role because of the breadth of the discipline in interpreting human behavior and social systems within the total context of human cultures; and because of their commitment to countering racism and ethnocentrism. The results of their research have practical implications for nutrition, health care, social service, technological innovation, intergroup relations, education, and thus, ultimately, for social change. For anthropological research to be meaningful, she emphasizes, it is necessary to apply the concept of culture in a way that does not ignore political and economic relationships. As she explains:

> On the one hand a focus on "culture"—hence on traditions, values, and at-
> titudes—rather than on class relations can be and is widely used to mask and
> distort the brutal realities of power and exploitation. On the other hand, how-
> ever, a focus on culture in the context of political economy discourages superfi-
> cial and mechanistic interpretations of group behavior, because it requires at-
> tention to the role of consciousness and ideology in social process. (1982:257)

She also argues for committed scholarship and "advocacy anthropology."
When combined with a broad historical orientation and an advocacy stance,
she writes,

> anthropological perspectives make it possible to examine ways in which the
> conflicts and ambivalence people experience in their daily lives express funda-
> mental socio-economic conflicts that are impelling change. They offer the pos-
> sibility for defining the potentials for action and the ambiguities that hinder
> it, as individuals and groups in part accept and in part resist the existing power
> relations that oppress them. Advocacy anthropology enhances the possibilities
> for delineating practical short-range steps and meaningful long-term goals for
> the problems urban people confront. Commitment makes it possible to work
> toward an effective—a practical—theory of social change. (1987:334)

Conclusion

Eleanor Leacock inspired—and continues to inspire—scholars and activists
in a wide arena. Her legacy includes a compelling body of work in anthropology and education, as well as in the anthropological subfields of ethnohistory, gender relations, and subsistence societies, unified in its advocacy for a
more equitable and just society. Education was a focal point of her research
because of its centrality in both reflecting social processes and ideologies and
its potential for transforming them. From her first publications, "Harrison Indian Childhood" (1949a) and "The Seabird Community" (1949b), in which she
described the social organization and child-rearing practices of a Northwest
Indian community, to her last, "Postscript: The Problems of Youth in Contemporary Samoa" (1993b), about gender relations, adolescence, and youth unemployment, Leacock's scholarship concerns the relationship of the individual to
society—sometimes expressed in her application of the concept of "levels of

integration"—and with cultural processes of change. Her approach is consistently couched in the framework of dialectics and the historically constituted circumstances in which individuals and groups find themselves.

Throughout her career she argued against biological (racism, sexism, sociobiology, innate aggression) and psychological (culture-and-personality, culture-of-poverty, the modern-traditional framework) determinism. In her many publications, she exposed the ethnocentrism of false dichotomies such as public/private, nature/culture, abstract/concrete, traditional/modern, and magical/scientific to uncover the embedded ideology in the presumption that these oppositions are universal. Moreover, because her research interests were tied to her intellectual and political commitments, she always aimed at educating an audience beyond anthropology and anthropologists.

Leacock's research on education and schooling created the foundation for the still unfinished reassessment of learning and education she proposed. Underlying her dialectical approach to the critical study of educational institutions is her insistence that children, like adults, function at a *social* and not an individual level of integration. The problems she described in unequal educational systems remain. The emphasis on precepts rather than concepts in teaching, and on rote rather than creative learning, persists. With some notable exceptions, the quality of resources and type of education still depend on students' social class and ethnic background.

Far more frequently than not, opportunities for self-affirmation and skills in problem solving and critical thinking remain middle-class, and often male, domains.[11] Similarly, the burdens on well-intentioned but often poorly trained teachers continue, as they struggle to teach in undersupplied but overcrowded classrooms. Their jobs have been made even more difficult by an added policing and social service role, for which they are ill prepared.[12] The battle for community control of the schools has been both won and lost.

Yet, not everything is the same. Collaborative learning is an educational goal in many classrooms. The cooperation Leacock admired in African schools as students shared scarce textbooks and pencils is now mirrored in American classrooms as students share computers. The new technologies, when used well, can allow equal access to educational and community resources. Schools have many more minority teachers and principals. Curriculum guides have

been changed to include people of color, and far fewer classroom bulletin
boards still exhibit an exaggerated blondness in those portrayed.

Leacock's own work in anthropology and education is a model of the advocacy anthropology she supported. *Teaching and Learning in City Schools,* in particular, is an example of the application of the dialectical and collaborative approach to ethnographic social research. Some of the improvements in schools
since the book's publication are, in part, the results of educational reforms
Leacock and others influenced by debunking the assumptions of the culture-
of-poverty theorists.

Not all the changes have been positive; in some aspects, schools have deteri-
orated. Among the new problems are skyrocketing violence, spiraling dropout
rates, the segregation of bilingual and special education, a misplaced overem-
phasis on technology and standardized tests, and increasing school privatiza-
tion. Leacock would have advised us to research these issues and to propose
solutions, cautioning, however, against the quick fix that is no fix, and against
the (mis)use of anthropologists and other social scientists to isolate problems
from the historical and particular context in which they arise. We do well to
heed her warning.

Notes

1. See Price 2005 for a discussion of the varied roles anthropologists were playing in
the war effort.

2. The FBI has not released her files (Price 2004:363).

3. For further discussion of Engels's application of Morgan's work, see Trautmann
(1987:251–255).

4. The *Jesuit Relations,* reports originally written annually by Jesuit missionaries in
Quebec and elsewhere in New France to their superiors in France, were assembled,
translated, and edited by Reuben Gold Thwaites at the end of the nineteenth century
(Thwaites 1896–1901). The reports are among the best sources of information for Native
American life in North America during the seventeenth century. Leacock kept volumes
from this massive scholarly work close at hand in her downtown Manhattan loft.

5. For a review of the continuing relevance of her contributions, see Mullings (1993)
and Casey and Curtis (2005).

6. In a symposium sponsored by the CUNY Working Class Anthropology Project and
the Brecht Forum in New York City, November 7–8, 1997, *History, Science, and Advocacy:
The Living Legacy of Eleanor Burke Leacock (1922–1987),* participants repeatedly commented
on Leacock's unique ability to combine theory and practice. I thank them—especially

William Askins, Geraldine Casey, Renee Llanusa-Cestero, Richard Lee, Annette Rubin-stein, Ethel Tobach, and Connie Sutton—and also Phyllis Gunther, Martha Livings-ton, June Nash, Ruby Rohrlich, Betty Rosoff, Anita Schwartz, Ethel Tobach, and Julius Trubowitz for sharing their memories of Leacock. I also thank the University of Ne-braska reviewers for their helpful comments.

7. For a complete bibliography of Leacock's publications, see Sutton (1993:141–149).

8. Regrettably, the series was never published for wider distribution. The titles of the individual readers indicate the themes she thought important for a unified theory of social science: 1. *Understanding, Perception, and Reality*; 2. *What Are Laws?—Concepts and Reality*; 3. *Unity, Diversity, and Levels of Integration*; 4. *Language, Understanding and Misun-derstanding*; 5. *The Emergence of Social Science*; 6. *Modern Social Science: The Analysis of Class in Relation to Political Power and Social Change*; 7. *Biology and Society: Society and Ideology as Lev-els of Integration*; and 10. *Theory, Data, and Analysis*. A total of ten volumes were planned; two were never completed.

9. The historical perspective, she wrote, "makes it possible to present basic prob-lems as first posed and as rephrased in different periods, thereby demonstrating a fundamental aspect of thought: its development over time in relation to specific, his-torical conditions . . . makes clear the somewhat fortuitous and arbitrary definition of the separate disciplines, and demonstrates the need for the integrated view of human behavior which has been lost though overspecialization . . . [and] avoids the problem of attempting to relate already fragmented fields and allows us to confront broad and fundamental issues directly" (1968, vol. 3:v).

10. Ethel Tobach, personal communication, February 1998.

11. For the role played by gender across social class lines, see Orenstein (1994).

12. For a well-documented example of the burdens placed on a contemporary urban school system, from the perspective of political economy, see Anyon (1997).

References

Adams, Jane, and D. Gorton. 2004. Southern Trauma: Revisiting Caste and Class in the Mississippi Delta. *American Anthropologist* 106(2):334–345.

Ahmed, Akbar S. 1980. *Pukhtun Economy and Society: Traditional Structure and Economic Development in a Tribal Society*. London: Routledge & Kegan Paul.

Allen, Frederick Lewis. 1952. *The Big Change: America Transforms Itself, 1900–1950*. New York: Harper & Brothers.

Anyon, Jean. 1997. *Ghetto Schooling: A Political Economy of Urban Educational Reform*. New York: Teachers College Press.

Archdeacon, Thomas J. 1983. *Becoming American: An Ethnic History*. New York: Free Press.

Arensberg, Conrad M. 1972. Culture as Behavior: Structure and Emergence. *Annual Review of Anthropology* 1:1–26.

———. 1983. Sol Kimball: Anthropologist of Our America. *Florida Journal of Anthropology* 9(1):7–11.

———. 1988[1937]. *The Irish Countryman: An Anthropological Study*. 2nd ed. Prospect Heights IL: Waveland.

Arensberg, Conrad M., and Solon T. Kimball. 1940. *Family and Community in Ireland*. Cambridge MA: Harvard University Press.

———. 1965. *Culture and Community*. New York: Harcourt, Brace, & World.

———. 2001[1940, 1968]. *Family and Community in Ireland*. 2nd ed., Cambridge MA: Harvard University Press, 1968. 3rd ed., Ennis, Ireland: CLASP, 2001.

Atwood, Mark. 1960. An Anthropological Approach to Administrative

Change: The Introduction of a Guidance Program in High School. PhD dissertation, Columbia University.

Baker, Lee D. 1998a. *From Savage to Negro: Anthropology and the Construction of Race, 1896–1954*. Berkeley and Los Angeles: University of California Press.

———. 1998b. Unraveling the Boasian Discourse: The Racial Politics of "Culture" in School Desegregation, 1944–54. *Transforming Anthropology* 7(1):15–32.

———. 2004. Franz Boas out of the Ivory Tower. *Anthropology Theory* 4(1):29–51.

Baldwin, James, and Margaret Mead. 1971. *A Rap on Race*. New York: Dell.

Barnouw, Victor. 1983. Coming to Print on Samoa. *Journal of Psychoanalytic Anthropology* 6:425–433.

Barth, Fredrik. 1959. *Political Leadership among Swat Pathans*. London: Athlone.

Bateson, Gregory. 1935. Music in New Guinea. *Eagle* 24:158–170.

———. 1936. *Naven*. Cambridge: Cambridge University Press.

———. 1971. Communication. In *The Natural History of the Interview*. Norman McQuown, ed. University of Chicago Microfilm Collection of Manuscripts in Cultural Anthropology, series 15, nos. 95–97.

———. 1972. *Steps to an Ecology of Mind*. New York: Ballantine.

———. 1976. For God's Sake, Margaret. *Co-Evolutionary Quarterly* 10:32–44.

———. 1991. *A Sacred Unity: Further Steps to an Ecology of Mind*. New York: HarperCollins.

Bateson, Gregory, and Margaret Mead. 1942. *Balinese Character: A Photographic Analysis*. Special Publications of the New York Academy of Sciences 2. New York: New York Academy of Sciences.

Bateson, Mary Catherine. 1984. *With a Daughter's Eye*. New York: Morrow.

Belo, Jane, ed. 1970. *Traditional Balinese Culture*. New York: Columbia University Press.

Benedict, Ruth. 1934a. Anthropology and the Abnormal. *Journal of General Psychology* 10:59–82.

———. 1934b. *Patterns of Culture*. Boston: Houghton Mifflin.

———. 1938. Continuities and Discontinuities in Cultural Conditioning. *Psychiatry* 1:161–167.

———. 1939. Some Comparative Data on Culture and Personality with Reference to the Promotion of Mental Health. In *Mental Health*. Forest Ray Moulton, ed., 245–249. American Association for the Advancement of Science, Publication no. 9. Washington DC: AAAS.

———. 1940. *Race: Science and Politics*. New York: Modern Age.

———. 1942a. Primitive Freedom. *Atlantic Monthly* 169:756–763.

———. 1942b. *Race and Cultural Relations: America's Answer to the Myth of a Master Race*. Problems in American Life, Unit no. 5. Washington DC: National Council for the Social Studies, National Association of Secondary-School Principals, National Education Association.

———. 1943a. Basic Plan for Rumania: Background and Suggestions for Psychological Warfare. Office of War Information. 16 pp. RFB Papers, Box 108, Vassar College Libraries Archives and Special Collections, Poughkeepsie NY.

———. 1943b. Recognition of Cultural Diversities in the Post-War World. *Annals of the American Academy of Political and Social Sciences* 228:107.

———. 1943c. Rumanian Culture and Behavior. Office of War Information. 63 pp. RFB Papers, Box 107, Vassar College Libraries Archives and Special Collections, Poughkeepsie NY.

———. 1943d. Transmitting Our Democratic Heritage in the Schools. *American Journal of Sociology* 48:722–727.

———. 1946a. *The Chrysanthemum and the Sword: Patterns of Japanese Culture*. Boston: Houghton Mifflin.

———. 1946b. The Growth of the Republic. MS prepared for the Grolier Encyclopedia, unpublished. 13 pp. RFB Papers, Box 54, Vassar College Libraries Archives and Special Collections, Poughkeepsie NY.

———. 1948. Patterns of American Culture. Lectures on American Life Series, Columbia University, February 21, 1948. 11 pp. RFB Papers, Box 58, Vassar College Libraries Archives and Special Collections, Poughkeepsie NY.

———. 1949. Remarks. In *Culture and Personality*. Stanfield Sargent and Marian W. Smith, eds. Proceedings of Interdisciplinary Conference, November 1947, 139. New York: Viking Fund.

———. 1952[1943]. *Thai Culture and Behavior*. Data Paper no.4, Southeast Asia Program. Ithaca: Cornell University. (Also available at the Institute for Intercultural Studies, New York, and RFB Papers, Box 110, Vassar

College Libraries Archives and Special Collections, Poughkeepsie NY.)

Benedict, Ruth, and Gene Weltfish. 1943. *The Races of Mankind*. Public Affairs Pamphlet no. 85. New York: Public Affairs Committee.

———. 1948. *In Henry's Backyard: The Races of Mankind*. New York: Henry Schuman.

Bennett, John W. 1946. Interpretation of Pueblo Culture: A Question of Values. *Southwest Journal of Anthropology* 2:361–374.

Berube, Maurice R., and Marilyn Gittell, eds. 1969. *Confrontation at Ocean Hill-Brownsville*. New York: Praeger.

Birdwhistell, Ray. 1970. *Kinesics and Context*. Philadelphia: University of Pennsylvania Press.

———. 1977. Some Discussions of Ethnography, Theory, and Method. In *About Bateson*. J. Brockman, ed. New York: Dutton.

Bix, Herbert P. 2000. *Hirohito and the Making of Modern Japan*. New York: HarperCollins.

Boas, Franz. 1887a. Museums of Ethnology and Their Classification. *Science* 9:587–589, 612–614.

———. 1887b. The Study of Geography. *Science* 9:137–141. Reprinted in Boas, 1940, *Race, Language, and Culture*, 639–647, and in Stocking, 1996, *"Volksgeist" as Method and Ethic*, 9–16.

———. 1895. Human Faculty as Determined by Race. *Proceedings of the American Association for the Advancement of Science* 43:301–347.

———. 1904. The History of Anthropology. *Science* 20:513–524.

———. 1911a. Introduction. In *Handbook of American Indian Languages*. Bureau of American Ethnology Bulletin 40:1–83. Washington DC: Government Printing Office.

———. 1911b. *The Mind of Primitive Man*. New York: Macmillan. Rev. ed., New York: Macmillan, 1938b. Reprint, New York: Macmillan, 1963.

———. 1912. *Changes in Bodily Form of Descendants of Immigrants*. New York: Columbia University Press.

———. 1928b. Foreword. In Mead, *Coming of Age in Samoa*.

———, ed. 1938a. *General Anthropology*. Boston: D. C. Heath.

———. 1945. *Race and Democratic Society*. New York: J. J. Augustin.

———. 1955[1927]. *Primitive Art*. New York: Dover.

———. 1962[1928a]. *Anthropology and Modern Life*. New York: W. W. Norton.

———. 1966a[1940]. The Aims of Anthropological Research. In Boas, *Race, Language, and Culture*, 243–259.

———. 1966b[1940]. *Race, Language, and Culture*. New York: Free Press.

Bock, Philip. 1980. *Continuities in Psychological Anthropology: A Historical Introduction*. San Francisco: W. H. Freeman.

Boon, James. 1986. Between-the-Wars Bali: Rereading the Relics. In Stocking, *Malinowski, Rivers, Benedict, and Others*, 218–247.

———. 1990. *Affinities and Extremes: Crisscrossing the Bittersweet Ethnology of East Indies History, Hindu-Balinese Culture, and Indo-European Allure*. Chicago: University of Chicago Press.

Bourguignon, Erika. 1991. Hortense Powdermaker, The Teacher. *Journal of Anthropological Research* 47:417–428.

Brady, Ivan, ed. 1983. Speaking in the Name of the Real. *American Anthropologist* 85:908–947.

Breitbart, Eric. 1997. *A World on Display*. Albuquerque: University of New Mexico Press.

Bryson, Lyman, and Louis Finkelstein, eds. 1942. *Science, Philosophy and Religion: A Symposium*. New York: Conference on Science, Philosophy and Religion in Their Relation to the Democratic Way of Life.

Burkholder, Zoë. 2005. Descending the Ivory Tower: Anthropologists and Public Education in New York City, 1939–1945. Paper presented at the Annual Meetings of the American Anthropological Association, Washington DC, December 2.

Burnett, Jaquetta Hill. 1968. Workflow versus Classroom Models of Academic Work. *Michigan Journal of Secondary Education* 9(2):14–23.

———. 1969. Ceremony, Rites and Economy in the Student System of an American High School. *Human Organization* 29(1):1–11.

Butler, Samuel. 1903. *The Way of All Flesh*. London: Grant Richards.

Caffrey, Margaret M. 1989. *Ruth Benedict: Stranger in This Land*. Austin: University of Texas Press.

Caplow, Theodore, and Reece J. McGee. 1958. *The Academic Marketplace*. New York: Basic Books.

Carrithers, Michael, and Caroline Humphrey, eds. 1991. Introduction. In *The*

Assembly of Listeners: Jains in Society. Cambridge: Cambridge University Press.

Cascy, Gerrie, and Ric Curtis. 2005. The Legacy of Eleanor Leacock and Contemporary Participatory Action Research: Alternative Approaches to the Study of Drugs and Crime in New York City. Paper presented at the Annual Meetings of the American Anthropological Association, Washington DC, December 1.

Cash, Wilbur J. 1941. *The Mind of the South.* New York: Knopf.

Cazden, Courtney B., Vera P. John, and Dell Hymes, eds. 1972. *Functions of Language in the Classroom.* New York: Teachers College Press.

Chambers, Erve. 1986. *Applied Anthropology: A Practical Guide.* Englewood Cliffs NJ: Prentice Hall.

Chapple, Eliot D., with the collaboration of Conrad M. Arensberg. 1940. Measuring Human Relations: An Introduction to the Study of the Interaction of Individuals. *Genetic Psychology Monographs* 22:3–147.

Chapple, Eliot D. 1970. *Culture and Biological Man: Explorations in Behavioral Anthropology.* New York: Holt, Rinehart & Winston.

———. 1979. *The Biological Foundations of Individuality and Culture.* Huntington NY: Robert E. Krieger.

———. 1980. The Unbounded Reaches of Anthropology as a Research Science, and Some Working Hypotheses. *American Anthropologist* 82:741–758.

Chapple, Eliot D., and Carleton Stevens Coon. 1942. *Principles of Anthropology.* New York: Henry Holt. Rev. ed., Huntington NY: Robert E. Krieger, 1978.

Cherneff, Jill B. R. 1991a. Introduction. In Cherneff, Legacy, 373–376.

———, ed. 1991b. The Legacy of Hortense Powdermaker. Theme issue, *Journal of Anthropological Research* 47(4).

Chicago Commission on Race Relations. 1922. *The Negro in Chicago: A Study of Race Relations and a Race Riot.* Chicago: University of Chicago Press.

Cohen, Yehudi. 1971. The Shaping of Men's Minds: Adaptations to Imperatives of Culture. In Wax et al., *Anthropological Perspectives on Education,* 19–50.

Cole, Douglas. 1999. *Franz Boas: The Early Years, 1858–1906.* Vancouver: Douglas and McIntyre.

Cole, Michael, Lois Hood, and Ray McDermott. 1978. *Ecological Niche Picking: Ecological Invalidity as an Axiom of Experimental Cognitive Psychology.* Laboratory of Comparative Human Cognition, Working Paper no. 14. New York: Rockefeller University.

Cole, Sally. 1994. Ruth Landes in Brazil: Writing, Race, and Gender in 1930s American Anthropology. In Landes, *City of Women,* vii–xxxiv.

———. 2003. *Ruth Landes: A Life in Anthropology.* Lincoln: University of Nebraska Press.

Covarrubias, Miguel. 1937. *The Island of Bali.* New York: Knopf.

Cremin, Lawrence. 1965. *The Genius of American Education.* New York: Vintage.

Darnell, Regna. 1990. *Edward Sapir: Linguist, Anthropologist, Humanist.* Los Angeles: University of California Press.

———. 1997. History of Anthropology in Historical Perspective. *Annual Review of Anthropology* 6:399–417.

———. 1998. *And Along Came Boas: Continuity and Revolution in Americanist Anthropology.* Amsterdam and Philadelphia: John Benjamins.

———. 2001. *Invisible Genealogies: A History of Americanist Anthropology.* Lincoln: University of Nebraska Press.

Darnell, Regna, and Frederic W. Gleach. 2002. Introduction. Special centennial issue, *American Anthropologist* 104(2):417–422.

Davis, Allison, Burleigh B. Gardner, and Mary R. Gardner. 1941. *Deep South: A Social Anthropological Study of Caste and Class.* Chicago: University of Chicago Press.

Dearborn, Mary. 1988. *Love in the Promised Land: The Story of Anzia Yezierska and John Dewey.* New York: Free Press.

de Munck, Victor C. 2002. Contemporary Issues and Challenges for Comparativists: An Appraisal. *Anthropological Theory* 2(1):5–19.

Deutsch, Martin. 1967. *The Disadvantaged Child: Selected Papers of Martin Deutsch and Associates.* New York: Basic Books.

Dewey, John. 1922. *Human Nature and Conduct.* New York: Henry Holt.

———. 1934. *Art as Experience.* New York: Minton Balch.

———. 1938. *Experience and Education.* New York: Macmillan.

———. 1940[1897]. My Pedogogic Creed. In *Education Today.* Joseph Ratner, ed. New York: G. P. Putnam's Sons.

———. 1944[1916]. *Democracy and Education.* New York: Free Press.

———. 1964[1899]. The School and Society. In *John Dewey on Education: Selected Writings.* Reginald D. Archambault, ed., 295–312. New York: Modern Library.

———. 1968. Creative Democracy—The Task before Us. In *The Philosopher of the Common Man: Essays in Honor of John Dewey to Celebrate His Eightieth Birthday.* New York: Greenwood.

de Zoete, Beryl, and Walter Spies. 1938. *Dance and Drama in Bali.* London: Faber & Faber.

Diamond, Stanley. 1969. *Primitive Views of the World.* New York: Columbia University Press.

———. 1971a. Epilogue. In Wax et al., *Anthropological Perspectives on Education,* 300–306.

———. 1971b. Tape's Last Krapp. Review of *A Rap on Race* by Margaret Mead and James Baldwin. *New York Review of Books,* December 2.

———, ed. 1980. *Theory and Practice: Essays Presented to Gene Weltfish.* The Hague: Mouton.

di Leonardo, Micaela. 2003. Margaret Mead and the Culture of Forgetting in Anthropology: A Response to Roscoe. *American Anthropologist* 105:592–595.

Dillon, Wilton S. 1980. Margaret Mead and Government. *American Anthropologist* 82:319–390.

Dollard, John. 1937. *Caste and Class in a Southern Town.* New Haven: Yale University Press.

Du Bois, W. E. B. 1899. *The Philadelphia Negro: A Social Study.* Series in Political Economy and Public Law, no. 14. Philadelphia: Published for the University of Pennsylvania.

Ebihara, May. 1985. American Ethnology in the 1930s: Contexts and Currents. In *Social Contexts of American Ethnology, 1840–1984.* June Helm, ed., 101–121. Washington DC: American Anthropological Association.

Eddy, Elizabeth M. 1969. *Becoming a Teacher: The Passage to Professional Status.* New York: Teachers College Press.

———. 1983. Review Essay: The Anthropology and Education Series, Solon T. Kimball, General Editor *Anthropology and Education Quarterly* 14(2):141–147.

———. 1985. Theory, Research, and Application in Educational Anthropology. *Anthropology and Education Quarterly* 16(2):83–104. Reprinted in *Education and Cultural Process: Anthropological Approaches.* 2nd ed. George Dearborn Spindler, ed., 5–25. Prospect Heights IL: Waveland, 1987.

Eddy, Elizabeth M., and William L. Partridge, eds. 1978. *Applied Anthropology in America.* New York: Columbia University Press.

Efron, David. 1941. *Gesture and Environment.* New York: Kings Crown. Reprinted with additions as *Race, Culture, and Gesture.* The Hague: Mouton, 1971.

Embree, Edwin R. 1943. The Educational Process as Applied in America. *American Journal of Sociology* 48:759–765.

Erikson, Erik. 1950. *Childhood and Society.* New York: W. W. Norton.

Feinberg, Richard. 1989. Margaret Mead and Samoa: Coming of Age in Fact and Fiction. *American Anthropologist* 91:656–663.

Foerstel, Leonora, and Angela Gilliam, eds. 1992. *Confronting the Margaret Mead Legacy: Scholarship, Empire, and the South Pacific.* Philadelphia: Temple University Press.

Fordham, Signithia. 1993. "Those Loud Black Girls:" (Black) Women, Silence, and Gender "Passing" in the Academy. *Anthropology and Education Quarterly* 24(1):3–32.

———. 1996. *Blacked Out: Dilemmas of Race, Identity, and Success at Capital High.* Chicago: University of Chicago Press.

Fordham, Signithia, and John U. Ogbu. 1986. Black Students' School Success: Coping with the "Burden of 'Acting White.'" *Urban Review* 18(3):176–206.

Frake, Charles. 1980. *Language and Cultural Description.* Stanford: Stanford University Press.

Fraser, Gertrude. 1991. Race, Class and Difference in Hortense Powdermaker's *After Freedom: A Cultural Study in the Deep South. Journal of Anthropological Research* 47:403–415.

Frazier, E. Franklin. 1939. *The Negro Family in the United States.* Chicago: University of Chicago Press.

Freed, Stanley A., and Ruth S. Freed. 1983. Clark Wissler and the Development of Anthropology in the United States. *American Anthropologist* 85(4):800–825.

Freeman, Derek. 1983. *Margaret Mead and Samoa.* Cambridge MA: Harvard University Press.

———. 1995. *Margaret Mead and the Heretic: The Making and Unmaking of an Anthropological Myth.* Baltimore: Penguin.

———. 1998. *The Fatal Hoaxing of Margaret Mead: A Historical Analysis of Her Samoan Research.* Boulder CO: Westview.

Fried, Morton. 1980. A Continent Found, a Universe Lost. In Diamond, *Theory and Practice,* 263–284.

Friedenberg, Edgar Z. 1969. What Are Our Schools Trying to Do? *New York Times Book Review,* Special Educational Supplement, September 4.

Fukui, Nanako. 1999. Background Research for *The Chrysanthemum and the Sword. Dialectical Anthropology* 24:173–180.

Gacs, Ute, Aisha Khan, Jerrie McIntyre, and Ruth Weinberg, eds. 1989. *Women Anthropologists: Selected Biographies.* Urbana: University of Illinois Press.

Gaster, Moses. 1915. *Rumanian Bird and Beast Stories.* London: Sidgwick & Jackson.

Gearing, Frederick O., and B. Allen Tindall. 1973. Anthropological Studies of the Educational Process. *Annual Review of Anthropology* 2:95–105.

Geertz, Clifford. 1973. *The Interpretation of Cultures.* New York: Basic Books.

———. 1980. *Negara: The Theater State in Nineteenth Century Bali.* Princeton: Princeton University Press.

———. 1988. *Works and Lives.* Stanford: Stanford University Press.

Geertz, Hildred. 1994. *Images of Power: Balinese Paintings Made for Gregory Bateson and Margaret Mead.* Honolulu: University of Hawaii Press.

Gilliam, Angela, and Lenore Foerstel. 1992. Margaret Mead's Contradictory Legacy. In Foerstel and Gilliam, *Confronting the Margaret Mead Legacy,* 101–156.

Gleason, Philip. 1983. Identifying Identity: A Semantic History. *Journal of American History* 69:910–931.

Goethe, Johann Wolfgang von. 1998. *Maxims and Reflections.* Peter Hutchinson, ed. Elisabeth Stopp, trans. London: Penguin.

Goffman, Erving. 1979. *Gender Advertisements.* Cambridge MA: Harvard University Press.

Goldfrank, Esther S. 1978. *Notes of an Undirected Life: As One Anthropologist Tells It.* New York: Queens College Press.

Goodall, Jane. 1986. *The Chimpanzees of Gombe: Patterns of Behavior*. Cambridge MA: Belknap.

Goodenough, Ward H. 2002. Anthropology in the 20th Century and Beyond. Special centennial issue, *American Anthropologist* 104(2):423–440.

Gordon, Deborah. 1992. The Politics of Ethnographic Authority: Race and Writing in the Ethnography of Margaret Mead and Zora Neale Hurston. In *Modernist Anthropology: From Fieldwork to Text*. Marc Manganaro, ed. Princeton: Princeton University Press.

Gould, Harold. 1971. Jules Henry, 1904–1969. *American Anthropologist* 73(3):788–797.

Grant, Nicole. 1995. From Margaret Mead's Field Notes: What Counted as "Sex" in Samoa? *American Anthropologist* 97:678–682.

Gravlee, Clarence C., H. Russell Bernard, and William R. Leonard. 2003. Heredity, Environment and Cranial Form: A Reanalysis of Boas's Immigrant Data. *American Anthropologist* 105(1):125–138.

Griffin, Patricia C. 1983. Field Work in Wales with Solon Kimball. *Florida Journal of Anthropology* 9(1):25–29.

Hagaman, Dianne. 1995. Connecting Cultures: Balinese Character and the Computer. In *The Cultures of Computing*. Susan Leigh Star, ed. Oxford: Blackwell.

Handler, Richard. 1986. Vigorous Male and Aspiring Female: Poetry, Personality, and Culture in Edward Sapir and Ruth Benedict. In *Stocking, Malinowski, Rivers, Benedict, and Others*, 127–155.

Harper, Kenn. 2000. *Give Me My Father's Body: The Life of Minik, the New York Eskimo*. New York: Simon & Schuster.

Harris, Marvin. 1968. *The Rise of Anthropological Theory*. New York: Thomas Crowell.

Hart, Mitchell B. 2003. Franz Boas as German, American, and Jew. In *German-Jewish Identities in America*. Christof Mauch and Joseph Salmons, eds. Madison WI: Max Kade Institute for German-American Studies.

Harwood, Ruth. 1965a. A Primary School for Boys in Chincha, Peru. Mimeograph. New York: Teachers College.

———. 1965b. A Primary School for Girls in Lima. Mimeograph. New York: Teachers College.

Henderson, L. J. 1936. *The Social Theory of Pareto*. Cambridge MA: Harvard University Press.

Henry, Jules. 1941. *Jungle People*. New York: J. J. Augustin.

———. 1949. Cultural Objectification of the Case History. *American Journal of Orthopsychiatry* 19:655–673.

———. 1951. The Inner Experience of Culture. *Psychiatry* 14:87–103.

———. 1952. Child Rearing, Culture and the Natural World. *Psychiatry* 15:261–271.

———. 1954a. The Formal Structure of a Psychiatric Hospital. *Psychiatry* 17:139–151.

———. 1954b. Laughter in Psychiatric Staff Conferences: A Sociopsychiatric Analysis. *American Journal of Orthopsychiatry* 24:175–184.

———. 1955. Culture, Education, and Communications Theory. In Spindler, *Education and Anthropology*, 188–207.

———. 1957. The Culture of Interpersonal Relations in a Therapeutic Institution for Emotionally Disturbed Children. *American Journal of Orthopsychiatry* 27:725–734.

———. 1960. A Cross-Cultural Outline of Education. *Current Anthropology* 1:267–305.

———. 1961. An Anthropologist's View of Curriculum Change. *Teacher's College Record* 62:541–549.

———. 1963. *Culture against Man*. New York: Random House.

———. 1965. Hope, Delusion, and Organization: Some Problems in the Motivation of Low Achievers. In *The Low Achiever in Mathematics*. OE Bulletin (U.S. Department of Health, Education and Welfare, Office of Education) 31:7–16.

———. 1966. A Theory for an Anthropological Analysis of American Culture. *Anthropological Quarterly* 39:90–109.

———. 1967. Sham. *North American Review*, May–June, 6–8.

———. 1971. *Pathways to Madness*. New York: Random House.

———. 1972. *On Education*. New York: Random House.

———. 1973. *On Sham, Vulnerability and Other Forms of Self-Destruction*. New York: Random House.

Henry, Jules, and Zunia Henry. 1944. *Doll Play of Pilagá Indian Children*. New

York: American Orthopsychiatric Association. Reprint, New York: Random House, 1974.

Herskovits, Melville. 1927. *The Negro and the Intelligence Tests*. Hanover NH: Sociological Press.

———. 1963[1911]. Introduction to Boas, *Mind of Primitive Man*.

Hier, Sean P., and Candace L. Kemp. 2002. Anthropological Stranger: The Intellectual Trajectory of Hortense Powdermaker. *Women's History Review* 11(2):253–271.

Hinsley, Curtis. 1981. *The Smithsonian and the American Indian: Making a Moral Anthropology in Victorian America*. Washington DC: Smithsonian Institution Press.

Holmes, Lowell Don. 1987. *Quest for the Real Samoa: The Mead/Freeman Controversy and Beyond*. South Hadley MA: Bergin and Garvey.

Howard, Alan. 1970. *Learning to Be Rotuman*. New York: Teachers College Press.

Howard, Jane. 1984. *Margaret Mead: A Life*. New York: Simon & Schuster.

Hyatt, Marshall. 1990. *Franz Boas, Social Activist: The Dynamics of Ethnicity*. New York: Greenwood.

Hymes, Dell, ed. 1974[1972]. *Reinventing Anthropology*. New York: Pantheon. Reprint, New York: Vintage, 1974. Reprint, with new introduction, Ann Arbor: University of Michigan Press, 1999.

———. 1982. To the Memory of Margaret Mead. In *Children in and out of School*. Perry Gilmore and Alan Glattmore, eds. Washington DC: Center for Applied Linguistics.

———. 1983. *Essays in the History of Linguistic Anthropology*. Amsterdam and Philadelphia: John Benjamins.

Ignatieff, Michael. 2001. *Human Rights Politics as Politics and Idolatry*. Princeton: Princeton University Press.

Isaia, Chief Malopa'upo. 1999. *Coming of Age in American Anthropology: Margaret Mead and Paradise*. Parkland FL: Universal Publishers.

Jensen, Gordon D., and Luh Ketut Suriyani. 1992. *The Balinese People: A Reinvestigation of Character*. New York: Oxford University Press.

Johnson, Charles Spurgeon. 1934. *Shadow of the Plantation*. Chicago: University of Chicago Press.

———. 1943. Education and the Cultural Process: Introduction to Sympo-
    sium. *American Journal of Sociology* 48(6):629–632.

John-Steiner, Vera, and Eleanor Leacock. 1979. Transforming the Structure of
    Failure. In *Educating All Our Children: An Imperative for Democracy*. Doxey
    A. Wilkerson, ed., 76–91. Westport CT: Mediax.

Joyce, James. 1939. *Finnegans Wake*. New York: Viking.

Kardiner, Abram, and Lionel Ovesay. 1951. *The Mark of Oppression: A Psychologi-
    cal Study of the American Negro*. New York: W. W. Norton.

Kelly, Lawrence C. 1985. Why Applied Anthropology Developed When It Did:
    A Commentary on People, Money and Changing Times, 1930–1945.
    In *Social Contexts of American Ethnology, 1840–1984*. June Helm, ed.,
    122–138. Washington DC: American Ethnological Society.

Kendon, Adam. 1990. *Conducting Interaction: Patterns of Behavior in Focused En-
    counters*. New York: Cambridge University Press.

Kent, Pauline. 1996. Misconceived Configurations of Ruth Benedict. *Japan
    Review* 7:33–60.

———. 1999. Japanese Perceptions of *The Chrysanthemum and the Sword*. *Dialec-
    tical Anthropology* 24(2):181–192.

Kimball, Solon T. 1955a. The Method of Natural History and Educational Re-
    search. In Spindler, *Education and Anthropology*, 82–88.

———. 1955b. Problems of Studying American Culture. *American Anthropolo-
    gist* 57(6):1131–1142.

———. 1955c. The Supreme Court Decision on Segregation: Educational
    Consequences. In Spindler, *Education and Anthropology*, 281–295.

———. 1956. American Culture in Saudi Arabia. *Transactions of the New York
    Academy of Sciences*, series 2, 18(5):469–484.

———. 1960a. Introduction. In van Gennep, *Rites of Passage*.

———. 1960b. Primary Education in Brazil. *Comparative Education Review*
    4(1):49–54. Reprinted and expanded as chapter 15 in Kimball 1974,
    189–199.

———. 1963. Communication Modalities as a Function of Social Rela-
    tionships. *Transactions of the New York Academy of Sciences*, series 2,
    25(4):459–468. Reprinted as chapter 10, Communication Behavior
    as a Function of Social Structure, in Kimball 1974, 113–123.

———. 1966. Individualism and the Formation of Values. *Journal of Applied*

Behavioral Science 2(4):465–482. Reprinted as chapter 11 in Kimball 1974, 125–138.

———. 1968. Arnold van Gennep. *International Encyclopedia of the Social Sciences* 6:113–114. New York: Macmillan.

———. 1972. Learning a New Culture. In *Crossing Cultural Boundaries.* Solon T. Kimball and James B. Watson, eds. San Francisco: Chandler.

———. 1974. *Culture and the Educative Process: An Anthropological Perspective.* New York: Teachers College Press.

———. 1975. Interaction Analysis Reformulated. Review of *Interaction and Social Structure: Approaches to Semiotics* by Orvis Collins and June M. Collins (The Hague: Mouton, 1973). *Semiotica* 14(2):189–196.

Kimball, Solon T., and James E. McClellan Jr. 1962. *Education and the New America.* New York: Random House.

Kimball, Solon T., and Marion B. Pearsall. 1954. *The Talladega Story: A Study of Community Process.* Tuscaloosa: University of Alabama Press.

Kimball, Solon T., and John H. Provinse. 1942. Navajo Social Organization in Land Use Planning. *Applied Anthropology: Problems of Human Organization* 1(4):18–25.

———. 1946. Building New Communities during War Time. *American Sociological Review* 11(4):396–409.

Kimball, Solon T., and Charles Wagley. 1974. Race and Culture in School and Community (Final Report: Project no. 2-0629; Grant no. OEG-0-72-3942). U.S. Department of Health, Education and Welfare, Office of Education, National Institute of Education.

Klineberg, Otto. 1935. *Race Differences.* New York: Harper & Brothers.

Kuper, Adam. 1973. *Anthropologists and Anthropology: The British School, 1922–1972.* London: Allen Lane.

Kurent, Heather Paul. 1982. Frances R. Donovan and the Chicago School of Sociology: A Case Study in Marginality. PhD dissertation, American Studies, University of Maryland.

Lamphere, Louise. 1989. Feminist Anthropology: The Legacy of Elsie Clews Parson. *American Ethnologist* 16:518–533.

Landes, Ruth. 1937. *Ojibwa Sociology.* New York: Columbia University Press. Reprint, New York: AMS Press, 1969.

———. 1938. *The Ojibwa Woman.* New York: Columbia University Press.

———. 1947. *The City of Women*. New York: Macmillan. Reprint, Albuquerque: University of New Mexico Press, 1994.

———. 1965. *Culture in American Education: Anthropological Approaches to Minority and Dominant Groups in the Schools*. New York: John Wiley & Sons.

———. 1968a. *The Mystic Lake Sioux: Sociology of the Mdewakantonwan Sioux*. Madison: University of Wisconsin Press.

———. 1968b. *Ojibwa Religion and the Midewiwin*. Madison: University of Wisconsin Press.

———. 1970a. *The Prairie Potawatomi: Tradition and Ritual in the Twentieth Century*. Madison: University of Wisconsin Press.

———. 1970b. A Woman Anthropologist in Brazil. In *Women in the Field*. Peggy Golde, ed., 119–139. Berkeley: University of California Press.

Lansing, J. Stephen. 1995. *The Balinese*. Fort Worth TX: Harcourt Brace College.

Lapsley, Hilary. 1999. *Margaret Mead and Ruth Benedict: The Kinship of Women*. Amherst: University of Massachusetts Press.

Leacock, Eleanor Burke. 1949a. Harrison Indian Childhood. In Smith, *Indians of the Urban Northwest*, 206–242.

———. 1949b. The Seabird Community. In Smith, *Indians of the Urban Northwest*, 195–205.

———. 1954. *The Montagnais "Hunting Territory" and the Fur Trade*. American Anthropological Association. Memoir 78.

———, with Louis Menashe, Helmut Gruber, and I. Leonard Leab. 1968. *Science Theory and Method: An Integrated Historical Introduction*. 8 vols. Brooklyn NY: Polytechnic Institute Department of Social Sciences.

———. 1969. *Teaching and Learning in City Schools*. New York: Basic Books.

———. 1970. Education, Socialization, and the "Culture of Poverty." In Rubinstein, *Schools against Children*, 192–210.

———, ed. 1971a. *The Culture of Poverty: A Critique*. New York: Basic Books.

———. 1971b. Theoretical and Methodological Problems in the Study of Schools. In Wax et al., *Anthropological Perspectives on Education*, 169–179.

———. 1972a. At Play in African Villages. *Natural History*, December, 60–66.

———. 1972b. Introduction. In Frederick Engels, *The Origin of the Family, Private Property and the State*. Eleanor Leacock, ed., 1–67. New York: International Press.

———, with Jacqueline Goodman. 1976. Montagnais Marriage and the Jesuits in the Seventeenth Century. *Western Canadian Journal of Anthropology* 6(3):77–91.

———. 1977. Education in Africa: Myths and Modernization. In *The Anthropological Study of Education*. Francis Ianni and Craig Calhoun, eds., 230–250. The Hague: Mouton.

———. 1978. Women's Status in Egalitarian Society. *Current Anthropology* 19(2):247–275.

———. 1980. Politics, Theory and Racism in the Study of Black Children. In Diamond, *Theory and Practice*, 153–178.

———. 1981. *Myths of Male Dominance*. New York: Monthly Review.

———. 1982. Marxism and Anthropology. In *The Left Academy: Marxist Scholars on American Campuses*. Bertell Ollman and Edward Vernoff, eds., 242–276. New York: McGraw-Hill.

———. 1985[1972]. Abstract versus Concrete Speech: A False Dichotomy. In Cazden et al., *Functions of Language in the Classroom*, 111–134.

———. 1987. Theory and Ethics in Applied Anthropology. In *Cities of the United States*. Leith Mullings, ed., 317–336. New York: Columbia University Press.

———. 1992. Anthropologists in Search of a Culture: Margaret Mead, Derek Freeman, and All the Rest of Us. In Foerstel and Gilliam, *Confronting the Margaret Mead Legacy*, 3–30.

———. 1993a. Being an Anthropologist. In C. Sutton, *From Labrador to Samoa*, 1–31.

———. 1993b. Postscript: The Problems of Youth in Contemporary Samoa. In C. Sutton, *From Labrador to Samoa*, 115–130.

Leacock, Eleanor, Nancie Gonzalez, and Gilbert Kushner, eds. 1975. *Training Opportunities for New Opportunities in Applied Anthropology*. Washington DC: American Anthropological Association.

Lee, Dorothy. 1949. Ruth Fulton Benedict (1887–1948). *Journal of American Folklore* 62:345–47.

Lee, Richard B., and Richard H. Daly. 1993. Eleanor Leacock, Labrador, and the Politics of Gatherer-Hunters. In C. Sutton, *From Labrador to Samoa*, 33–46.

Leemon, Thomas A. 1972. *The Rites of Passage in a Student Culture: A Study of the Dynamics of Transition*. New York: Teachers College Press.

Lesser, Alexander. 1981. Franz Boas. In Silverman, *Totems and Teachers*, 1–34.

Lewin, Kurt. 1951. *A Dynamic Theory of Personality*. New York: McGraw-Hill.

Lewis, Herbert S. 1999. The Misrepresentation of Anthropology and Its Consequences. *American Anthropologist* 100:716–731.

Lewis, Oscar. 1970. *Anthropological Essays*. New York: Random House.

Li An-che. 1937. Zuñi: Some Observations and Queries. *American Anthropologist* 39:62–76.

Liss, Julia. 1996. German Culture and German Science in the *Bildung* of Franz Boas. In Stocking, *"Volksgeist" as Method and Ethic*, 155–184.

Locke, Alain, ed. 1925. *The New Negro*. New York: Albert and Charles Boni.

Locke, Alain, and Bernhard J. Stern, eds. 1942. *When Peoples Meet: A Study in Race and Culture Contacts*. New York: Committee on Workshops, Progressive Education Association.

Lummis, Douglas. 1980. Ruth Benedict's Obituary for Japan: A New Look at *The Chrysanthemum and the Sword*. *Kyoto Review* 12:34–68.

Lynd, Robert S., and Helen Merrill Lynd. 1929. *Middletown, a Study in Contemporary American Culture*. New York: Harcourt, Brace.

MacDonald, Kevin. 1998. *The Culture of Critique: An Evolutionary Analysis of Jewish Involvement in Twentieth-Century Intellectual and Political Movements*. Westport CT: Praeger.

Mahon, Maureen. 2000. The Visible Evidence of Cultural Producers. *Annual Review of Anthropology* 29:467–492.

Mahony, Mary Ann. 1996. Review of *The City of Women* by Ruth Landes. H-Net, April.

Malinowski, Bronislaw. 1927. *Sex and Repression in Savage Society*. London: Routledge & Kegan Paul.

———. 1935. *Coral Gardens and Their Magic*. 2 vols. London: George Allen & Unwin.

Marcus, George E., and Michael Fischer. 1986. *Anthropology and Cultural Critique: An Experimental Moment in the Social Sciences*. Chicago: University of Chicago Press.

Maslow, Abraham H., and J. J. Honigman. 1970. Synergy: Some Notes of Ruth Benedict. *American Anthropologist* 72:320–333.

Mason, Otis Tufton. 1894. *Women's Share in Primitive Culture*. New York: D. Appleton.

McMillan, Robert. 1986. The Study of Anthropology, 1931 to 1937, Columbia University and the University of Chicago. PhD dissertation, History, York University, Toronto, Canada.

McPhee, Colin. 1947. *A House in Bali*. London: Victor Gollancz.

———. 1955. Music and Children in Bali. In *Children and Contemporary Cultures*. Margaret Mead and Martha Wolfenstein, eds. Chicago: University of Chicago Press.

Mead, George Henry. 1934. *Mind, Self, and Society*. Chicago: University of Chicago Press.

Mead, Margaret. 1927. Group Intelligence Tests and Linguistic Disability among Italian Children. *School and Society* 25:465–468.

———. 1928. *Coming of Age in Samoa*. New York: Morrow.

———. 1930a. *Growing Up in New Guinea*. New York: Morrow.

———. 1930b. *Social Organization of Manu'a*. Bernice P. Bishop Museum Bulletin 76. Honolulu: Bernice P. Bishop Museum.

———. 1932. *The Changing Culture of an Indian Tribe*. New York: Columbia University Press.

———. 1934. *Kinship in the Admiralty Islands*. Anthropological Papers 34, pt. 2: 183–358. New York: American Museum of Natural History.

———. 1935. *Sex and Temperament in Three Primitive Societies*. New York: Morrow.

———. 1938–49. *The Mountain Arapesh*. 5 vols. Anthropological Papers. New York: American Museum of Natural History.

———. 1942. *And Keep Your Powder Dry*. New York: Morrow. Reprint, New York: Berghahn, 2000.

———. 1943. Our Educational Emphasis in Primitive Perspective. *American Journal of Sociology* 48:633–639.

———. 1949. *Male and Female*. New York: Morrow.

———. 1951. *The School in American Culture*. Cambridge MA: Harvard University Press.

———. 1956. *New Lives for Old: Cultural Transformation—Manus, 1928–53*. New York: Morrow.

———. 1958. Thinking Ahead: Why Is Education Obsolete. *Harvard Business Review* 36:23–30.

———, ed. 1959a. *An Anthropologist at Work: Writings of Ruth Benedict*. Boston: Houghton Mifflin.

———. 1959b. *People and Places*. Cleveland: World.

———. 1968. Concluding Remarks. In *Science and the Concept of Race*. Margaret Mead, Theodosius Dobzhansky, Ethel Tobach, and Robert Light, eds. New York: Columbia University Press.

———. 1972. *Blackberry Winter*. New York: Morrow.

———. 1976. Towards a Human Science. *Science* 191:903–909.

———. 1977. *Letters from the Field, 1925–1975*. New York: Harper & Row.

———. 1978a. The Evocation of Psychologically Relevant Responses in Ethnological Field Work. In Spindler, *The Making of Psychological Anthropology*.

———. 1978b. The Sepik as a Cultural Area. *Anthropological Quarterly* 51:69–75.

———. 1979. *Margaret Mead, Some Personal Views*. Rhoda Metraux, ed. New York: Walker.

Mead, Margaret, and Paul Byers. 1968. *The Small Conference*. The Hague: Mouton.

Mead, Margaret, and Frances Cooke Macgregor. 1951. *Growth and Culture: A Photographic Study of Balinese Childhood*. New York: G. P. Putnam's Sons.

Mead, Margaret, and Rhoda Metraux, eds. 1953. *The Study of Culture at a Distance*. Chicago: University of Chicago Press.

———. 1978. *An Interview with Santa Claus*. New York: Walker.

Mintz, Sidney. 1981. Ruth Benedict. In Silverman, *Totems and Teachers*, 141–170.

Modell, Judith S. 1983. *Ruth Benedict: Patterns of a Life*. Philadelphia: University of Pennsylvania Press.

———. 1999. The Wall of Shame: Ruth Benedict's Accomplishment in *The Chrysanthemum and the Sword*. *Dialectical Anthropology* 24:193–215.

Moore, Alexander. 1967. *Realities of the Urban Classroom: Observations in Elementary Schools*. New York: Anchor Doubleday.

———. 1973. *Life Cycles in Atchalán: The Diverse Careers of Certain Guatemalans.*
New York: Teachers College Press. Rev. ed., Los Angeles: Ethno-
graphics Press, University of Southern California, 1999.

———. 1984. Obituary, Solon Toothaker Kimball (1909–1982). *American Anthropologist* 86(2):386–393.

———. 1991. Discipline or Profession: Anthropology and Its Guilds. *Reviews
in Anthropology* 18:115–125.

———. 1998. *Cultural Anthropology: The Field Study of Human Beings.* 2nd ed.
San Diego: Collegiate Press.

Morawski, J. G. 1986. Organizing Knowledge and Behavior at Yale's Institute
of Human Relations. *Isis* 77:219–242.

Morgan, Lewis Henry. 1963[1877]. *Ancient Society.* Eleanor Leacock, ed. New
York and Cleveland: World.

Mullings, Leith P. 1993. Race, Inequality, and Transformation: Building on
the Work of Eleanor Leacock. *Identities* 1(1):123–129.

Murray, Stephen O. 1994. *Theory Groups and the Study of Language in North America.* Amsterdam and Philadelphia: John Benjamins.

Nader, Laura. 1997. The Phantom Factor: Impact of the Cold War on Anthropology. In *The Cold War and the University: Toward an Intellectual History
of the Postwar Years* by Noam Chomsky et al., 107–146. New York: New
Press.

———. 2002. Missing Links: A Commentary on Ward H. Goodenough's
Moving Article "Anthropology in the 20th Century and Beyond."
Special centennial issue, *American Anthropologist* 104(2):441–449.

Neville, Gwen Kennedy. 1987. *Kinship and Pilgrimage: Rituals of Reunion in American Protestant Culture.* New York: Oxford University Press.

———. 1994. *The Mother Town: Civic Ritual, Symbol and Experience in the Borders of
Scotland.* New York: Oxford University Press.

Newman, Denis, Peg Griffin, and Michael Cole. 1989. *The Construction Zone.*
New York: Cambridge University Press.

Newman, Louise. 1996. Coming of Age, but Not in Samoa: Some Reflections
on Margaret Mead's Legacy for Western Liberal Feminism. *American
Quarterly* 48:233–272.

New York Times. 1953. Columbia Is Dropping Dr. Weltfish, Leftist. April 1: Section L, 1, 19.

Ogbu, John. 1992. Understanding Cultural Diversity and Learning. *Educational Researcher* 21(8):5–14.

Orans, Martin. 1996. *Not Even Wrong: Margaret Mead, Derek Freeman, and the Samoans.* Novato CA: Chandler & Sharp.

Orenstein, Peggy. 1994. *Schoolgirls: Young Women, Self-Esteem & the Confidence Gap.* Garden City NY: Doubleday.

Park, George, and Alice Park. 1989. Ruth Schlossberg Landes. In Gacs et al., *Women Anthropologists,* 208–214.

Parsons, Elsie Clews. 1906. *The Family.* New York: G. P. Putnam's Sons.

Pathé, Ruth E. 1989. Gene Weltfish. In Gacs et al., *Women Anthropologists,* 372–381.

Patmore, Derek. 1939. *Invitation to Roumania.* London: Macmillan.

Patterson, Thomas C. 2001. *A Social History of Anthropology in the United States.* New York: Berg.

Pelissier, Catherine. 1991 The Anthropology of Teaching and Learning. *Annual Review of Anthropology* 20:75–95.

Perry, Helen Swick. 1982. *Psychiatrist of America: The Life of Harry Stack Sullivan.* Cambridge MA: Belknap.

Piers, Gerhart, and Milton Singer. 1953. *Shame and Guilt: A Psychoanalytic and Cultural Study.* Springfield IL: Charles C. Thomas. Reprint, New York: W. W. Norton, 1971.

Pollak, Richard. 1997. *The Creation of Dr. B: A Biography of Bruno Bettelheim.* New York: Simon & Schuster.

Pollmann, Tessel. 1990. Margaret Mead's Balinese: The Fitting Symbols of the American Dream. *Indonesia* 49:1–36.

Powdermaker, Hortense. 1924. From the Diary of a Girl Organizer. *The Amalgamated Illustrated Almanac—1924,* 46–47. New York: Amalgamated Clothing Workers of America, Education Department.

———. 1933. *Life in Lesu: The Study of a Melanesian Society in New Ireland.* New York: W. W. Norton.

———. 1939. *After Freedom: A Cultural Study in the Deep South.* New York: Viking. Reprint, Madison: University of Wisconsin Press, 1993.

———. 1941. Review of *Race: Science and Politics* by Ruth Benedict. *American Anthropologist* 43:474–475.

———. 1943a. The Channeling of Negro Aggression by the Cultural Process. *American Journal of Sociology* 48(6):750–758.

———. 1943b. Review of *When Peoples Meet: A Study in Race and Culture Contacts* by Alain Locke and Bernhard J. Stern. *American Anthropologist* 45:476.

———. 1944a. The Anthropological Approach to the Problem of Modifying Race Attitudes. *Journal of Negro Education* 13:295–302.

———. 1944b. *Probing Our Prejudices.* New York: Harper & Brothers.

———. 1945. An Anthropologist Looks at the Race Question. *Social Action* 11(2):5–13.

———. 1950. *Hollywood, the Dream Factory: An Anthropologist Looks at the Movie-Makers.* Boston: Little, Brown.

———, ed. 1953. *Mass Communications Seminar.* New York: Wenner-Gren Foundation for Anthropological Research.

———. 1962. *Copper Town: Changing Africa, the Human Condition on the Rhodesian Copperbelt.* New York: Harper and Row.

———. 1966. *Stranger and Friend: The Way of an Anthropologist.* New York: W. W. Norton.

———. 1967. An Agreeable Man. Letter to the Editor. *New York Review of Books,* November 9, http://www.nybooks.com/articles/11916, accessed November 2, 2005.

Powdermaker, Hortense, and Joseph Semper. 1938. Education and Occupation among New Haven Negroes. *Journal of Negro History* 23:200–215.

Price, David. 2004. *Threatening Anthropology: McCarthyism and the FBI Surveillance of Activist Anthropologists.* Durham NC: Duke University Press.

———. 2005. Anthropology as Weapon: The Use and Abuses of Anthropology at the OSS's Research and Analysis Division. Paper presented at the Annual Meetings of the American Anthropological Association, Washington DC, December 2.

Radin, Paul. 1987[1933]. *The Method and Theory of Ethnology.* South Hadley MA: Bergin & Garvey.

Raines, Theron. 2002. *Rising to the Light: A Portrait of Bruno Bettelheim.* New York: Knopf.

Randall, John Herman. 1953. John Dewey, 1859–1952. *Journal of Philosophy* 50:5–13.

Rapp, Rayna. 1993. Eleanor Leacock's Contribution to the Study of Gender. In C. Sutton, *From Labrador to Samoa*, 87–94.

Rappaport, Roy A. 1986. Desecrating the Holy Women. *American Scholar* 55:313–347.

Redfield, Robert. 1941. *The Folk Culture of Yucatán*. Chicago: University of Chicago Press.

Reed, Gay. 1993. Deprovincialization: Margaret Mead on Education. Paper presented at the Annual Meeting of the American Educational Studies Association, Chicago.

Reik, Theodor. 1941. *Masochism in Modern Man*. Margaret H. Beigel and Gertrud M. Kurth, trans. New York: Farrar & Rinehart.

Richie, Alexandra. 1998. *Faust's Metropolis: A History of Berlin*. New York: Carroll & Graf.

Rigdon, Susan. 1988. *The Culture Façade: Art, Science, and Politics in the Work of Oscar Lewis*. Urbana: University of Illinois Press.

Rockefeller, Steven C. 1991. *John Dewey: Religious Faith and Democratic Humanism*. New York: Columbia University Press.

Roscoe, Paul. 2003. Margaret Mead, Reo Fortune, and Mountain Arapesh Warfare. *American Anthropologist* 105:581–591.

Rubinstein, Annette T., ed. 1970. *Schools against Children: The Case for Community Control*. New York: Monthly Review Press.

Sapir, Edward. 1934. The Emergence of the Concept of Personality in a Study of Cultures. *Journal of Social Psychology* 5:408–415.

———. 1994. *The Psychology of Culture: A Course of Lectures*. J. Irvine, ed. Berlin: Mouton de Gruyter.

Schmidt, Dwight Leigh. 1983. Memories of Solon T. Kimball. *Florida Journal of Anthropology* 9(1):31–36.

Schneider, David. 1983. The Coming of a Sage to Samoa. *Natural History*, June, 4, 6, 10.

———. 1995. *Schneider on Schneider: The Conversion of the Jews and Other Anthropological Stories*. Richard Handler, ed. Durham: Duke University Press.

Schneider, Jo Anne. 2001. Introduction: Social Welfare and Welfare Reform. *American Anthropologist* 103(3):705–713.

Shankman, Paul. 1996. The History of Samoan Sexual Conduct and the Mead-Freeman Controversy. *American Anthropologist* 98:555–567.

Silverman, Sydel, ed. 1981. *Totems and Teachers: Perspectives on the History of Anthropology*. New York: Columbia University Press. 2nd ed., published as *Totems and Teachers: Key Figures in the History of Anthropology*. Walnut Creek CA: AltaMira Press, 2003.

———. 1989. Hortense Powdermaker (1896–1970). In Gacs et al., *Women Anthropologists*, 291–296.

———. 2004. Hollywood and American Anthropology at Mid-Century. Unpublished paper.

Smith, Marian W., ed. 1949. *Indians of the Urban Northwest*. New York: Columbia University Press.

———. 1959. Boas' "Natural History" Approach to Field Method. In *The Anthropology of Franz Boas*. Walter Goldschmidt, ed., 46–60. American Anthropological Association. Memoir 89.

Sparks, Corey S., and Richard L. Jantz. 2002. A Reassessment of Human Cranial Plasticity: Boas Revisited. *Proceedings of the National Academy of Sciences* 99(23):14636–14639.

Spindler, George D., ed. 1955. *Education and Anthropology*. Stanford CA: Stanford University Press.

———, ed. 1974. *Education and Cultural Process: Toward an Anthropology of Education*. New York: Holt, Rinehart, & Winston.

———, ed. 1978. *The Making of Psychological Anthropology*. Berkeley: University of California Press.

Steward, Julian H., et al. 1956. *The People of Puerto Rico: A Study in Social Anthropology*. Urbana: University of Illinois Press.

Stocking, George W., Jr. 1968. *Race, Culture and Evolution: Essays in the Historiography of Anthropology*. New York: Free Press.

———. 1974a. Benedict, Ruth Fulton. In *Dictionary of American Biography*, Supplement 4 (1946–1950): 70–73.

———, ed. 1974b. *The Making of American Anthropology, 1883–1911*. New York: Basic Books.

———, ed. 1986. *Malinowski, Rivers, Benedict, and Others: Essays on Culture and Personality*. History of Anthropology vol. 4. Madison: University of Wisconsin Press.

———. 1992. *The Ethnographer's Magic and Other Essays in the History of Anthropology*. Madison: University of Wisconsin Press.

———, ed. 1996. "*Volksgeist*" *as Method and Ethic: Essays on Boasian Ethnography and the German Anthropological Tradition.* History of Anthropology vol. 8. Madison: University of Wisconsin Press.

———. 2001. *Delimiting Anthropology: Occasional Inquiries and Reflections.* Madison: University of Wisconsin Press.

———. 2002. Introduction. In *American Anthropology, 1921–1945: Papers from the "American Anthropologist."* George W. Stocking Jr., ed. Lincoln: University of Nebraska Press.

Sullivan, Gerald. 1999. *Margaret Mead, Gregory Bateson, and Highland Bali: Fieldwork Photographs of Bayung Gedé.* Chicago: University of Chicago Press.

Suryani, Luh Ketut, and Gordon D. Jensen. 1992. *Trance and Possession in Bali: A Window on Multiple Personality, Possession Disorder, and Suicide.* New York: Oxford University Press.

Sutton, Constance, ed. 1993. *From Labrador to Samoa: Theory and Practice of Eleanor Burke Leacock.* Arlington VA: American Anthropological Association.

Sutton, Nina. 1995. *Bruno Bettelheim: The Other Side of Madness.* David Sharp, trans. London: Duckworth.

Suzuki, Peter T. 1985. Ruth Benedict, Robert Hashima, and *The Chrysanthemum and the Sword. Research: Contributions to Interdisciplinary Anthropology* 3:55–69.

———. 1999. Overlooked Aspects of *The Chrysanthemum and the Sword. Dialectical Anthropology* 24:217–231.

Szwed, J. F. 1974. An Anthropological Dilemma: The Politics of Afro-American Culture. In Hymes, *Reinventing Anthropology,* 153–181.

Thompson, Clara. 1950. *Psychoanalysis: Evolution and Development.* New York: Hermitage House.

Thwaites, Reuben Gold, ed. 1896–1901. *The Jesuit Relations and Allied Documents, 1610–1791: Travels and Explorations of the Jesuit Missionaries in New France, 1610–1791. The original French, Latin, and Italian texts, with English translations and notes.* 73 vols. Cleveland: Burrows Brothers.

Toulmin, Stephen. 1984. The Evolution of Margaret Mead. *New York Review of Books* 31(19; December 6):3–9.

Trautmann, Thomas R. 1987. *Lewis Henry Morgan and the Invention of Kinship.* Berkeley: University of California Press.

Tyack, David, and Elisabeth Hansot. 1990. *Learning Together: A History of Coeducation in American Schools*. New Haven: Yale University Press.

Vacaresco, Helene. 1908. *The Bard of the Dimbovitza: Roumanian Folk-songs*. Carmen Sylva and Alma Strettell, trans. Rev. ed., London: Harper & Brothers.

Valentine, Charles. 1968. *Culture and Poverty*. Chicago: University of Chicago Press.

Valentine, Lisa, and Regna Darnell, eds. 1999. *Theorizing the Americanist Tradition*. Toronto: University of Toronto Press.

van Gennep, Arnold. 1960. *Rites of Passage*. Chicago: University of Chicago Press.

van Ginkel, Rob. 1992. Typically Dutch: Ruth Benedict on the National Character of Netherlanders. *Netherlands Journal of Social Sciences* 28:50–71.

Van Willigen, John. 1986. *Applied Anthropology: An Introduction*. South Hadley MA: Bergin & Garvey.

Varenne, Hervé. 1984. Collective Representation in American Anthropological Conversations about Culture. *Current Anthropology* 25:281–300.

———. 2000. Introduction: America According to Margaret Mead. In Mead, *And Keep Your Powder Dry*.

Varenne, Hervé, and Ray McDermott. 1998. *Successful Failure: The Schools America Builds*. Boulder CO: Westview.

Visweswaran, Kamala. 1997. Histories of Feminist Ethnography. *Annual Review of Anthropology* 26:591–621.

Vygotsky, Lev. 1987. *The Collected Works of L. S. Vygotsky*. Vol. 1: *Problems of General Psychology* (including *Thinking and Speech*). Robert W. Rieber and Aaron S. Carton, eds., Norris Minick, trans. New York: Plenum.

Wade, Nicholas. 2002. A New Look at Old Data May Discredit a Theory on Race. *New York Times*, October 8, F2–F3.

Wagley, Charles. 1977. *Welcome of Tears: The Tapirapé of Central Brazil*. New York: Oxford.

Ware, Caroline F. 1935. *Greenwich Village, 1920–1930: A Comment on American Civilization in the Post-war Years*. New York: Columbia University Press.

Wax, Murray. 1956. The Limitations of Boas's Anthropology. *American Anthropologist* 58:63–74.

Wax, Murray, Stanley Diamond, and Fred O. Gearing, eds. 1971. *Anthropological Perspectives on Education*. New York: Basic Books.

Weiner, Annette. 1995. Culture and Our Discontents. *American Anthropologist* 97:14–21.

Weltfish, Gene. 1930. Prehistoric North American Basketry Techniques and Modern Distributions. *American Anthropologist* 32:435–495.

———. 1936a. *Caddoan Texts. Part 1: Pawnee South Bend Dialect*. Publications of the American Ethnological Society, vol. 17. Washington DC: American Ethnological Society. Reprint, New York: AMS, 1974.

———. 1936b. The Vision Story of Fox Boy: A South Pawnee Text. *International Journal of American Linguistics* 9(1):44–75.

———. 1945. Science and Prejudice. *Scientific Monthly* 61:210–212.

———. 1953. *The Origins of Art*. Indianapolis: Bobbs Merrill.

———. 1956. The Perspective for Fundamental Research in Anthropology. *Philosophy of Science* 23:63–76.

———. 1959. The Question of Ethnic Identity: An Ethnological Approach. *Ethnohistory* 6:321–346.

———. 1960a. The Anthropologist and the Question of the Fifth Dimension. In *Culture in History: Essays in Honor of Paul Radin*. Stanley Diamond, ed., 160–180. New York: Columbia University Press.

———. 1960b. The Ethnic Dimension of Human History: Pattern or Patterns of Culture. In *Selected Papers of the Fifth International Congress of Anthropological and Ethnological Sciences*. Anthony F. C. Wallace, ed., 207–218. Philadelphia: University of Pennsylvania Press.

———. 1962. Some Main Trends in American Anthropology in 1961. *The Annals of the American Academy of Political and Social Sciences* 339:171–176.

———. 1965. *The Lost Universe*. New York: Basic Books.

———. 1967. Project: New Vistas on Work and Leisure: Statement of Purpose, April. ACIM Publication 1(2). Morristown NJ: American Civilization Institute of Morristown.

———. 1968a. The Aims of Anthropology: An American Perspective. *Current Anthropology* 9:305–306.

———. 1968b. Project: New Vistas on Work and Leisure: Progress Report—1968. ACIM Publication 1(3). Morristown NJ: American Civilization Institute of Morristown.

———. 1979. The Anthropology of Work. In *Toward a Marxist Anthropology*. Stanley Diamond, ed., 215–256. The Hague: Mouton.

———. 1980. Franz Boas: The Academic Response. In *Anthropology: Ancestors and Heirs*. Stanley Diamond, ed., 123–147. The Hague: Mouton.

Weltfish, Gene, and Alexander Lesser. 1932. Composition of the Caddoan Linguistic Stock. *Smithsonian Miscellaneous Collections* 87(6):1–15.

Weltfish, Gene, and Harry Wenner. 1970. New Vistas on Work and Leisure: An Innovative Program for Relevant Education of School and Community. Morristown NJ: American Civilization Institute of Morristown.

Westbrook, Robert B. 1991. *John Dewey and American Democracy*. Ithaca: Cornell University Press.

White, Leslie. 1963. *The Ethnography and Ethnology of Franz Boas*. Texas Memorial Museum Bulletin 6. Austin: Texas Memorial Museum.

———. 1966. *The Social Organization of Ethnological Theory*. Houston: Rice University Press.

Whyte, William Foote, and Kathleen King Whyte. 1984. *Learning from the Field: A Guide from Experience*. Beverly Hills CA: Sage.

Williams, Brackette F., and Drexel G. Woodson. 1993. Hortense Powdermaker in the Deep South. Introduction. In Powdermaker, *After Freedom*, ix–xi.

Williams, Vernon J., Jr. 1995. Franz Boas and the African American Intelligentsia. *Western Journal of Black Studies* 19(2):81–89.

———. 1996. *Rethinking Race: Franz Boas and His Contemporaries*. Lexington: University of Kentucky Press.

Wilson, Robin. 2003. The "Feminization" of Anthropology. *Chronicle of Higher Education* 49(32; April 18):A13.

Wolf, Eric. 1971. Hortense Powdermaker, 1900–1970. Obituary. *American Anthropologist* 73:783–786.

———. 1972. American Anthropologists and American Society. In Hymes, *Reinventing Anthropology*, 251–263.

———. 1999. *Envisioning Power: Ideologies of Dominance and Crisis*. Berkeley: University of California Press.

Wolf, Eric R., and Joseph G. Jorgensen. 1970. Anthropology on the Warpath in Thailand. *New York Review of Books*, November 19:26–35.

Woo, Elaine. 1999. Obituary: Virginia Durr; Aristocrat Ostracised for Early
    Civil Rights Work. *Los Angeles Times*, February 26, A36.
Wyatt, Donald. 1976. The Student Clique System of a Desegregated High
    School and Its Influence on the Instructional Process. PhD disserta-
    tion, University of Florida.
Yanagisako, Sylvia, and Carol Delaney, ed. 1995. *Naturalizing Power*. New York:
    Routledge.
Yans-McLaughlin, Virginia. 1986. Science, Democracy, Ethics. *History of An-
    thropology* 4:184–217.
Yon, Daniel A. 2003. Highlights and Overview of the History of Educational
    Ethnography. *Annual Review of Anthropology* 32:411–429.
Young, Virginia Heyer. 2005. *Ruth Benedict: Beyond Relativity, Beyond Pattern*.
    Lincoln: University of Nebraska Press.
Zechenter, Elizabeth M. 1997. In the Name of Culture: Cultural Relativity and
    the Abuse of the Individual. In Universal Human Rights versus Cul-
    tural Relativity. Terence Turner and Carole Nagengast, eds. Special
    Issue. *Journal of Anthropological Research* 53(3):319–347.
Zumwalt, Rosemary. 1992. *Wealth and Rebellion: Elsie Clews Parsons, Anthropolo-
    gist and Folklorist*. Urbana: University of Illinois Press.

Contributors

Jill B. R. Cherneff is a research scholar with the UCLA Center for the Study of Women. She is also presently a research associate in anthropology at the Natural History Museum of Los Angeles County, where she is at work on an assessment of the collection of Philippine materials. She was guest editor of "Special Issue: The Legacy of Hortense Powdermaker," *Journal of Anthropological Research* (1991b).

Regna Darnell is a professor of anthropology and director of First Nations Studies at the University of Western Ontario. Her books include *Invisible Genealogies: A History of Americanist Anthropology* (Nebraska, 2001), *And Along Came Boas* (1998), and *Edward Sapir: Linguist, Anthropologist, Humanist* (1990). She co-edits Nebraska's *Critical Studies in History of Anthropology* and *Histories of Anthropology Annual*. She is a fellow of the Royal Society of Canada and a member of the American Philosophical Society.

Richard Handler is a professor of anthropology at the University of Virginia. He received his PhD in cultural anthropology from the University of Chicago in 1979. His book, *Critics against Culture: Anthropological Observers of Mass Society*, was published by the University of Wisconsin Press in 2005. He is currently the editor of *History of Anthropology*.

Eve Hochwald is a practicing anthropologist who conducts research in educational and workplace settings. She is particularly interested in the impact of new technologies on social organization. She received her PhD in 1984 from the City University of New York Graduate Center, where she was a student of Eleanor Leacock.

Ray McDermott is a cultural anthropologist and professor of education at Stanford University. With Hervé Varenne, he is the author of *Successful Failure: The School America Builds* (Westview). His most recent work offers a critique of the very idea of genius.

Alexander Moore is a professor of anthropology at the University of Southern California. He was born in Manila of American parents and educated at Harvard and Columbia, where his mentor was Conrad Arensberg. Although his doctoral fieldwork took place in Guatemala, his first book, *Realities of the Urban Classroom: Observations in Elementary Schools* (Doubleday Anchor, 1967), dealt with New York City. During nine years on the faculty at the University of Florida, he was closely associated with Solon T. Kimball.

Juliet Niehaus holds a PhD in anthropology and a master's degree in social work. She left academia in 1998 to pursue a career in horticultural therapy, a profession using gardening and nature-related activities to help people with disabilities. She is currently director of education and horticultural therapy at Tucson Botanical Gardens.

Virginia Young is now retired from the University of Virginia. She received her PhD in 1953 from Columbia University. Her research interests are subordinate cultures; biculturalism, especially among African and Chinese Americans; and the Caribbean. Her newest book is *Ruth Benedict: Beyond Relativity, Beyond Pattern* (Nebraska 2005).

Index

In the Critical Studies in the History of Anthropology series

Invisible Genealogies: A History of Americanist Anthropology
Regna Darnell

The Shaping of American Ethnography:
The Wilkes Exploring Expedition, 1838–1842
Barry Alan Joyce

Ruth Landes: A Life in Anthropology
Sally Cole

Melville J. Herskovits and the Racial Politics of Knowledge
Jerry Gershenhorn

Leslie A. White: Evolution and Revolution in Anthropology
William J. Peace

Rolling in Ditches with Shamans:
Jaime de Angulo and the Professionalization of American Anthropology
Wendy Leeds-Hurwitz

Irregular Connections:
A History of Anthropology and Sexuality
Andrew P. Lyons and Harriet D. Lyons

Ephraim George Squier and the Development of American Anthropology
Terry A. Barnhart

Ruth Benedict: Beyond Relativity, Beyond Pattern
Virginia Heyer Young

Looking through Taiwan:
American Anthropologists' Collusion with Ethnic Domination
Keelung Hong and Stephen O. Murray

Visionary Observers: Anthropological Inquiry and Education
Jill B. R. Cherneff and Eve Hochwald